THE ORGANIZATION
& ADMINISTRATION
OF
PASTORAL
COUNSELING
CENTERS

THE ORGANIZATION & ADMINISTRATION

OF

PASTORAL COUNSELING CENTERS

John C. Carr
John E. Hinkle
David M. Moss III

Abingdon
Nashville

THE ORGANIZATION & ADMINISTRATION
OF PASTORAL COUNSELING CENTERS

Copyright © 1981 by Abingdon

Library of Congress Cataloging in Publication Data

Main entry under title:
  The Organization and administration of pastoral counseling centers.
  Bibliography: p.
  Includes indexes.
  1. Pastoral counseling centers—Addresses, essays, lectures. I. Carr, John
Crosby. II. Hinkle, John E. III. Moss, David M.
  BV4012.25.O74   253.5   80-22416

ISBN 0-687-29430-4

Acknowledgment is made for permission to reprint the following: Excerpts from
"Pastoral Psychotherapy, The Fee-for-Service Model, and Professional Identity," by
John B. Houck and David M. Moss, originally published in the *Journal of Religion and
Health*, 16:3 (1977); "The 'Robin Hood' Policy: Ethical and Practical Issues Growing
Out of the Use of Fee Scales in Pastoral Counseling Centers," by John E. Hinkle, Jr.,
originally published in *The Journal of Pastoral Care*, 31:2 (1977). In complete form:
"Supervision of Pastoral Psychotherapy," by Blaine B. Rader, originally published in
The Journal of Pastoral Care, 31:3 (1977).

MANUFACTURED BY THE PARTHENON PRESS AT
NASHVILLE, TENNESSEE, UNITED STATES OF AMERICA

This book is dedicated with deep affection to Carroll A. Wise, person, pastor, teacher, author, and therapist-counselor. We honor his passion for authentic, caring, freeing, growth-enhancing relationships; his own strong sense of personal and pastoral identity; his concept of ministry through relationships; his unsurpassed contributions to the field of Pastoral Psychology and Counseling as author, teacher, and organizer; and his continuing concern for others. Without his life and influence this book would not have been written. It is therefore most appropriately dedicated to him. "Well done, thou good and faithful servant" (Matt. 25:21).

C O N T E N T S

PART V: EVALUATION AND RESEARCH

F O R E W O R D

The growth of pastoral counseling centers during the past twenty years has been phenomenal, not only in the number of centers established, but in the increase in the number of staff members employed by the centers. This growth is proof that many persons, even some not actively religious, seek help from a pastor when facing trouble. It is also an indication of the tremendous need for pastoral counseling in our communities. The use and growth of such centers expresses a confidence and hope to which pastors are responding. Clearly a new arm of the church is being established.

The situation places certain responsibilities on the pastors who see this as a viable field of service. The first is that they establish within themselves a strong and viable pastoral identity. Pastors who move into this work out of dissatisfaction with the parish may find themselves equally unhappy if their pastoral identity is not strong and clear.

The second responsibility is that the pastor acquire a high level of proficiency in pastoral counseling and psychotherapy. Many pastors today have disciplined themselves through study and supervision and are as well trained as many other professional workers. Although there is an abundance of books seeking to assist pastors in their training, the values and limitations of reading have become well recognized. Clinical training under supervision is required, and centers have been set up to provide the answer to this need.

The third responsibility of pastors entering this field is to become proficient in matters of administration and finance. These are some of the harsh but real facts of life which must be wrestled with. Strangely enough, and to the best of our knowledge, here is the first book which seeks to help pastors with these problems. Although it cannot be claimed that reading this book will make a pastor a good center administrator, it can help a great deal. The editors of this book have gathered together a group of competent and experienced writers. They write out of their daily experience and in a manner helpful to the pastor seeking to develop or administer a pastoral counseling center. The material deals with many of the issues faced in the organization and/or administration of pastoral counseling centers, such as proper business and clinical practices, legal and financial issues, selection of consultants, personnel, and staff, training issues, and many more. It is high time a book like this appeared and the editors and authors are to be congratulated on plowing some new ground.

Carroll A. Wise

P R E F A C E

This book developed for the purpose of assisting pastors in conceiving, planning, organizing, and administering pastoral counseling centers. The value of this work grows out of: (1) the need of persons in this society for pastoral counseling services; (2) the need for a societal structure that emerges from and supports the values inherent in pastoral counseling to provide the proper base for delivery of such services; (3) the need of pastoral counselors for peer review and interprofessional consultation; and (4) the need for training in counseling to equip other able and interested pastors for fuller participation in the counseling task.

The need for pastoral counseling services could be documented in many ways. A 1975 nationwide Gallup Poll has shown that 57 percent of the respondents want their own church or synagogue *to establish a counseling service.* For persons with a college education and a business or professional occupation, the figure rose to 64 percent favoring such a serivce. (Gallup Report #114, *Religion in America,* Princeton, New Jersey, 1975.) These figures come as no surprise in view of the well-established fact that 43 percent of those persons seeking help with emotional problems turn first to the clergy. Further evidence of this need comes from clergy themselves. The usefulness of training in pastoral counseling for ministers engaged in parish work is rated as second in importance only to biblical studies (and sometimes even at the same level as, or ahead of, biblical studies). One twenty-year study of pastors' ratings concludes that the high proportion (45%) of seminary graduates rating pastoral psychology and counseling as most helpful for their present work is a clear indication of its importance to their ministries. (S. Wong, "A Descriptive Study of Garrett Graduates," Garrett Theological Seminary, unpublished, 1971.)

Additionally, pastoral counseling centers are needed because they both grow out of and express a set of values appropriate to the personal as well as spiritual growth of individuals, couples, and families. Centers organized in accordance with these values can effectively deliver pastoral counseling services which meet the needs of persons for personal and spiritual growth. Such centers can deliver the pastoral counselor from the conflict of interests felt so often by the perceptive parish priest or pastor: the conflict between the needs of an individual parishioner or family and the needs of the parish program. These and other factors account for the phenomenal growth in the number and size of pastoral counseling centers in recent years.

This book is designed for the many well-intentioned church leaders who are aware of these factors but do not properly understand how to organize and administer pastoral counseling centers effectively. Many centers have started and failed needlessly. Centers currently in operation can be made even more effective if they will do a careful review of their present operation based on the material in the following chapters.

In an undertaking of this magnitude, gratitude flows in many directions. Persons who have heard about the development of this book have expressed appreciation to the editorial committee who first conceived it and provided the initial impetus, namely, Richard Augspurger, John Carr, Emily Demme Haight, Richard Guest, Stephen Nahrwold, and myself. The willingness of John Carr to fulfill the role of coordinating editor at that initial stage was a decisive factor in the original decision to develop the manuscript. Subsequently, the thoughtful investments of David Moss helped bring this project to fruition. Moss was assisted by T. David Brent, The University of Chicago Press, Frank M. Ross, Candler School of Theology, and Jean Levenson of Darby Press, Atlanta. John Patton, Georgia Association of Pastoral Care, and William North, Care and Counseling, St. Louis, also aided in the closure of this project.

The work of the editors has been made bearable by the strong affirmative responses of those persons who were asked to prepare chapters. I am grateful to them and to the Editorial Committee for their cheerful cooperation and personal warmth throughout this endeavor. Pamela Holliman Cox, Rachel Howland Kraps, and Marilyn Carr deserve special mention for their careful work in preparing the typed manuscript—as do my own family for their forebearance of my workaholism, without which the seminars would not have been taught, the consultation not done, and the first drafts not written.

Finally, to the staff colleagues, board members, consultants, students, and counselees of the Indiana Counseling and Pastoral Care Center, Indianapolis—friends who taught me how to administer a pastoral counseling center—my ongoing appreciation. Thank you.

John E. Hinkle, Jr.

INTRODUCTION

David M. Moss III, John C. Carr,
and John E. Hinkle, Jr.

A s Dr. Wise's Foreword points out, this anthology seeks to "plow some new ground" in the field of pastoral care. Wise's statement is reinforced by the fact that the American Association of Pastoral Counselors (AAPC) sponsored its first national workshop on the organization and administration of pastoral counseling centers as recently as 1974.[1] Held in Chicago, that workshop led to a series of research projects which form the backdrop of the next fifteen chapters.

As these projects were conducted, we discovered a host of issues that pastoral counselors and psychotherapists had left untouched or unanticipated since the Association was formed decades ago. Consequently we turned to colleagues across the United States and Canada for the construction of an anthology which might offer pragmatic and theoretical guidelines for specialized ministers joining together to create or refine pastoral counseling centers. This book is the product of those efforts and of the original seminars taught by Dr. Hinkle. While it cannot be considered a final and definitive source, it is the first of its nature to be published.

The book is divided into five sections. However, some of the chapters within those sections might very well have been included or digested in others. For example, Hinkle's chapter on pastoral counseling center training standards could have been placed in Part IV and that section might have increased in scope. The reader will also notice some repetition and an occasional difference of opinion or professional perspective. Perhaps a prime illustration of the latter is the different perspectives on supervision and/or consultation set forth by Haight, Christensen, Siskind, and Lindemann in chapters 9, 10, and 11. The Editorial Committee has attempted to limit replication, but some duplication seems unavoidable since most authors share common commitments. The various contributors have organized their material in different fashions, drawing from experience and research that brings a unique quality to each chapter. Out of respect for their individual perspectives, no attempt has been made to homogenize their styles or positions, for their diversity adds to rather than detracts from the readability of this anthology.[2]

In our opinion, respect for various professional perspectives cannot be emphasized enough. It is at the core of what "ministry" means to those who have dedicated their lives to the health care services. This commitment has an ancient tradition from which all of us draw. Since the Western movement of Judeo-Christian ministry, clergy have often been referred to as "bridge-builders" (fr. L *pontifus*). With the crystallization of AAPC this tenor of service has intensified. As pastors develop their ability to provide psychological assistance, the value of interdisciplinary dialogue becomes apparent and the mutuality of ministry is further clarified. This professional awareness enables us to focus on our strengths and, at the same time, recognize our limitations—the fact that our ministry can be aided by other disciplines.

For centuries proponents of faith, mental health, and medicine have gathered, united, fragmented, and rejoined during various crises. Currently that union must be embraced in the interests of the totality of selfhood. A wholistic view of humanity necessitates reflection, dialogue, expansion, and interdisciplinary reciprocity. Contributors to this volume support such a process and agree with Piaget's "three cardinal ideas" regarding the complementarity of disciplines invested in "the cure of souls": "(1) that of the *production of new structures*;

18

(2) that of *equilibrium*, but in the sense of regulation and self-regulation (and not merely the balance of forces); and (3) that of *exchange* in the sense of material exchange, but equally . . . the exchange of information"[3] (italics added).

Ultimately, this means an extension of our insights with those of attorneys, physicians, nurses, and morticians, as well as branches of psychology that have much to offer to those willing to receive. Recent changes in the American Psychological Association (the establishment of Division 36: "Psychologists Interested in Religious Issues") and alterations in the membership standards of the American Association of Marriage and Family Therapy (acceptance of degrees in theology as equivalent to other graduate degrees) are clear indications of this willingness. Our individual responses should be just as pronounced. This does not necessarily mean a confusion of "church and state" but an *affinity* that is open, direct, and lucid. Such dialogues would naturally include certain areas of law and education, two important professional spheres of our culture that have already experienced some bridge-building by, or rather with, AAPC.

If the meaning of "church" is to grow in our culture, then this bridge-building must continue with other members of professional communities that have gifts to share with the pastoral psychology movement. Eliot's words seem apt: "What life have you if you have not life together? There is no life that is not community. . . ."[4] Like ourselves, our clients seek such life—a meaningful form of living that is "constructed" of soul, body, and culture.

While we could further elaborate on the importance of interdisciplinary dialogue and wholistic ministry, such comments have been postponed until the companion volume to this book is completed. The content of this first book is our immediate concern, particularly the subject matter of its five major sections, or parts. To reference Carroll Wise again, these chapters grow out of the "daily experience" of "competent" professionals who are committed to establishing "a new arm of the church." For instance, in Part I, Hinkle and Carr attempt to provide an evaluative description of the various institutional models which have evolved during the gestation and growth of pastoral counseling during the last thirty years. They address such elementary issues as: What is a pastoral counseling center? How does it come into being? Guest takes us through the process of developing a pastoral counseling center "starting from the ground up." His chapter is also attentive to the staff and board members of existing centers and offers a theoretical framework which clarifies several consistent elements that are sometimes vague or unspecified in the development and/or maintenance of such an agency. The final chapter in Part I is, in some respects, a preface to Bruehl's contribution to the outset of Part II. Both Hinkle and Bruehl reflect a deep concern for training standards in pastoral counseling centers, especially centers invested in AAPC's consistent efforts to insure quality control.

Part II will be beneficial for those who are responsible for designing and refining the administrative procedures of a center. The chapter by Moss on the fee-for-service model and the one by Hinkle on fee-setting principles are, in certain ways, provocative and open-ended. Although well researched, they do not provide solutions to the economic topic so long debated by pastoral counselors—namely, the various issues involved in a minister charging a fee for pastoral care. We hope enough stimulation is provided so that the reader will be able to formulate useful conclusions about what is appropriate for his or her context and understanding of pastoral psychotherapy. The final chapter in this section dovetails into Carr's discussion of business practices. In it Augspurger deals with legal concerns. Thus, these four chapters collectively provide a good pragmatic base for the following three sections.

Part III is devoted to clinical, consulting, and referral procedures. The authors lucidly speak to the issues of establishing a clinical practice, as well as the consultation and referral procedures which make it possible for a center to realize effective service. Haight provides an overview, while Christensen, Siskind, and Lindemann set forth positions based on years of experience as consultants and supervisors of pastoral counselors. As we said earlier, this is a section of the book which reflects diversity mostly due to the professional disciplines from which the authors have emerged—psychiatry, clinical psychology, and social work. In the concluding chapter of this section, Alley and Moss add a number of well-reasoned suggestions about referral processes which we believe to be quite useful in the development of a pastoral counseling center, regardless of the model it is based on.

Quality pastoral counseling grows out of adequate training, supervision, and consultation. These activities are nearly impossible in sufficient intensity apart from the existence and effective operation of a pastoral counseling center. Consequently, Part IV on supervision and training is not an extra but rather an essential component of the whole, speaking as it does to the issue of how people are trained to do the work which manifestly needs to be done in centers and parishes. Hinkle, Rader, Grant, and Moss address themselves to this issue in a way which opens up the possibilities created by the growth of pastoral counseling centers for seasoning, leavening, and illuminating the total ministry of the churches of our continent. Reading these chapters, one becomes aware that clinical service and training for pastoral counseling go hand in hand, that one is not complete without the other.

The final section, Part V, "Evaluation and Research," contains a single chapter and might well have been entitled "Epilogue." Chapter 15 is a composition by three psychotherapists who have devoted a great deal of attention to the merits of research in pastoral counseling centers. Nahrwold has condensed a great deal of literature by reviewing several studies which are paradigmatic, while Florell and Moss have digested some basic psychometric procedures as a way of providing some intellectual and practical tools which can frequently assist professionals in their assessment of the effectiveness of the therapeutic services they deliver. At the outset, Moss expands on the rationale for this chapter, underscoring the fact that all of the previous chapters grew out of research projects carefully conducted in the interests of improving pastoral assistance. However, given the nature of this book and the Editorial Board's interest in addressing a broad audience, most of the technicalities of these projects have been indirectly summarized rather than elaborated on in any detailed manner.

Naturally, it is our hope that each chapter in its own particular way will serve as a useful touchstone for those invested in the institutional and theological maturation of the pastoral psychology movement.

Notes

1. Although the American Association of Pastoral Counselors is the body to which most U.S. pastoral counselors belong, some pastoral counselors and some pastoral counseling centers are oriented to the American Association for Clinical Pastoral Education. In Canada, the Canadian Association for Pastoral Education has recently developed standards for training specialists in pastoral counseling and accrediting Supervisors in Pastoral Counseling Education.

2. An exception to this rule has been the editing of language which *seems* "sexist." This is a problem that has become quite sensitive for many writers in the fields of psychology and religion. However, it is sometimes very hard to avoid the linguistic difficulties related to gender, particularly pronouns. We have handled the issue with care, since some denominations still do not favor the ordination of women to the ministry. Obviously, our Editorial Board does not wish to contribute to that resistance. Every contributor to this volume is an advocate of sexual equality and is acutely aware of the need for qualified females in the pastoral counseling movement. So, to those who spot our linguistic oversights, we say *Pace!* We tried.

3. Jean Piaget, *Main Trends in Inter-Disciplinary Research* (New York: Harper & Row, 1973), p. 13.

4. T. S. Eliot, "The Rock," *Collected Poems: 1909–1935* (New York: Harcourt, Brace & World, 1962), p. 101.

P A R T

ONE

ORGANIZATION

1

An Overview of
Pastoral Counseling and Center Models
John E. Hinkle, Jr. and John C. Carr

This chapter attempts to provide a brief description of ten models which might be followed in establishing and administering a pastoral counseling center. Structures are determined by goals, context, and attitude toward such issues as fees, fund-raising opportunities and methods, the community's religious attitudes and its level of ecumenical commitment, clinical standards, demand for services, and stage of development. As a result, there is considerable overlap between the various models described, although each has enough of its own unique components to warrant separate review. Other combinations of components might well result in further expansion of the present list of clearly identifiable models. The models described, however, constitute an exhaustive list of those known to be in operation or, in the case of Models I and J, seen to be potential bases of professional pastoral counseling services. [1]

For each model an attempt has been made to provide a brief description of the context, the constituency served, the lines of administrative and clinical responsibilities, and the financial policies followed.

Models

A. Parish Staff Counselor
B. Parish-Based Pastoral Counseling Service
C. Community-Based Pastoral Counseling Center

D. Pastoral Counseling Group Practice
E. Satellite Pastoral Counseling Service
F. Seminary/University Counseling Services
G. Hospital Outpatient Pastoral Counseling Services
H. Judicatory Counseling Service
I. Denominational Social Service Agency
J. Pastoral Counseling in Church Information Centers

We regard Models C, D, and G as the best options for a middle and upper class suburban or urban context because they maximize the potential for high quality service and ecumenical involvement. Moss' chapter on the fee-for-service model will underscore this point in more detail. Other models might be used at an early stage of development, leading eventually to one of these three "ideal" models. Other models are also appropriate in contexts where development of one of the models is not feasible for socioeconomic or other reasons, or the goal is that of providing a limited range of services.

Model A. *Parish Staff Counselor*

As a member of a parish staff, the professional pastoral counselor serves as counselor-to-the-parish. The minister is a specialist who:

1. provides individual, marital, and group therapy to persons who come referred by other staff members or on self-referral. The therapist may do the counseling or refer them elsewhere for therapy appropriate to their needs;
2. provides consultation to other staff members when the specialist's expertise is requested (or when it is needed even though not requested);
3. relates to appropriate committee structures and programs of the parish.

Accountability is to denominational structures and to the senior pastor, with appropriate supervision and/or consultation by

25

a competent mental health professional (e.g., AAPC Diplomate or Fellow, a Psychiatric or Psychological Consultant, an AAMFC Supervisor, etc.).

The constituency served is the membership of the parish, although the pastoral counselor may be available to non-members of the parish on the basis of established policies, perhaps using such criteria as a referral source, seriousness of the problem, place on the waiting-list, residence in the community served by the parish and related factors.

Fees would probably not be charged for initial evaluative sessions, but there would be fees on a nominal *or* ability-to-pay basis for therapy beyond evaluation. Collected fees would be deposited in a special account to be used for the development of the counseling service.

This model can be used to provide limited service to an existing constituency. No structures need to be established as all the functions of planning and overseeing the service are carried out by existing groups and committees. Since decisions are made by persons already related to each other in a parish, goal-setting and establishment of criteria for use in evaluating the service may be facilitated. Moreover, the parish benefits directly from the impact of the counseling service on other aspects of its life. For example, staff development, education, worship, and program development are likely to be affected.

This model is, however, a relatively closed system and can become somewhat ingrown and faddish. It may lead to some polarization of the congregation's general structures due to poorly handled transference in the therapy provided. The greatest risk is that the pastoral counselor may begin to see people because they are paying the counselor's salary, rather than on the basis of informed clinical judgment as to the appropriateness of working with the specific individual, couple, or family. Obviously, highly competent pastoral counselors will be aware of this risk and will attempt to establish safeguards for their clinical functioning which take cognizance of the reality that no one therapist is able to work with everybody who comes for help, and that there are many problems which cannot be resolved through counseling in the context of a parish.

In a large parish this model can be extremely useful. The emphasis of the counseling service needs to be on short-term therapy and referral, preventive mental health, crisis intervention, and consultation with other staff members.

Model B. Parish-Based Pastoral Counseling Service

In this model, the pastoral counselor functions both as counselor-to-the-parish and counselor-to-the community. Administrative accountability is to an autonomous board of directors (representing a cross-section of the parish's membership) appointed by the parish's governing body.

Professional responsibility is to an advisory committee which includes mental health professionals, one of whom would be the service's psychiatric consultant. The advisory board is appointed by the board of directors.

The constituency served is primarily the parish, but chains of referral would also be developed in the community which would bring some clients from sources other than parish-staff and parish-member referrals. In any case, no attempt would be made to restrict services to parish members.

The service could be paid for by the fees of clients served except for such subsidization as (1) the housing and equipping of the service in the church building; (2) the provision, from the parish budget, of scholarship funds to subsidize those clients unable to pay at the level determined by the fee scale (i.e., who are under extraordinary pressure). It needs to be made clear, in the parish and in the community, that the counseling provided is on a sliding-scale fee basis.

The risks involved in the use of this model are similar to, but not as great as, those described in Model A. It is a somewhat more open system, with greater potential for developing referral chains in the community, and for utilizing and contributing to the community's total mental health facilities.

The model provides a useful option in a community where the need for pastoral counseling services is apparent, where the parish is sensitive to and has adequate resources to meet the need, and where ecumenical interaction is such that Models C, D, or G. are not feasible. By using a nondenominational approach to client intake and staffing of the service, Model B can become a catalyst for the development of closer ecumenical relationships in the community and the eventual development of an administrative structure involving the total community, or at least a significant segment.

Model C. Community-Based Pastoral Counseling Center

In this model, the pastoral counselor functions as counselor-to-the-community and the service is established on an ecumenical basis, including as broad a range of ecclesiastical and mental health organizations as possible.

Administrative responsibility is vested in a board of directors elected by the sponsoring groups and possibly by individuals who have qualified for voting privileges by donating funds in order to become "sustaining members." In the case of sponsoring groups, the number of board members is determined by a combination of criteria, including the size of the organization and the extent of its financial commitment. Where there is a sustaining membership provision, those who undertake this kind of support are given the right to elect (at an annual meeting) board members who are their representatives, or directors-at-large.

Professional responsibility is vested in an advisory board which includes a variety of mental health professionals, and one of whom is the center's psychiatric consultant. The advisory board members are appointed by the board of directors.

In this model, service is available to anyone from the community and its environs on a fee-for-services-rendered basis. The long-term goal is to make the service able to provide for its cost from fees charged to its clients, except for the subsidization provided through membership fees and through housing the service at minimal or no cost in church buildings. For the sake of clients who would be reluctant to enter a church building, it might be advisable to have some counseling done in a nonecclesiastical setting.

Fees are determined by a fee scale. Sometimes a reduction is made for clients referred from sponsoring or supporting parishes and other funding institutions. In other words, membership fees subsidize the fees of these clients. In addition, they help to fund capital expenditures and expansion, and to subsidize educational programs.

As previously indicated, this model may evolve out of the others. Models A, B, and E, and perhaps I and J, could eventually develop to the stage represented by Model C. Alternatively, this model may be called into being by an existing ministerial association, council of churches, or ecumenical task force and can become a focal point for the ecumenical commitment of these kinds of organizations.

This model's advantages include broad-based involvement of the people and institutions of the community as providers and recipients of an essential service, with effective deployment and use of community and ecclesiastical resources. Its structures require an innovative and creative program of development and maintenance which may, at first, seem more difficult than those required in some of the other models, but which results in a higher degree of community involvement with mental health goals.

Model D. Pastoral Counseling Group Practice

In this model two or more pastoral counselors work in a collegial relationship with each other on the basis of contracts established between them and a number of parishes. Parishes provide office space in which counseling may be done, and publicize the services available to their constituency and in the communities they serve. Pastoral counselors are assigned to do counseling in the church building for a specified number of days each week.

Clinical and administrative responsibility rests with the professional members of the group practice. All positions are filled through an electoral process for a specified term. Peer review is provided by an elected professional standards committee. Counselors are expected to contract for supervision or consultation appropriate to their professional development, making use of the skills of group members or of professionals outside the group.

A director is appointed to coordinate the therapy work done at each site serviced by the group. The person relates to an advisory committee representing the parish, or cluster of parishes being serviced, and provides a liaison between the advisory committee and the administrative structures of the group practice. In addition to this, the director consults with the advisory committee on matters such as maximizing the use of the counseling service in the community (developing referral chains) and improving the facilities in which counseling is being done. Finally, the person is available to the constituent organizations as a consultant, and as need arises and the director is comfortable doing so, as a liturgist and preacher. An annual meeting of representatives of the advisory committee from each site is held to review the work of the group and to advise with regard to future planning.

The service is available to anyone from the community on a fee-for-services-rendered basis. (See Model C and chapter 5 on business practices for details.) Normally, no fee reduction is available to members of sponsoring bodies.

In the Group Practice model, the fee scale needs to be drafted in such a way as to provide a reasonable income for the pastoral counselors providing the service. They are essentially private practitioners whose income is directly related to the fees paid by the clients whom they see. That is, each pastoral counselor is paid a percentage of the fee income generated by the person's work. The percentage is determined by the amount of administrative responsibility undertaken in the group. Thus, a center director might receive 95 percent of the counseling income personally generated, whereas a pastoral counselor who only does counseling might receive 70 percent. Each pastoral counselor pays all of his own expenses out of his income, including the cost of supervision.

This model is attractive to aggressive counselors with confidence in their professional competence. As Moss' chapter notes, it has some historical affinities to the missionary movement of the early twentieth century and runs the concomitant risk of a kind of imperialism which is neither clinically acceptable nor ecclesiastically advantageous. Moreover, it may tend to require a fee structure which is higher than that required in other models, and thus needs a significant base in suburban communities which have high socioeconomic populations.

Centers established using this model may have their origins in a denominational or ecumenical movement from within the community or in the initiative of pastoral counselors looking for a context in which to work. Ecumenical and community involvement are a *sine qua non*, with accrual of benefits already enumerated under Model C.

Model E. Satellite Pastoral Counseling Service

A congregation, a cluster of congregations, or a judicatory may contract with an existing pastoral counseling center for the services of one or more of its staff members for a specified amount of time each week.

Services would be available to a constituency determined by the nature of the contract (see Models A, B, C, F, G, and H). They would be paid for in one of two ways:

1. The center charges the organization being serviced for the time and expenses of the pastoral counselor. The

local sponsoring organization recovers its expenses through congregational or judicatory budgets and fees charged to clients.

2. The center charges the clients served on the same basis as that used in its own facilities and charges the pastoral counselor's travel and accommodation expenses to the local sponsoring organization.

The pastoral counselor is administratively and clinically responsible through the structures established within the counselor's center. This counselor or the center's director may meet for liaison purposes with a local advisory committee.

This model affords a relatively low overhead method by which high quality clinical service may be provided in a community. The advantages of some of the other models can be incorporated into the contract with the center providing the service. A prime example is involvements in the parish or community as a consultant to parish clergy or to educational programs. There is, of course, some loss of local control over and involvement in administrative and clinical policies of the counseling service provided. The sponsoring parish or ecumenical group is a "receiver" more than an active participant in the provision of services. Establishment of this model can be an effective way of developing a more fully integrated model which affords opportunity for effective involvement of the community in the service provided.

Model F. *Seminary/University Counseling Services*

In a seminary or university context the pastoral counselor functions as a counselor to students, staff, faculty and their families. The person may be designated as "pastoral counselor" or as "chaplain" to the community served, but membership in that community (or referral by one of its members) is a prerequisite for obtaining the pastoral services. The chaplain might function, in addition to providing counseling services, as a liturgist for the university or seminary community or as an initiator or teacher of formal or informal courses and seminars. Much of this work is short-term, with crisis intervention and referral a major focus. The services, if available primarily or only to members of the community, are available at a nominal fee, sometimes without fee.

Clinical and administrative or academic responsibilities need to be defined clearly so that administrative functions—activities such as grade-setting, in the case of students or professional advancement, in the case of faculty and staff—do not destroy the potential for confidentiality between the pastoral counselor and individual clients in the community. Professional responsibility is to a psychiatric or pastoral consultant (who might also provide ongoing supervision) and to an advisory board of mental health professionals appointed by the institution's administration.

Model G. Hospital Outpatient Pastoral Counseling Services

A hospital may develop an outpatient pastoral counseling service as an extension into the community of its in-house chaplaincy service. Thus, the services of pastoral counselors trained in pastoral psychotherapy (individual, marital, family, and group) become available to the community served by the hospital on a fee-for-services-rendered basis.

In-house hospital chaplaincy may be supported by a portion of the daily patient fee, by contributions from local churches, or by a combination thereof; but we regard it as unethical for the in-house chaplaincy service to provide outpatient pastoral care and counseling when it is supported, in whole or in part, by in-house patient fees.

The potential for two-way referral between medical and pastoral staff is enhanced in this model, with development of personal relationships through common institutional involvement. The outpatient pastoral counseling service is also a catalyst for consultation between parish clergy and hospital and community health professionals.

As a consequence, the outpatient pastoral counseling service may function as a section of the hospital's pastoral care division. Community involvement is enhanced by having an advisory committee that is representative of the community's churches. The pastoral counselors may participate with the in-house chaplaincy section of the division in the provision of continuing education opportunities in pastoral care for parish clergy. They may also plan and lead courses, retreats, workshops, and seminars, such as parent effectiveness training courses (P.E.T.), marriage enrichment retreats, premarital counseling courses, and death education seminars.

Initiative for the development of this model may come from the hospital chaplaincy staff or from the community, but it is important to its success that the active participation of the clergy and parishes of the community be solicited.

Model H. Judicatory Counseling Service

Increasingly, church judicatories are providing specialized pastoral counseling for the professional church workers and their families. The increasing mental health problems of religious professionals have made this an essential element in the judicatory's exercise of its episcopal responsibility. The pastoral counselor who provides this care may do so in an office at the judicatory headquarters, at a career counseling center, or by traveling about the geographic region serviced by the judicatory.

Professional confidentiality is a major issue in the exercise of this ministry and needs to be protected meticulously. The judicatory pastoral counselor needs to be "out among" the religious professionals of the judicatory, as a pastor is "out among" the people of the community, in a way that develops the trust necessary for effective preventive, remedial, and referral work. However, the counselor needs to take care not to be identified with those structures in the ecclesiastical framework which have influence over appointments and advancement. If the person is functioning as an agent of disciplinary structures—such as, in evaluating candidates for professional religious work, or in assessing psychological factors in cases where ecclesiastical charges have been laid—the counselor needs to make this specific in the contract with the person being evaluated.

Although administratively related to the ecclesiastical authority providing these services, the judicatory pastoral counselor needs to be professionally responsible to an independent advisory board of mental health professionals, including a psychiatric and/or pastoral consultant.

One way of cementing the confidentiality of this relationship with clients is to charge a fee. The bulk of the cost of providing judicatory pastoral counseling services is, however, generally provided out of the judicatory budget through assessment to local congregations or through special bequests or gifts.

Model I. Denominational Social Service Agency

Some denominations have traditionally been heavily invested in the provision of social service agencies (e.g., Lutheran Welfare, Salvation Army, Catholic Charities) through which material help and some counseling have been made available in the community. The addition of a trained pastoral counselor to the staff of such church agencies could do much to effect an integration of pastoral care and social action. In such a context, marital and family therapy would probably constitute a large share of the pastoral counselor's caseload. In addition to the work with agency clients, the pastoral counselor would serve as a consultant to other agency personnel on the religious and psychodynamic aspects of the work which they are doing.

The counselor's salary would be provided out of the agency's budget, with minimal fees charged to clients, assuming that the clientele of such agencies will normally be in the lower income brackets and that client fees would not provide revenues sufficient to pay the cost of the services. Although administratively responsible to the agency's director and board, the pastoral counselor in such a context is provided with a consultant to whom he is professionally responsible.

The difficulty with this model is that the dependency often resulting from the social service approach of meeting human needs is at odds with the ideal of autonomy which we believe is essential in professional pastoral counseling. The pastoral counselor in such a context can, however, be alert to opportunities to help some clients move beyond dependency and can help them learn how to make use of professional pastoral counseling.

Model J. Pastoral Counseling in Church Information Centers

Some denominations have established centers with the primary purpose of providing educational programs for their own constituency and/or the community-at-large (e.g., the Paulist Fathers' Catholic Information Centers). In such a context, a pastoral counselor might do some highly effective work in the field of preventive mental health (e.g., in the premarital counseling, marriage enrichment, and P.E.T. programs often organized by such centers), as well as providing therapy and referral services to those who go to such centers indirectly seeking counseling. Often, those who seek "educational" opportunities or who undergo religious conversion are trying to shore up weakening defense systems without acknowledging their need for therapy.

The pastoral counselor's role, in such a context, would be defined as a constellation of educational and therapeutic goals, with administrative responsibilities to the center director and board, and professional responsibilities to a psychiatric or pastoral consultant. Financial policies and fee structures, in such a context, may follow those of the Parish-Based or Community-Based models (B or C). No restriction or limitation would be placed on the service's availability.

The potential for identifying mental health needs which might otherwise go unnoticed is a major advantage in this model. The actual quantity and quality of personality change taking place directly as a result of work done in such a context is probably minimal, with a major emphasis being placed on education and referral.

Conclusion

As we said at the outset, this chapter is intended to provide a brief description of ten standard models which might be utilized in the organization and maintenance of a pastoral counseling center. Those models have been labeled: (A) Parish Staff Counselor, (B) Parish-Based Pastoral Counseling Service, (C) Community-Based Pastoral Counseling Center, (D) Pastoral Counseling Group Practice, (E) Satellite Pastoral Counseling Service, (F) Seminary/University Counseling Services, (G) Hospital Outpatient Pastoral Counseling Services, (H) Judicatory Counseling Service, (I) Denominational Social Service Agency, and (J) Pastoral Counseling in Church Information Centers. In many respects they form a base for the following chapters. They are particularly important to keep in mind as one reads about practical and legal concerns in Part II. However, a note of caution should be underscored here: The models do not rest on a pretense of rigidity. Along with the other contributors to this volume, we are sensitive to environmental factors which may blend, veto, or radically revise any or all of these ten designs. We hope that the reader will recall our encouragement of adaptation as each section unfolds what might be called "the grammar and syntax" of the pastoral psychology movement.

Notes

1. While the models and concepts of this chapter have been carefully reviewed by AAPC colleagues, they were also presented at an interdisciplinary forum in an unpublished paper: David M. Moss, "Interdisciplinary Dialogue and Pastoral Counseling Center Models," American Psychological Association's Presidential Panel: Psychologists Interested in Religious Issues, Montreal, 1980.

C H A P T E R

2

Community Resources and the Process of Pastoral Counseling Center Development

Richard E. Guest

A pastoral counseling center like any other organization has a life cycle. The duration of the cycle may vary from a few weeks to many decades. Whether it is long or short there are certain identifiable phases within its life cycle. These phases can be generally described as planning, development, maintenance, and cessation. The planning phase begins when the concept of a center is first considered and predominates until either a center is created or the idea is abandoned. Planning also continues afterward as a function of development and maintenance, although during these phases it is more adaptive than formative.

Development is the process of creating an actual organization. It draws upon the information derived from planning as an (albeit flexible) blueprint. Successful development requires: a sensitivity to community needs and resources; and an ability to creatively match community needs and resources in the process of diagnosing such needs; tailoring services to needs; informing the community of the service; establishing and maintaining relationships with individuals and structures within the community; reevaluating and correcting.

Maintenance can be regarded as a chronological extension of the development process. It begins when an organization is established and the organizational thrust shifts from inception to survival and prosperity. Like development, it requires a creative sensitivity to the community. It also requires a sensitivity to the internal processes of the center and an ability to adapt the center to the combined dictates of its environs, internal processes, and personnel. Finally, cessation of a pastoral counseling center occurs whenever it no longer continues to operate, for whatever reason. However, evaluation must occur throughout the organization's life cycle. Evaluation allows for adaptive changes which are necessary if the organization is to survive.

This chapter is devoted to an analysis of the planning and development phases of the center's life cycle. In general, the same process which occurs during these initial phases continues throughout the organization's entire life cycle, although as the center becomes established emphasis tends to shift from innovation to continuation and adaptation of services.

Comments in this chapter are specifically focused on the development of a Community-Based center (see Model C, chapter 1) because this model involves virtually all the relationships which are present between any existing center and its environs. Hence, what is said regarding development of a Community-Based center can be applied and adapted to most forms of centers.

From the standpoint of development, the Group Practice (D) and Satellite (E) models may be treated simply as special cases of the Community-Based center. The Parish-Based (B) and institutionally-related (F, G) models can be conceptualized as Community-Based models within a restricted environment. The Parish-Staff (A) and Judicatory (H) models have highly restricted application and, while general developmental principles still apply, are often structured according to specific needs and perceptions of the sponsoring body. Application of the material in this chapter to Denominational Social Service (I) and Church Information Center (J) models will vary widely depending upon the philosophies which govern the individual centers of these two types.

The Planning Phase

Any group contemplating the establishment of a counseling center needs to consider the following questions. Is there a need within the community for such a center or service? Can the kind of institution which is envisioned meet existing needs; or, can it realistically be developed in a way which will meet those needs? If the answer to either question is no, then attempts to develop a center are probably a waste of time.

Assuming that preliminary evidence indicates a need for the type of services which a pastoral counseling center provides, then a systematic approach to organizational development is indicated. The initial phase of this process is not unlike that employed in marketing research. The prospective center, to avoid hit-or-miss chances of success, needs to be aware of the kind of market which exists for its services. Although centers may vary tremendously in form and practice, all centers which succeed solve certain basic problems. All successful pastoral counseling centers provide services which are regarded by their communities, or certain parts of their communities (churches, clientele, etc.), as sufficiently valuable to warrant support, financial and otherwise. From an organizational development point of view, the first administrative task related to developing a pastoral counseling center is to determine what services are desired by the community to an extent which will engender adequate support for the center. Once such a determination is made, then programs can be developed to meet identified needs.

However, determining needs of the community is only a part of the planning phase. The other major task is to determine whether the identified needs, and the programs which are indicated by them, fall within the sphere of services which a center provides. For example, if the churches in a community wish to start a legitimately needed crisis intervention center geared especially to drug-related problems among adolescents, and if the personnel they want to hire for the center are primarily interested in long-term therapy and have little

41

expertise or interest in drug-related crisis intervention, then the prospective center faces a serious initial problem. Either the churches must find new center personnel whose interest is similar to their own, or they must change the objectives of the proposed center. In the latter case a reassessment of community needs may be required to determine whether sufficient need exists for such a treatment center.

In essence, the process of determining the feasibility of a center is simply a matter of deciding whether the needs of the community coincide with the services a center is prepared to provide. In reality, it is a complex process. It requires the use of diagnostic and relational skills analogous to those utilized in therapy.

A variety of investigative methodologies may be employed to determine community needs. Perhaps the most obvious is a simple questionnaire survey. Questionnaires can be mailed to community residents asking them to indicate whether they have sought counseling; if so, what kind; and if they would use the services of a pastoral counseling center. Questionnaires should be anonymous to encourage candid responses. Church rolls are a good source of names for the mailing. It should also be remembered that many persons who utilize pastoral counseling centers are not formal members of any congregation. A mailing to church members may be supplemented by mailings to other persons in the community if there are sources of other names available. If this is done, care should be taken to avoid duplicating mailings.

It should also be remembered that any item which is mailed to potential clients has two effects. The overt effect is, of course, to gather data to determine the feasibility of establishing a pastoral counseling center. The covert effect of the mailing upon the recipient needs to be considered also. For most people, receiving such a questionnaire will constitute their first contact with a pastoral counseling center. Just as their responses convey information to the investigator the letter and questionnaire also convey information upon which potential clients form opinions.

The mailing should honestly convey the information the investigator wishes to present, should represent the center concept fairly, and should be written in such a way that it communicates concern and acceptance and avoids insulting and argumentative implications. For mailings to church members one good technique is to prepare a form letter which participating churches can send to parishioners on their own stationery. Such a letter might take the form of the one below.

Dear Member,

Your pastor and the (insert name of appropriate governing body, such as Administrative Board, Session, Vestry, etc.) are taking this opportunity to seek your opinion on a matter which concerns us. We feel that there may be a need for pastoral counseling resources in (insert name of community) which exceeds the capacity of our local churches and their pastors.

We now have the opportunity to develop an ecumenical (if it is intended to be ecumenical) counseling center in our community which would provide counseling by highly skilled ministers with specialized training in psychology and counseling. These pastoral counselors would be available to assist persons who are depressed, anxious, having marriage or family problems, having difficulty adjusting to bereavement or divorce or are suffering from other problems of an emotional/spiritual nature.

Should the need for such services warrant establishing a center, it would not take the place of the counseling done by your pastor. He (or she) would continue counseling as he (or she) does at present, and additional training in pastoral counseling would be available to him (or her) through the center. The primary responsibility of counselors at the center would be to counsel with persons whose problems require the additional expertise that professional counselors can provide.

To assist us in determining whether such a center would be desirable in our community, would you please fill out the enclosed questionnaire and return it to the church office (or other designated place). Please do not sign your name. Your answers will be completely anonymous.

Thank you very much.

Sincerely,

Pastor
Chairman of Administrative Board (or other appropriate official)

The questionnaire which accompanies the letter should solicit information relevant to the establishment of the center in that particular community. In general, it should seek the kind of information requested in the model questionnaire below.

Pastoral Counseling Center Survey

1. Do you feel that (name of community) would benefit from a pastoral counseling center?_____

2. If you felt the need for counseling, would you be likely to utilize a pastoral counselor?_____

3. Have you ever sought counseling in the past?_____

   If yes, what kind of counselor did you see? Please check appropriate answer(s):
   ____minister
   ____psychiatrist
   ____psychologist
   ____social worker
   ____other_____

   If yes, what kind of counseling did you seek? (check appropriate answer[s])
   ____marriage counseling
   ____individual counseling
   ____family counseling
   ____other_____

   If yes, how long did counseling continue? (check appropriate answer[s])
   ____one session
   ____two or five sessions
   ____six to ten sessions
   ____eleven to twenty-five sessions
   ____more than twenty-five sessions

   If yes, how much did the counselor charge:_____

   If yes, were you satisfied with the counseling? (check appropriate answer)
   ____yes
   ____partially
   ____no

4. Do you have friends who you believe would utilize a pastoral counseling center?_____

5. If you presently were seeking counseling to whom would you turn? Please indicate your preference in the spaces below by placing a "1" next to the counselor you would seek out first, a "2" next to your second choice, and a "3" next to the one you would seek out third.

   ____my own minister
   ____pastoral counseling specialist
   ____psychiatrist
   ____psychologist
   ____social worker
   ____other_____

6. Do you have any additional comments about our community's need for a pastoral counseling center? You may use the space below to answer. Please feel free to attach additional sheets as necessary._____

_____

_____

_____

_____

If a questionnaire such as the one above is used, results will be more meaningful if it is possible to differentiate between the answers received from active church supporters and inactive members. For example, if five hundred questionnaires are returned and two hundred support a center but three hundred do not, it would be helpful to know if the three hundred are predominantly active or inactive members. If the survey indicates that active members of the community congregations support a pastoral counseling center, then it may be worth pursuing further even if inactive members oppose it. To differentiate between the two groups, separate mailings may be used. Questionnaires sent to members of one group may be identified by a slight change in questionnaire format or by devices such as an inconspicuous ink mark on one corner of the questionnaire.

Another method of differentiation is the inclusion of questions which explore the respondent's level of church involvement. For example:

How frequently do you attend church?
____every week
____three weeks out of four
____about twice a month
____once a month or less
____almost never

How many hours a week do you spend engaging in church activities (including Sunday worship)?
____more than five
____two to five
____one
____almost none

How would you describe your participation in church activities?
____very active
____moderately active
____minimally active
____inactive

If questions such as these are used, the researcher must be cognizant of the possibility of biasing respondents' answers (including their willingness to return the questionnaire) by possible judgmental implications about the relationship between their "performance" as church members and their feelings about a center. My own preference is to use separate mailings or other unobtrusive techniques where possible. In my judgment this tends to minimize one source of defensiveness on the part of respondents.

While questionnaires are a relatively economical source of data, they are seldom adequate as a sole source of information. For that reason other sources of data are normally desirable. Intensive investigation of community needs and resources involves a variety of observational and interview processes. These are frequently more difficult and require more creativity, but they often yield especially valuable information. For example, in developing support for a center it is invaluable to have some knowledge about which key persons in the community power structure will be sympathetic to a center and which concerns will be of the greatest significance to them. Since concerns often result from an individual's (or his family's) experience in counseling or therapy, the individual may be reticent to discuss them, hence this kind of information is not readily available. It therefore behooves the center developer to cultivate good relationships with community persons who are likely to help him or her learn this kind of strategically useful information. It hardly needs to be stated that such knowledge must be kept scrupulously confidential by the developer. Its value is in identifying key issues in the community to which members of the power structure are *sensitively attuned*. This kind of information is highly useful in devising developmental strategies.

This raises a pertinent point about program development vis-à-vis community needs. It is not enough to simply identify therapeutic needs within a community. It is also important to particularly identify those needs to which clientele will *respond*. For example, in a particular rural western town with which I am acquainted, the prevailing ethos exerted great pressure on individuals, particularly males, to be stoic and individualistic. Although there were a considerable number of problems apparent to a knowing observer, problems for which family therapy or long-term individual therapy were indicated, relatively few individuals or families sought treatment from the local mental health clinic. However, two astute staff members at the clinic observed that a large number of mothers were experiencing disciplinary problems with their school-age children.

Their observations led them to initiate a series of public forums devoted to the problems of rearing children. Parents responded enthusiastically to these forums (and frankly surprised the author by the extent to which they were willing to publicly reveal their problems). This was a need to which people were attuned and one which they perceived. They responded readily to the resources offered them. Eventually the forum became a referral channel through which many parents sought more extensive treatment. Thus, through sensitivity to a community's perceived need, the clinic was able to provide a service which met that need and also became a bridge to services which met previously unacknowledged needs. A crucial task for the developer of a center is that of gaining an understanding of those needs which the community feels most acutely, and, within the limits of the center's resources and identity, developing programs to meet those needs.

Besides the above-mentioned techniques of questionnaires, interviews, and unobtrusive investigation, there are a number of other resources which should be explored when developing a center. Probably the most obvious resource is the community's clergy. A pastoral counseling center, by virtue of its very identity, is an extension of the ministry of local churches and their pastors. Solid relationships with local pastors, is, in my opinion, de rigueur. On philosophical grounds, a center which operates with antagonism or disregard for the local religious community must be considered suspect. On pragmatic grounds, a center which alienates the religious community foolishly deprives itself of its most important referral source as well as a potential source of supplemental funds. Time spent building and maintaining strong relationships with local pastors and local churches is essential for the ecumenically based center. If the local council of churches or ministerial alliance formally supports the center, so much the better.

Besides the direct support which local pastors can provide, they are also a source of information about the community. They are important resources who can identify key persons or organizations through which the center can gain support and guidance. Judicatory relationships, too, are important. At the very least, center staff need the endorsement of their respective denominational bodies. In some instances denominations may provide direct tangible support. Other professionals who typically are helpful in providing support, information, and referrals include physicians, attorneys, educators, funeral directors, and mental health professionals. In a given community other key persons may become apparent to the observant developer.

The planning phase of center development can be summarized as a series of progressive steps beginning with early consideration of developing a center and moving through information-gathering procedures to strategizing. These steps are summarized below.

1. Identify the community where a center may be developed.
   A. Identify the actual community.
   B. Determine the catchment area which it naturally serves (i.e., What are the political, social, economic, and geographic boundaries of the catchment area?).
2. Identify the community's existing *needs*. To what extent are they presently being met?
3. Identify the community's *resources*.
4. Identify the *power structure* (i.e., who controls the resources?).
5. Determine what *needs a center can effectively serve*. Do they appear to warrant the establishment of a center?
6. Identify the *resources which can be utilized by the center*. Determine tentative ways to utilize them.
7. Based on the above, decide if it is feasible to attempt to develop a center.
8. If the decision is affirmative, *determine a strategy* for developing a center in a manner which will:
   A. meet community needs,
   B. effectively utilize community resources,
   C. be consistent with the precepts of a center, and

D. utilize the most effective center structural model (see chapter 1).

The Development Phase

When evolving a strategy for the development process of a center, it is important to remember that development is just that: *a process*. The process begins with the earliest contact between center-related persons and the community, and continues until the center no longer exists in the community. It behooves the center director and board to keep their organizational antennae sensitively attuned to community needs.

Stated simply, development is the process of evolving an organization in such a way that it and its environment mutually benefit from their relationship. Broadly speaking, there are two objectives in the development process: to provide the best possible service to the environment, and to do so in a way which enables the organization to prosper.

If the planning work has been done well, development is already underway. As mentioned earlier, gathering data for planning has other functions as well. Astute developers utilize their data-gathering contacts from the outset to lay a foundation for the center. While they are obtaining information from individuals and organizations in the community, they are also *conveying* information to them. This is a process which cannot be avoided. Like it or not, they are regarded as representatives of the prospective center. Opinions are formed about the proposed center, whether accurately or inaccurately, on the basis of their demeanor and their perceived competence, as well as the facts which they relate. If they are wise, they will see that they do not convey information haphazardly.

Effective developers are professional in their relationships. They are ethical and direct in their interactions. They are careful to present information honestly. They should not attempt to define policies which are not yet clarified. They also must believe in the organization they are developing. Their own integrity and enthusiasm are key factors in the initial reception of the center. If they maintain a stance of integrity and realistic enthusiasm from the outset, they avoid creating unnecessary resistance.

There is no specific formula for developing an organization. It is a process of creating a mutually beneficial relationship between the community and the center. If this is to occur successfully, the center needs to be clear about what it is and is not. If it represents itself as a family counseling center, then it must have personnel who are competent family counselors. The same is true for other types of treatment, such as crisis intervention, long-term therapy, etc.

It must be wary of institutional omnipotence. Rarely is a center able to provide both crisis intervention and depth-psychotherapy, for example, since the two approaches tend to be mutually exclusive. It is important for the center to be well defined in the minds of its board and administrative personnel. This permits developers to give a clear message to the community regarding the kind of services which it can and cannot provide. For example, if the community is misinformed that a center will offer crisis intervention when it is not prepared to do so, then the stage is set for some serious community relations problems when the center fails to respond to crisis situations as expected.

There are a broad variety of services which a center can offer. A representative list would include such services as: conjoint marital therapy, family therapy, individual brief psycho-therapy, long-term individual therapy, group marital and group individual therapy, crisis intervention, issue-centered counseling, marriage enrichment programs, consultation services, community and church educational programs, training for pastors, and others. Which services will and will not be offered is a function of the objectives and resources of the center. Before attempting to develop services, it is important to work through the goals and objectives of the center with its governing body.

51

The end result should be a clear statement of the center's philosophy, its objectives, and its policies. As the center develops they may be changed as necessary, but they should be established from the beginning.

One format which may be used for this process is a steering committee. Consisting of enthusiastic clergy, professionals, and citizens, the committee should be formed to direct the initial phases of the development process. The committee may wish to retain an organizational consultant to assist it. It is important for the committee to agree on the nature of the center they are creating. Thus, one of the first tasks is a goal-setting process to tentatively define the center. A block of time (three hours is a suggested minimum) needs to be set aside during which the committee members can meet together. At this meeting formative steps are to be taken in establishing center policies and priorities. Additional sessions may be required before the center's policies are sufficiently defined to allow concrete steps toward further development.

There are a variety of ways to conduct this goal-setting process. For example, with the committee gathered together, divide it into groups of not more than eight people. Ask each group to prepare a statement beginning with the words: "The purpose of the (name of center) is to. . . ." Allow approximately twenty minutes for the groups to evolve statements, then reassemble the entire committee. Have each group present its goal statement and allow the group to negotiate until a consensus is reached. If a director has been hired, he or she should be present and should give input during this negotiating process.

Once consensus is reached, again divide into the same groups for consideration of the community needs which relate to the center. Ask the group to define the needs and prioritize them. Information gathered during the earlier planning phase should be made available to the groups. Approximately thirty minutes should be allowed, although more may be required. Again, reassemble the entire committee and repeat the consensus process.

Once prioritized needs have been defined, analyze them in the context of the center's philosophy. Where conflicts exist some needs may be discounted as beyond the purview of the center. In other instances specific needs may serve to clarify the goal statement and to prompt revisions in it. At this stage it is important to include input from the director and/or other professional resource persons to clarify the realistic limits of the needs the center can serve. Here the committee must rely heavily on the professional opinion of its director and/or consultant(s).

The above process continues until the committee has clarified which kinds of services it will provide and which it will not. The details of policy determinations should be avoided at this juncture.

The steering committee's next task, if it is satisfied with the workability of the proposed center, is to effect the transition to a formal organization. During the transitional interim it will continue to function as an *ad hoc* decision-making body. It will continue to cultivate support within the community and to move toward organizational solidarity. Working experiences with the steering committee will suggest persons who would function well as adminstrative board members.

One generally useful model for the administrative structure involves the creation of two bodies—an administrative board and an advisory board. The administrative board should be of workable size (i.e., approximately twelve members). The advisory board, which can be much larger, should include mental health professionals, clergy, prominent townspeople, and related professionals (e.g., physicians, attorneys, educators and institutional representatives from other centers, contributing organizations, and judicatory bodies, etc.). Its purpose is to recommend to the board and to be sensitive to the broad scope of issues which relate to the center.

The administrative board, in which decision-making authority is vested, should include persons with administrative ability, sympathy for the purposes and ideal of the center, and professional and financial expertise. It should include as *ex officio* members the center's attorney, accountant, professional consultants (e.g., psychiatric, organizational, etc.), and director.

Aside from their formal responsibilities, the members of these boards also have other important functions. They serve as interpreters of the center to the community. The public relations function which they perform is of inestimable value. A related function concerns the finances of the center. In order to establish a center, a board should produce sufficient funds to operate the center for two years, drawing upon community and other resources. Once established, the board should continue to raise sufficient supplemental funds to keep the center operating. When board members are being selected, it is important to include persons who are able to perform these functions.

Once the administrative and advisory boards are operating, the center can begin to function in earnest. The board can begin to evolve specific policies for the operation of the center. Fund-raising, which was a peripheral issue during previous phases, can be begun in earnest by the board. Once an adequate financial base (plus physical facilities, personnel, etc.) is established and policies are defined, the center can begin full-scale operations.

Concluding Comments

As experienced administrators and organizational developers will have recognized, the process described above is an idealized process. Rarely, and perhaps never, will the actual development situation coincide exactly with the generalized model of development. In some situations, based on the realities of the community, it is advantageous to begin offering counseling services at an existing parish location before much of the development process is completed. In other situations an agency may have already done much of the preparatory groundwork and be prepared to move directly into the establishment and administration of a center. In some instances there may be no need for a steering committee. Each situation has its own unique needs and resources.

The model suggested here is intended as a general framework, to be adapted to the specific circumstances of the community. Nonetheless, the basic elements of analysis, responsive development, evaluation, and adaptive change are crucial to the effective development of a center regardless of the complexity or simplicity of the setting.

Developmental Resources

AAPC, 3000 Connecticut Avenue, N.W., Suite 300, Washington, D.C. 10008, publishes a list of certifed consultants in all phases of counseling center operation. Send $1.00 with request for list of counseling center consultants.

Biddle, William W. and Biddle, Loureide J. *The Community Development Process*. New York: Holt, Rinehart & Winston, 1965. An excellent presentation of the overall, systematic process of community development.

Buckley, Walter. *Sociology and Modern Systems Theory*. Englewood Cliffs, N. J.: Prentice-Hall, 1967. Chapters 4 and 5. Good presentation of the processes of organizational development. More theoretical than pragmatic but principles are pragmatically applicable.

Ecklein, Joan Levin and Lauffer, Armand A. *Community Organizers and Social Planners*. New York: Wiley, 1962. A casebook of community development applications. Companion volume to Perlman and Gurin (below).

Lawrence, Paul R. and Lorsch, Jay W. *Developing Organizations: Diagnosis and Action*. Reading, Massachusetts: Addison-Wesley, 1969. Helpful (but technical) outline of diagnosis, design, and intervention processes in developing organizations.

Perlman, Robert and Gurin, Arnold. *Community Organization and Social Planning*. New York: Wiley, 1972. Companion volume to Ecklein and Lauffer (above). Good theoretical presentation of development process. See especially chapters 6-9.

Schein, Edgar. *Process Consultation: Its Role in Organizational Development.* Reading, Massachusetts: Addison-Wesley, 1969.

Schindler-Rainman, Eva and Lippit, Ronald. *The Volunteer Community.* Washington, D.C.: NTL Learning Resources, 1971. Excellent treatment of issues in working with volunteers and voluntary agencies. (See also chapters 4 and 5 of Perlman and Gurin for an additional perspective on working with voluntary organizations.)

CHAPTER

3

The Place of Training
in a Pastoral Counseling Center

John E. Hinkle, Jr.

Throughout this anthology, the issue of "quality control" is consistently emphasized. This concern is the result of a basic equation: quality pastoral counseling generates the demand for an ever-increasing quantity of pastoral counseling. An effective pastoral counseling center staff, no matter how large, finds itself eventually unequal to the task of meeting the community's need for services. Thus, the demand for trained professionals to staff pastoral counseling centers is self-intensifying. As this relatively new profession expands, the development of programs to meet the growing demand for trained professionals becomes an important focus in the administration of pastoral counseling centers.

When center administrators consider initiating a training program, a cluster of issues emerges: How will the training program affect and interact with the ongoing business of the center? What factors are important in deciding whether or not to establish a training program? What type and level of program would be appropriate? How would the program best be financed? What new administrative tasks would the program create? This chapter deals with five major training issues as they confront the administrator: (1) the interaction between service and training; (2) the initial decisions concerning a training program; (3) training program operations; (4) strategies for financing; and (5) administrative tasks.

The training question surfaces early in the life of a counseling center. A variety of factors are involved, chief among them the needs of the center constituents, the staffing needs of the center itself, and the strong motivation of many pastors to seek increased skills in counseling. The options of the pastoral counseling center with regard to the training question range on a continuum in which the emphasis at one extreme is heavily on training programs—to the exclusion of counseling services as a primary end—and at the other extreme is heavily on counseling and consulting services to the exclusion of training. The distinction of training as opposed to service is valuable for the purposes of this chapter, even though it is somewhat artificial since training is, after all, a service. The distinction between administrative (in this instance, financial) and professional perspectives forms the basis for the distinction between training and service: Training is the only service offered by pastoral counseling centers which will not easily pay its own way.

Having drawn the training-service distinction on administrative-financial lines, however, it becomes important to point out the interrelationships between the two from a professional standpoint. First of all, the training of professional counselors inevitably involves the practice of counseling by the trainees. This may not be so in the very early stages of training, but part of any program eventually must involve counseling done by the trainees. Thus, any extended counselor training program will, by definition, offer services as well as training. In addition, many trainees find that they need to receive counseling themselves, either as part of their training or in conjunction with it. It would be impossible, then, to train ministers in pastoral counseling to the level of professional functioning without the occurrence of counseling, both by and for the trainees.

Second, quality counseling involves ongoing training. A professional level of service can scarcely be maintained in a pastoral counseling center unless the staff involves itself in ongoing training (an exception to this would be Model D. Group Practice, described in chapter 1). The normal clinical-professional processes of any center (supervision, consultation, staffing, counseling, etc.) are such that participation in these experiences results in a staff training process. As an example, the community-oriented pastoral counseling center would be the most likely to demonstrate an especially strong training dimension in its ongoing clinical process.

Third, a center's involvement in a formal training program expands and enhances the staff training process. A professional staff which is involved in both service and training functions will deliver a higher quality of service over a longer period of time. Through teaching, supervising, and other training activities, clinicians receive feedback and refreshment for their own delivery of counseling services. The educational and training processes in which these clinicians are involved enhance the likelihood that they will also continue their own professional growth and development in a focused and sustained way.

Fourth, in committing itself to the offering of quality services, a counseling center precipitates conditions in which the need for training is most pronounced. Quality counseling services, as mentioned above, generate more work for the center staff. As community demand for services and the pressure for increasing staff builds, so does the pressure for training persons who are potential staff members. Centers which are initiated under the concept of delivering a professional level of service may only come to the full recognition of their need to train additional staff people after a period of successful service to their community.

The training process is also potentially negative in effect. The demand for resources—especially time and energy—on the training side of the center's fthe center's service as well. The effort by allowing too little time for the clinical functioning of the professional staff. An inappropriately liberal use of interns and counselors-in-training could lower the overall quality of the center's service as well. The administrator acts here to balance the involvement of staff and trainees so as to move toward an area of maximum potential.

As a brief section summary, it would seem appropriate to note that training and service, whatever the emphasis of the individual center, are in the long run all but inseparable. Further, they are mutually supportive from the perspective of good clinical practice. Participation in a training program enhances the professional and personal growth of the staff person, facilitating the delivery of quality services. It seems clear that the decision to offer quality services and the decision to engage in training are closely related.

The Initial Decisions Concerning a Training Program

The decision about whether or not a counseling center will offer training should grow out of a careful consideration of five general factors: (1) the mission, purpose, and objectives of the agency; (2) the administrative and clinical model of the center; (3) the resources of the center; (4) the availability of trainees and counselors; and (5) the needs of the constituency.

The first consideration is the concept of "mission" or "purpose" under which the center is established and maintained. What is the center meant to accomplish? Would a training program be an appropriate and effective means of achieving the center's objectives? Answers to these questions and some of their ramifications are intricately related to the ten models overviewed in chapter 1.

For instance, the administrative and clinical model of the center should be taken into account in considering whether to train or not to train. Models C, F, G, and I have the best opportunity to accumulate adequate resources to offer extended training programs, with models B, D, and H also offering significant potential. Models F, C, H, and I would be most likely to see training as part of their basic mission.

Naturally, a choice of models is closely tied to the resources of a center. Included here would be not only finances but also personnel, affiliations with other institutions like churches, seminaries, hospitals, and so on. A major issue is a pragmatic estimation of what the center's resources are in contrast with what will be required for the establishment of a training program. Also included are the needs of the potential trainees. The training needs of rural parish pastors will differ from those of hospital chaplains. The needs of the constituency are important not only in the decision of whether or not to offer training but also in the decision about the type of training to offer.

Closely related to a center's resources is the availability of potential trainees. A successful training program requires reasonably accurate estimates of the numbers of trainees who are not only available and interested but also capable. If the estimate is low, the center may not be able to recruit enough candidates to justify the establishment of a training program.

The center must consider the needs of its constituency in deciding whether or not to train. As Guest's chapter points up, a center which plans to serve only a small local community will feel less impetus to establish a training program than a center which plans to serve a much larger or expanding community.

Training Program Options

Having decided to initiate training, the pastoral counseling center is faced with the need to make a qualitative decision: What sort(s) of training program(s) should be implemented? Presently the range of program options fall into four general categories. The first category covers training for parish or institutional pastoral care. The next category concerns training for pastoral counseling in the parish. The third is training for professional pastoral counseling in a clinical setting. The final category includes training in pastoral psychology or psychotherapy as a professional specialty, including Ph.D. and postgraduate levels of training.

In selecting the training program(s) appropriate to the individual center, it is again important to consider the five factors discussed above, namely, mission, model, resources, trainee availability, and need. The same considerations which cause center personnel to offer training will provide important clues about the type of training most appropriate to that center. Consider, as an example, a center based in a large urban hospital. If its mission encompasses the patients in the hospital, it will want to implement a program which will meet the needs of that inpatient constituency. With adequate resources and the availability of staff and potential trainees, the center might initiate a program for institutional pastoral care. If the center's mission encompassed the larger urban community, with sufficient resources, staff, and trainees, the center might wish to implement training for professional pastoral counseling in the hospital setting but oriented toward the community, i.e. an outpatient program. A flexible administrative model could allow the center to maintain both programs simultaneously. In contrast, a center located in a rural area with limited resources might refrain from involvement with potentially expensive operations yet still initiate programs aimed at increasing area pastors' effectiveness, both in counseling and in pastoral care in the parish setting. The decision, then, concerning the type of training most appropriate to the center will grow out of further consideration of the same issues which formed the basis for the center's original commitment to the training process.

Training programs in pastoral care fall into one of these general formats: (1) short-term workshop experiences; (2) longer term, moderately intensive, one-day-a-week programs; and (3) formal, full-time programs. Of these three, the first two formats are rather straightforward from an administrative point of view. As such they shall receive little attention here, although such neglect is not meant to imply a lack of potential. They are, however, relatively uncomplicated. Even more important for the purposes of this chapter, such programs are easily made financially self-supporting, thus qualifying them, according to the administrative perspective outlined earlier, as "service" rather than "training."

The best-known of the formal, full-time programs are those in Clinical Pastoral Education (CPE). In fact, while it is true that some CPE supervisors offer training in pastoral counseling, and that a few pastoral counseling centers offer non-CPE training in pastoral counseling, the vast majority of formal, full-time training in pastoral care is done in CPE programs. The single major exception to this would be seminary courses in pastoral care. Centers interested in pursuing this training format might, therefore, consult the CPE literature. Most centers, however, prefer to provide other types of training since CPE programs are already widely available in institutional pastoral care settings.

In offering training programs in counseling to parish pastors, the center must be particularly sensitive to the wide range of attitudes, abilities, and educational backgrounds that are likely to be represented by the prospective trainees. Programming here may range from introductory material in pastoral care and counseling in the context of mental health issues, to more advanced training in parish-based pastoral counseling for pastors who have had some introduction to a dynamic-developmental view of personality and who have had some training in interpersonal relationships.

In preparing this chapter I decided to include some initial results of a study which deserves further research but offers important suggestions regarding the tremendous potential of a presently underutilized educational medium, closed circuit educational television. This study grew out of a program involving five hundred twenty-five pastors representing twenty denominations in twenty-five communities scattered throughout a large mid-western state. The participating pastors viewed video taped presentations on closed circuit television concerning pastoral care and mental health, and participated in small group discussion at their viewing sites, both prior to and following the presentation. Thirty mental health professionals also participated. At least one mental health professional was present as a facilitator in each of the twenty-five small groups. A central objective of this series was the development of a context in which pastors could become professionally related to, or personally acquainted with, at least one mental health professional in their own community. An objective of the program was to determine whether such relationships would become liaisons across which supervision, consultation, information, and referrals would pass. A second primary objective of the series was to introduce parish pastors to some of the concepts and terminology of pastoral counseling and referral. The series was intended to encourage both appropriate referrals to local mental health professionals and involvement in pastoral care training on the part of the parish pastor.

A follow-up study measuring the attitudes of pastors who participated in the series indicated that as a result of involvement in the series, pastors made significantly more referrals, had more knowledge of how to refer, had more knowledge of how to decide to refer, and had gained more confidence in their ability to know when to give spiritual counsel, what their own limits were, and what problems to refer for psychological counseling.

One psychiatric consultant who participated in the series as a group facilitator received a total of twelve appropriate referrals from participating pastors in the three months subsequent to the series. At other sites around the state, pastors continued to meet with mental health professionals for consultation and training beyond the duration of the eight-week television series.

Administratively, such a program is nothing if not challenging. Arranging for the use of the media services, recruiting and coordinating personnel, designing organizational charts and brochures, all these tasks—with which many center administrators are unfamiliar in such a context—must be completed for a statewide constituency. Yet the potential for effective training at both the consciousness-raising and behavior change levels is quite remarkable.

A second level of parish-based pastoral counselor training may occur within the facilities of the center itself. Programs of this nature typically include lectures, case seminars, case conferences, interpersonal relations groups, and individual or group supervision. Participants usually meet one day a week for periods of from ten to thirty weeks.

In such programs pastors present counseling experiences from their parish-based counseling. Theoretical input may be provided by specialists in a variety of mental health fields as well as by the center staff. Attention can be given to the unique contextual issues of parish-based, as contrasted with center-based, pastoral counseling. Pastors seem to respond well to this combination of theory, supervised counseling, and peer review.

Regardless of the mode, however, a primary objective of the center that is offering training in parish-based pastoral counseling may be that of offering training options to pastors at various levels of experience, education, and involvement. This strategy makes training available to pastors in a way that will increase their effectiveness in the parish. At the same time, a pastor may choose to use the various training options as intermediary steps toward a higher level of specialization in professional pastoral counseling.

Training in Professional Pastoral Counseling for a Clinical Setting

A center may decide to offer a training program for pastors which would be sufficiently comprehensive so that those who complete the program would be qualified to serve in the center as full- or part-time professional staff members. Training to this level of expertise involves a set of experiences similar to that mentioned above for advanced parish-based pastoral counseling. Beyond that, however, it includes a focus on the clinical context of counseling and a rather extensive utilization of counseling experiences in the center as a basis for education. A comprehensive program would entail at least six types of training experiences: (1) client contact, (2) individual supervision of client contact, (3) group supervision of client contact, (4) consultation in interprofessional case conferences, (5) interpersonal relations groups, and (6) personal psychotherapy.

The initial client contact phase of the training requires careful monitoring and management. The center attempts to assign a counselor-trainee to work with a client whose need level is appropriate to the skill level of the trainee. This method of counselor-training requires initially extensive supervision by the center staff. As an example, the beginning counselor-trainee may spend one hour in supervision for each hour in counseling. A center might even require, as a matter of good clinical practice, that the trainee's first counseling experiences take place in the presence of a supervisor (e.g., in group therapy or in conjoint intake sessions). Only as the trainee gradually gains experience can the counseling-supervision ratio be increased. Eventually, as many as four client-hours might be covered in one hour with a supervisor, but it is crucial that such a step not be taken hurriedly.

Group supervision of the trainee's client contact is an important, even essential, part of a training program at this level. The wealth of feedback and guidance which an experience of group supervision provides cannot be obtained alone in sessions with a single supervisor. Yet individual supervision allows for a more specific and detailed focus. I believe, as do most contributors to this anthology, both modes of supervision are needed.

Interprofessional case conferences are important to the program. These conferences involve the presentation of clinical material on a regular basis—at least once a month. Interprofessional case conferences provide the counselor with the breadth of consultation necessary for a well-rounded view of the client. Psychological, sociological, and psychiatric viewpoints are essential to a full understanding of treatment options. The counselor-trainee's regular participation in such case conferences contributes to the quality of the training as well as the counseling service the trainee provides.

The interpersonal relationship group (IPR) is necessary to the training of the counselor-trainee in several ways. For one, it enables the trainee to get detailed and in-depth feedback from other persons about the trainee's manner of relating, contrasting the impact of the trainee's behavior as over against intention. The group also serves as a forum where trainees can work out personal relationship issues in a peer group with professional leadership. This in turn facilitates case conference functioning, for the IPR group serves as a context in which to deal with conflicts between trainees, conflicts which might otherwise divert or monopolize the case conference agenda. Thus the interpersonal relations group provides two important benefits: (1) feedback for the trainee so that there is congruence between intention and impact in therapeutic and other relationships; and (2) an arena in which relationships among trainees can be worked out so that tensions do not become static or disruptive in case conference functioning. The trainee also benefits from the experience-based learning in group dynamics and group process which this option provides.

This training process is sufficiently intense and comprehensive so as to raise a variety of personal as well as professional issues for the trainee. Each of the training experiences is designed to both surface and also focus on issues which will hinder the trainee's professional development. With few exceptions, trainees in a comprehensive program see the necessity of personal psychotherapy as part of the training process. It is important that personal therapy not be a program requirement, as that would undermine one of the most important prerequisites of successful therapy: that the individual sees the need for the therapy and actively seeks to initiate it. The trainee's supervisor, however, scrutinizes the nature of countertransference issues which arise. If these issues cannot be handled adequately in a supervisory context, the supervisor then recommends therapy for the trainee. It is essential to the training process, however, that therapy be of sufficient intensity that the trainee is unable to avoid personal issues that will hinder professional development and performance. Likewise, counseling skills can be more fully developed when the trainee has experienced the therapeutic relationship from the client's perspective.

As a final comment on the training process at this level, it is important to note the value of supervisory-level consultation. This term is used to denote a meeting of all the supervisors (including administrative) who are working with a particular trainee. Such consultations take place on a regular basis (preferably weekly). The purpose of the supervisory staff conference is the maintenance of consistency in, and the coordination of the variety of experiences for, the trainee in the interest of maintaining educational quality. This structure enables staff members to deal consistently with a given counselor-in-training on specific issues. This practice enhances significantly the impact of the training program on the trainee. It is important, however, that the trainee be informed that confidentiality extends not only to the supervisor but also to this supervisory staff conference as well. It is also important that the supervisory staff conference resist the tendency to become a collusion against the trainee.

Training for Specialization in Pastoral Psychology or Psychotherapy

In considering programs beyond the level of training necessary to qualify the individual as a professional pastoral counselor, two types of training are pertinent.

The first type of training concerns supervision. According to the standards of the American Association of Pastoral Counselors, those counselors who have met the Fellow-level requirements in AAPC need an experience in the supervision of their supervision in order to achieve the status of Diplomate. Thus the center may decide to provide an opportunity for

Diplomates, or other properly credentialed mental health professionals, to offer this supervision of supervision for Fellow-level counselors. Training programs at this level are best carried out in affiliation with seminary or university degree programs.

The center administration may also provide training programs for the center's professional-clinical staff members. Such training experiences are paid for by the center rather than by the staff. In this way the staff members are able to maintain and increase their skills, thus raising the overall quality of service offered by the center. On-site training experiences are provided by bringing in specialists from various areas to present workshops or staff retreats. The center may also provide funds for staff members to seek continuing professional development on a short-term basis away from the center. Ongoing, on-site experience is effective but is only feasible if the necessary professionals are available locally. The content of such programming could be tailored both to the needs of the individuals involved as well as to the developmental or program needs of the center (e.g., training in marriage and/or family counseling).

Strategies for Financing Training Programs

A training program becomes more difficult to finance as its expense and duration increases. Of the training programs mentioned in this chapter, easily the most difficult to finance is the program for professional pastoral counselors in the clinical setting. Here the investment is the greatest, both in professional time and in money. For this reason the focus of this section will be on developing strategies for financing such a program. The principles behind these strategies may be applicable to other training programs as well.

Consider the list of experiences for these counselors-in-training: client contact, intensive interpersonal relations groups, individual supervision, and personal therapy. Each of these experiences requires extensive personal attention to the trainee on the part of one or more highly skilled professionals. Any income derived from the trainee's client contact is outweighed many times over by the expense incurred in the other experiences. Also, most trainees, being ministers, are not likely to have extensive financial resources upon which to draw. In sharp contrast, consider the financial aspect of labs, workshops, or lectures: here one professional works with many others simultaneously, thus lowering the cost per individual. Even the limited incomes one associates with pastors can survive the collective cost of such a program.

In an effort to deal with the financial difficulties, the center may concentrate on three areas: (1) the length of the training period, (2) the amount of the trainee's client contact, and (3) the center's fee structure. Each of these areas offers possibilities for facilitating financial equilibrium, but each also has serious drawbacks which demand careful consideration.

Consider first the trainee who is advanced enough in counseling skills to begin rendering service immediately. This prodigy takes on practically a full caseload the first week and more than pays for the professional training (which, of course, is minimal) from the fees for services rendered.

That such a creature may exist is possible; sightings, however, are rare. The vast majority of counselors-in-training are not financially self-supporting during the course of a normal training period.

The center may, however, choose to employ training periods of sufficient length that the trainee develops to the point of carrying a client load which will allow repayment of costs incurred during early stages of training. Thus the trainee will continue to render service on behalf of the center for a period of time after training is completed. The center is reimbursed, as it were, for earlier expenses from the fees for the trainee's services.

The biggest single difficulty with this strategy is rather straightforward: the trainee grows angry—often, justifiably so—when not reimbursed adequately for increasingly professional work. This problem is mitigated by contracting for the length of the training period and the rationale behind it before the trainee enters the program. It is also important that the amount of time included in the training period be reasonable and fair to all concerned.

If there is a sufficiently great demand for the center's counseling services, the center may increase the amount of client contact on the part of the trainees. Potential counselees are then given the choice between electing to be seen sooner by a counselor-in-training rather than wait for a senior staff member. This strategy protects the counselees interests and increases the income from the fees for the trainees' services, thus helping to defray the cost of training.

The danger here is that the overall quality of service offered by the center may suffer significantly from the input of the relatively inexperienced and unskilled trainees. Such a strategy puts a great deal of pressure on supervisory and case conference sessions. This strategy, however, if employed with adequate safeguards, is quite appropriate to situations in which the constituency's need for services outstrips the center's capacity to serve.

Another means of funding the training program involves restructuring the center's fee scale so that it will cover part or all of the training costs. The most obvious drawback is that restructuring the fee scale raises the cost of the center's services. Such a move may conflict with the center's sense of obligation to provide counseling services regardless of the client's ability to pay. More directly, it may threaten the center's existence, as in the case where the center serves a community with a marginal socioeconomic base. Structuring program costs into the fee scale, then, is most appropriate in a community with an average or higher socioeconomic base. Counselees would be less hard-hit by higher fees, and the strategy would be less likely to conflict with the center's sense of mission to such a community.

Administrative Tasks

A number of administrative tasks are associated with the training process. These are: (1) recruitment, (2) selection, (3) contracting, (4) orientation, (5) trainee's initial client contact, (6) ongoing administration and clinical supervision, (7) evaluation, (8) certification, and (9) alumni relations. These tasks form a checklist of the most important administrative duties associated with the training process.

The recruitment of clergy candidates for training at a center is carried out in a variety of ways. Some programs have recruitment channels that are linked with those of other agencies—hence they occur more or less automatically. For example, if the center is providing a clinical setting for the M.Div. or D.Min. program of a theological seminary, candidates for training will appear as a result of the recruitment processes of the academic institution. If the center has subcontracted with some larger agency for such training, recruitment for certain programs may be a minor issue, with the emphasis falling upon the selection from among recruits of those candidates who have potential for training in pastoral counseling. When such channels of recruitment are not available, however, the center staff turns to denominational officials, alumni of similar training programs, board members, and other constituents, for the nomination of clergypersons who might be in need of such training.

Upon receipt of such a nomination, the center sends letters to the nominees indicating that they have been suggested as being interested in the pastoral counseling training program. It is also well to indicate in the letter that center representatives will be contacting the nominees by phone in a certain number of days in order to talk personally with them. Following the phone conversations the center administrator may mail specific information which describes aspects of the program that may be of particular interest to each nominee.

The next step is that of determining the applicants' potential for training and of discovering what level of training fits their individual interests and capacities. One successful procedure involves having two staff members interview each candidate for intensive training, dividing the responsibilities as follows: one staff member conducts a personality evaluation and writes up a summary of the results. A second staff member conducts an interview focused on the level of theoretical and practical counseling skill that the applicant has already attained. Results of that interview are also written up. Both interviewers then present the results to the full center staff. The staff then makes a decision regarding admission or nonadmission of nominees to training.

If the staff elects to deny admission to a prospective trainee, the denial may be made tentative with the possibility of acceptance at a later time if the applicant meets certain conditions in the interim. If the staff elects to admit the applicant, the next step in the process is to orient the applying person to the program of training appropriate to personal interests, background, and capacities.

Once the program has been presented to the trainee, a contracting phase is obtained. The trainee is asked to surface personal expectations and goals for the training program while the supervising staff members spell out further staff intentions for this person in the context of a particular training program. The contracting takes place in a variety of formal and informal settings within the training program, and is carried on between the trainees and the various professionals involved in the training process. A staff session is held with each trainee early in the program for the purpose of solidifying and reaching consensus concerning the trainee's learning contract.

Orientation processes are specific to the program and to the center involved. Once the recruitment, selection, orientation, and initial contracting is complete, the trainee enters into the structured educational program with other trainees. The ongoing administration and clinical supervision of the training program requires typical maintenance functions so that the program staff, administrative staff, trainees, and counselees meet when and where they should with the facilities they need and the themes designated in order to meet the specified goals of the center's training programs.

Ongoing evaluation is essential to good training. It is important to set aside specific periods of evaluation. The center may set up a mid-year evaluation at which time each trainee is given feedback about the progress already made and the issues needing attention during the remainder of the training year. A final evaluation is conducted near the end of the training period. These evaluations involve a review of the trainees' personal and professional development over the year with attention given to troublesome dynamic issues, such as ability to relate appropriately to peers, supervisors, professionals from other disciplines, or administrators. These evaluation issues do not replace the careful evaluation of therapeutic functioning which takes place in the counseling setting. Each staff member does a brief write-up on each student for the use of an interviewing team, which conducts a face-to-face evaluation with each trainee. The results of the evaluation interview may be recorded and kept on file as a reference source for those who wish to apply for membership in professional organizations which require clinical assessments of a counselor's skills by supervisors and training colleagues.

One issue that arises with reference to training programs of this type is the issue of academic or professional credit. Trainees in any training programs in pastoral counseling centers are provided with academic credit through the center's affiliation with seminaries and/or universities. Since trainees in such programs usually look to the AAPC for professional endorsement, the counselor-trainees and their supervisors keep records of the number of hours spent in various types of supervision and case consultation concerning various types of clients for use in making application to AAPC.

The practice of a center giving out certificates for the completion of certain courses is questionable. Such certificates are easily misused by the recipient to misrepresent the level of skill attained. The giving of such certificates is to be avoided.

Rather, the center should encourage persons who have received training to apply to a professional group such as the AAPC for appropriate certification. The professional processes endorsed and accredited by a wider group of professional peers is the best mechanism for assessing and certifying the continual upgrading of skills and professional competence.

Before closing I think it is important to add a note about the maintenance of ongoing relationships with pastors who have participated in training programs. A newsletter or other regular mailing concerning continued activities at the center, or with news of additional training events, is often helpful in this regard. Alumni respond well to suggested readings in various areas of the pastoral care/pastoral counseling field. As a result of such continuing relationships, center staff members will be called on to assist the pastors with educational events in their churches. Such preventive work is of value for the benefit it brings to the parishioners. Such contacts with parishioners serve also to strengthen the center's relations with its alumni. In this regard it is sometimes advisable to invite pastors to participate in the initial staff conference when the pastor is the referring source, if the referred parishioner agrees. These and many other methods may be utilized to facilitate the valuable relationships between the center and its alumni-constituents.

The outgrowth of such continuity is closely related to the philosophy and theology which undergirds the pastoral psychology movement. In the posture of a mature religious outlook, the link between colleagues "bound" to a commitment of intra/interpersonal harmony necessitates the sharing of responsibilities—responsibilities on a host of levels, many of which begin at the administrative level of a training center. The next two chapters, while more specific in their approach to subjects covered earlier, reiterate this colleagiality both directly and indirectly. Clearly, without such an esprit de corps it is doubtful that this book or anything like it would have much meaning for ministers invested in the development of therapeutic skills to help others help themselves.

PART

TWO

PRACTICAL AND LEGAL STANDARDS

C H A P T E R

4

The American Association of Pastoral Counselors and Pastoral Counseling Center Standards

Richard G. Bruehl

A book of this nature, a "text" of models and constructs, opinions and experiences, naturally lends itself to a discussion of professional organizational standards and membership. In the field of pastoral counseling and psychotherapy, the major certifying organization for such specialized ministry is the American Association of Pastoral Counselors (AAPC). When it was formed in 1964, one of AAPC's major concerns was the development and continued refinement of pastoral counseling centers. Listed in the AAPC *Handbook* is a central purpose of "accrediting pastoral counseling centers and approving training programs in pastoral counseling."[1] Obviously, this commitment entails a number of pragmatic factors which we will review in this chapter. However, some general comments might offer the reader a useful inroad into the five chapters of this section, Part II.

Pastors specializing in counseling and therapeutic ministries have demonstrated a special affinity for ecumenical and other church-related counseling centers. Such centers, somewhat unique among the mental health disciplines, provide settings for the practice of the art and science of pastoral counseling which are congruent with the traditional concept of ministry as integrally linked to an ongoing corporate body. In many communities the pastoral counseling center is the primary investment of its associated churches in the pastoral caring function of outreach.

Further, the center serves as an important link between the religious community and the related secular resources in the mental health fields. And finally, the value of colleagial relationships among staff, and increasingly clients, promotes a quality of care and support which is of high value to those who serve and are served by a center.

A second reason for the development of the pastoral counseling center is the need to achieve support for a new speciality in the field of ministry. While some few large churches can generate sufficient internal financial resources to support a counseling ministry, for most this is not possible. It is far easier to spread out the cost of providing such a service among several interested congregations than it is to depend on one for total support. In many communities it has been found that the establishment of a pastoral counseling service is the first ecumenical activity which has endured over time. Certainly this fact underscores both the vitality of the pastoral counseling movement as it seeks to meet a significant segment of the need for personal counseling and therapeutic services and, perhaps as no other area of ministry, the power of the concern for wholeness to draw persons of widely varying theological and churchly backgrounds together in a common cause.

A third and final factor which has contributed to the development of pastoral counseling ministries in a center setting is the efficiency of the concept. As a group, pastors and churches are perhaps more sensitive than most groups in our society to the burdens which private health care places upon significant segments of our population. As a result, most pastoral counselors have attempted to provide their services at the highest level of quality for the lowest possible cost. The center structure, often utilizing existing but heretofore unused space in churches and deriving at least a baseline of financial support from its associated religious community, offers an opportunity to provide services at a cost which would be difficult or impossible in other organizations.

Hence, for these and perhaps other more obscure historical

reasons, the pastoral counseling center has emerged in the past fifteen to twenty years as a primary vehicle for the practice of a specialized ministry. It further seems likely, if present trends continue, that such centers will become even more firmly entrenched as a primary setting for the work of the pastoral counselor.

The AAPC in Relation to Pastoral Counseling Centers

The AAPC functionally relates to pastoral counseling centers in three formal modes. Through one of its standing committees, Centers and Training, the organization provides standards, consultation and review, and accreditation procedures. Having adopted a set of standards for pastoral counseling centers, developed by a reasonable consensus of experienced professionals in the field, AAPC offers emerging and established centers an objective target to which to aspire and around which to organize their development. In short, one who wishes to know what pastoral counselors feel an effective center should look like has only to review the "Standards" for an answer. [2]

In addition to providing guidelines through its formal standards for pastoral counseling centers, the Centers and Training Committee has developed an informal brokerage service of consultants. Of particular use to centers in the early stages of formation, but potentially helpful to established centers as well, the *Directory of Consultants for Pastoral Counseling Centers* lists over sixty persons distributed throughout the country, representing a wide variety of training and experience, capable of providing effective consultation to centers in their formative and more developed stages. [3] The *Directory* provides specific information on consultants' addresses, telephone numbers, special interests and qualifications and, in most cases, suggested fees. Without question, in the opinion of the writer—an opinion validated by numerous experiences—the single most valuable investment for a new center is a consultative relationship with an individual of experience and vision, and the flexibility to apply this knowledge to a specific local situation. Guidance from such a person or persons can save a local center from untold grief and pain and can significantly increase the probability that the venture in question will be a successful one.

A second formal relationship between the AAPC and local pastoral counseling centers is the provision of a review and accreditation process. After one year of continuous operation, a pastoral counseling center becomes eligible for provisional accreditation and after three years is eligible for full accreditation by AAPC.

Some have questioned the value of accreditation but reflection provides some persuasive answers. In the first place, the accreditation of a center immediately associates it with an authority which transcends the local community. For whatever value such recognition may have for the local center, an ongoing association with a national body of increasing size and significance in effect says to the community, "we have been examined by a group of our peers, have been found to meet the standards which they have set for such centers as ours, and have been found to be in compliance with these standards."

In addition to the public relations value of accreditation, the time may soon be coming when having been through a rigorous examination by a national body will spell the difference between recognition and use or neglect. No one at this point, for example, can foretell the precise shape of federal health care legislation, but most seem agreed that if and when it comes, it will favor those professional groups and services demonstrating a high degree of responsibility in the rendering of their services. One important aspect of proving the accountability of the service organization will be its relationship to a national accrediting body.

Finally, the accreditation of the pastoral counseling center ties it in a special way to its mother professional group and in doing so strengthens that body. For whatever purposes, whether it be dealing with the government, church officials, or other professional groups, the whole profession of the special ministry of pastoral counseling is strengthened by the formal association of those organizations, many of which are large and formidable powers in their own right, with the national body representing all specialized pastoral counseling practitioners.

An examination of the process of seeking accreditation reveals still more benefits to a center. The first step in the accreditation procedure, for instance, is the completion of the application form and its submission to the chairperson of the Centers and Training Committee. While this paperwork may be to some an annoyance which seems to detract from more vital aspects of professional functioning, many have reported that organizing the material has given them a clearer concept of their own operations, a kind of self-study.

Assuming the paperwork to be in order, the chairperson of the Centers and Training Committee initiates the organization of a site visiting team in consultation with the regional committee chairperson in whose region the center is located. A team of three professional pastoral counselors is then assigned the task of visiting the center to review its structure and function. The teams, usually over a one-and-a-half to two-day period, review business practices; clinical process, including supervision and consultation; the handling of administrative relationships among the center staff and between the staff and board of directors; and discuss in depth the long-range planning of the center to achieve the specific goals indicated by the board and staff.

While the primary purpose of the on-site review of a center requesting accreditation is evaluation, practice shows that it generally includes a strong component of consultation as well. As the team listens, observes, questions, and reflects upon its communications with the center staff and board, new insight begins to emerge, just as in a constructive counseling experience at a personal level. Typically, center directors are appreciative of the opportunity to have a group of peers, with similar commitments and yet who are not emotionally invested in the particular center under review, to consult with.

Further, in this regard, it is the policy and hope of the AAPC and its committee that these visits be part of a two-party dialogue between the centers on the frontline of the profession and the national organization. Just as the center learns from the team, so too the AAPC is helped to clarify its goals, purposes, and identity as well as its weaknesses. Thus it is in these situations, as well as in the membership review committees, that AAPC ceases to be merely a remote objective entity and becomes a personal communication network of people working for the relief of needless human suffering and aspiring to nurture all people in their growth in the image of God.

The results of the on-site visit discussed immediately above are organized by the team in a written evaluation which describes the details of the visit and the findings of the committee, and makes a recommendation for or against accreditation. The center is provided with a copy of the final draft of the report, and the other copies are kept on permanent file in the national office. This report serves as the recommendation to the national Centers and Training Committee which first acts on the report and finally submits it to the AAPC Council for acceptance or rejection. The Council remains the final authority in the accreditation of a center with the center maintaining the right of appeal of any decision, first to the Centers and Training Committee and then to the Council.

At the present time nearly twenty centers have achieved accreditation while a number await the completion of the process. In addition four centers have been accredited as service centers and approved as pastoral counseling training centers. See AAPC *Directory* for a current listing of those centers.

Standards for Pastoral Counseling Centers

In November 1975, the AAPC Council approved new standards for pastoral counseling centers. These standards, adopted by the general membership, will provide guidelines for center development and evaluation for some time to come. To arrive at the recommendations to the Council, the Centers and Training Committee did extensive research involving well over one hundred directors of pastoral counseling centers in order to obtain as close to a consensus as possible for the present state of opinion regarding what ought to be required of centers seeking accreditation from the AAPC. The result is a document which both upholds some basic principles and at the same time makes some major adjustments in the formal "Standards for Pastoral Counseling Centers."

The purpose of the final section of this analysis of the relationship between the AAPC and Pastoral Counseling Centers is to explore the standards in depth. While no attempt will be made to restate the norms in detail, the basic rationale behind the document as well as specific critical changes will be discussed. It is hoped that the reader will thus gain a clear picture of current AAPC expectations of pastoral counseling centers.

Part I of the new standards restates the support of the association for pastoral counseling centers, recognizing them as "an important extension of the life of the religious community." The introductory section further underscores the role of pastoral counseling centers in "prevention, education, evaluation, referral, and psychotherapy" in the field of "personal and interpersonal relations and wholeness." The latter phrase was substituted for "mental health" because it more adequately reflects the unique pastoral and theological concern underlying the pastoral counseling movement.

In Part I specific standards are outlined. Several changes of particular import are summarized in the following paragraphs. First, the new norms attempt to clarify the complementary relationship between the professional staff and the board of the center. Professional and clinical standards are clearly defined as being the province of the professional staff while the board is charged with the responsibility for finance, education of the community, hiring of qualified personnel, and the interpretation of community needs to the staff. In addition, the board is supported in its retention of the oversight and determination of the general policy of the center. Recognizing that each of these sets of decisions arise out of a give-and-take process, the standards attempt to clarify the specific authorities to be granted to both staff and board.

A second major change involves an issue important to centers located in less populated areas of the country. Whereas previously the standards called for two pastoral counselors to be employed by a center, the current revision, while restating the desirability of such a "dynamic duo," allows for a minimal staff of one pastoral counselor and one "counselor from another professional discipline fully qualified and certified." This change, receiving broad consensual support in our research, encourages persons in areas sparsely populated with pastoral counselors to develop pastoral counseling centers using the resources at hand. In the opinion of the writer a center is unquestionably strengthened by the presence of two qualified persons from the same profession. It can also be argued that some very effective services utilizing two professional people from different disciplines have been developed.

A change related to the one described immediately above requires that the director of a pastoral counseling center hold Fellow or Diplomate status in the AAPC. Previously, only Diplomates were approved as center directors. This change recognizes the development of a fairly large pool of persons in the Fellow category who are fully qualified by training, experience, and education to direct the activities of pastoral counseling programs and broadens significantly the number of available persons from whom leadership may be drawn.

Addressing the long-standing requirement that a center develop responsible administrative policies, the new standards articulate the meaning of this norm. "Responsible policies" in the areas of personnel, administration, fees, record-keeping, referral communication, privileged communication, and supervision are now defined to mean the formulation, in writing, of guidelines appropriate to the specific center in question. The goal underscored in this section is that a person working within a particular setting will apply consistently and nondiscriminatingly the basic policy determined by the staff and board to all persons seeking service from the center. Further emphasized is the need for consistency and fairness in the handling of the various personnel issues which arise in any organization. Publication, understanding, and a commitment to written policies can help avoid many troublesome administrative and clinical issues which will inevitably arise.

In the matter of fees-for-service, the new standards seek to change what previously, for some centers, could have been a self-destructive policy. While recommending a sliding fee scale and underscoring the historic principle that pastoral counseling centers ought to provide a service to anyone regardless of the ability to pay, a recognition of the practical limits of this ideal is stated. Under the circumstance when a center has absorbed all of the persons it can at a low- or no-fee level, adequate referral procedures are recommended. Hence, while a pastoral counseling center cannot be expected to jeopardize its existence by accepting all persons for service without concern for their ability to support it, pastoral counseling centers are charged with the duty of seeing to it that clients whom it cannot serve are directed to appropriate agencies or persons where their needs can be met.

Previously the "Standards for Pastoral Counseling Centers" required psychiatric consultation as part of its ongoing service plan.[4] While the revised standards maintain the principle of pastoral counselors working cooperatively with other professionals, centers are now required to use consultants which best fit the particular needs of the center, whether from psychiatry, psychology, social work, pastoral theology, or other medical specialties. Consultation of a regular, ongoing variety protects both the clients and staff of the center by maintaining a continuous flow of information regarding clients seen by a center, and if such consultation is competent, ought to contribute positively to the quality of service available in the center. Thus, both staff and boards are asked to assess the resources available in their communities to determine those persons who have the most to offer in their field and who seem ready to make the greatest contribution to the specific orientation and goals of the center in question.

It goes without saying that part of the responsibility of the staff to its clients remains the evaluation of the need for specific services offered only by other professional persons, whether consultants of the center or not. Hence, one would not use a theological consultant if the counselor detects symptoms which might be indicative of a brain tumor.

The section on specific standards ends with the requirement that the pastoral counseling center has formally committed itself to the "Code of Ethics" contained in the AAPC *Handbook.* Further, the center is asked to be prepared to demonstrate its compliance with that code.

The third and fourth sections of the standards document details accreditation procedures and the process for the maintenance of accreditation. A formal procedure for the appeal of decisions made by an accreditation team is also outlined. Major significant changes in these sections include the following:

1. Reduction from two years to one year of continuous operation as the time when a center may apply for *provisional accreditation.*
2. Reduction from *five* years to *three* as the period required before a center may receive full accreditation.
3. Clarification of the process of maintaining accreditation to include: (a) payment of the annual membership fee, and (b) filing an annual report with both the regional and national committees on Centers and Training containing number of persons served, number of satellite centers in operation (if any), dates of board meetings held, report of

financial solvency, actions brought against the center, and other pertinent information.

4. Provision for a site visit at least every seven years after a self-study (for which guidelines will be provided).

5. Detailing and clarification of violations eventuating in the loss of accreditation and the provision for a formal process for handling such situations, to protect the rights both of the center and AAPC.

To the reader, especially if he or she is relatively uninitiated in the work of the AAPC, the changes detailed above and, indeed, the whole matter of standards may appear as another reel of red tape. However, it is the feeling of the Centers and Training Committee that these standards are indeed life-giving in that they provide a clear structure which demands responsibility yet offers considerable freedom to each center to organize itself in ways which best fit its circumstances and needs.

Summary and Conclusion

The AAPC historically has had a special affinity with the development of pastoral counseling centers as a community resource. Such centers are viewed as legitimate and important extensions of the church's ministry to "all sorts and conditions of men and women." The organization in both its membership, center standards, and review processes incarnates its commitment to developing excellence in the field of pastoral counseling.

Through its published "Standards for Pastoral Counseling Centers," coordination of consultation activities, and processes for accreditation and maintenance, the AAPC both promotes and undergirds the important frontline work of its individual members and affiliated agencies. In this way, the AAPC most clearly demonstrates its commitment to its central goals: the provision of a high quality of service for persons in emotional and spiritual difficulty and the stimulation of personal growth toward wholeness within the context of an overriding pastoral, theological, and religious concern.

Notes

1. *Handbook of the American Association of Pastoral Counselors* (New York: American Association of Pastoral Counselors, 1978), p. 1.

2. *AAPC Handbook,* pp. 32-33.

3. All materials mentioned in this paper are available from the central office of the AAPC, 3 West 29th Street, New York, New York 10001.

4. *AAPC Handbook,* p. 32.

C H A P T E R

5

Business Practices
in Pastoral Counseling Centers
John C. Carr

It is a basic assumption of this chapter that "business practice" and "clinical practice" in a pastoral counseling center are integrally related the one to the other, and that both are oriented to the specificity of *"pastoral* counseling." The psychological effects of business practices on the expectations of clients as they enter therapy and as the therapy proceeds is not to be taken lightly and, where the needs of the sponsoring body and/or the counseling or support staff dictate business practices which may be at odds with optimal clinical functioning, this reality needs to be recognized and taken into account. The need for economic stability, including the survival of the center, may dictate business policies which are tangential to a policy dictated by clinical judgment, but if it does, then that needs to be understood clearly.

The "Code of Professional Ethics" of the AAPC clearly states that: "The pastoral counselor stands ready to render service to individuals and communities in crisis, without regard to financial remuneration, when necessary."[1] This same principle is enunciated in the AAPC "Standards for Pastoral Counseling Centers": "It shall be the goal of the center to render service to all persons and not to deny service because of the inability to pay."[2] At the same time the AAPC standards state that: "A Center must give evidence of a sound financial structure and plan for long range financing."[3]

Although there is potential contradiction in these statements, and in the actual business practices of the centers studied for the purpose of compiling this paper, the basic principle which emerges involves responsible stewardship on the part of the client, the individual pastoral counselor, and/or the pastoral counseling center in which he or she works, and the religious community (or communities) to which the pastoral counseling service is related.

Income Sources

It seems to be taken for granted that pastoral counselors will receive a major proportion of the financial support for their work from the fees charged to their clients. There is even a trend for fees to be charged for extended counseling by parish pastors and parish staff counselors whose salary is paid by the parish. In the latter case, fees charged sometimes go to the church treasurer for inclusion in general parish revenue.

There are three basic economic issues that a pastoral counseling center must confront. First, there is the implementation of the bipolar principle that people ought not be turned away because of a lack of ability to pay and that everybody ought to pay according to his ability. Second, there is the matter of a decision regarding the extent to which the total center budget will be paid for out of fees from clients. Third, there is the question of whether training programs are to be financed, that is, to what extent is cost of training a student paid for by fees or tuition charged to the trainee? The reader may find it useful to reflect on each of these issues separately, but one has to keep in mind how interrelated they are.

Determination of Client Fees

The most popular way of determining client fees would seem to be a fee schedule based on gross family income and size of family. Sometimes clients are shown the schedule and asked to indicate what the appropriate fee would be. Sometimes they are asked to provide information on income and family size on their application form or when they call for an appointment. In some instances, the fees are then negotiated by a business manager. More often the counselor obtains this information, and contracts for the fee, in the initial interview.

In some instances, the fee schedule is taken as virtually inflexible, with any claim by clients that they cannot meet the suggested fee being regarded as resistance to therapy. In other instances, the schedule is seen as a basis for negotiation, with the possibility of fees being charged which are lower than those stipulated. When this is done, in some cases, the cost of the "subsidy" thus provided may be absorbed by special donations from individuals or congregations. In other cases, the "subsidy" is not accounted for as a subsidy but is just "written off." In general, however, the assumption is made that one can construct a fee schedule which, with a normally distributed population, will generate the revenue needed to run the center.

There does not seem to be any foolproof formula for constructing a fee schedule. Schedules are drafted, tested over an initial period to see if they generate the required income, revised upwards if necessary, and certainly revised upwards in relation to increased fixed costs. It is important to estimate the average income level of the community to be served, however, and to take account of the possibility that potential clients may be in a higher or lower income bracket than the community average. This is especially true for pastoral counseling centers serving small communities or rural areas and, in the case of rural areas, the question of how one calculates "gross" income can be somewhat complex.

In a suburban context, either as a basis for drafting a fee schedule or as a basis for negotiating fees without a formal schedule, the formula of $1 per session (weekly) per $1,000 annual income is often used, as it is in church stewardship campaigns.

Where a fee schedule is used, some determination needs to be made with respect to the minimum fee acceptable and the maximum fee. In some cases, these are infinitely variable with weekly fees ranging from $1–$100 plus. In others, the range is from $5–$10 weekly to $40–$50 weekly. At the top end of the scale, referral to private practice therapists becomes possible without economic hardship for the clients, and it may well be that pastoral counselors need to suggest that option to such clients. Some would raise questions concerning the ethics of a pastoral counseling center client paying a fee equivalent to private practice fees, especially when he or she is a trainee, but the ethical issue at stake is really a more basic one—that of the center's commitment to provide adequate supervision and consultation so that all clients receive quality care. If the pastoral counseling center has made that commitment, it need not apologize for charging "private practice level fees" to those who can afford it.

Some characterize the fee schedule approach as a "Robin Hood" or take-from-the-rich-to-care-for-the-poor style of operation. Others speak of it as an operationalization of the well-known principle that "all the world is a bell-shaped curve." However, the use of a fee schedule in a pastoral counseling center can also be linked with a biblical/theological emphasis. At the heart of current ecclesiastical stewardship is an emphasis on proportional participation in the ministry of reconciliation and healing which a Christian congregation exercises in its community. There is a sense in which, whether he or she is receiving counseling in individual, conjoint, family, or group therapy, the center's client makes a commitment to finding meaning which involves more than just personal growth and development. The client becomes part of a community in which love for self, love for neighbor, and love for God are inseparably connected. There are, however, some issues which should be faced, and these are raised by Moss and Hinkle in later chapters.

Where services other than the weekly therapy hour are provided (e.g., testing, staffing of the intake evaluation before a consultant and/or other staff members, etc.), some determination needs to be made concerning how the center's clients are to pay for these services. They can be regarded as general overhead costs, hence paid for out of the general revenues, or they can be regarded as costs which need to be attached specifically to the particular clients in relation to whom they are incurred. If the latter is the case, then they need to be included in the fee schedule, and there are at least two ways of doing this.

First, there can be specific charges for each component of the intake procedure. These may be scaled to income and size of family or may reflect the actual cost of the service. This method has a great deal of flexibility. The second is more formalized because the cost of the components of the intake procedures are lumped together and the client is assessed a charge for the intake, either scaled to income and size of family or determined by actual costs.

In either instance, many pastoral counseling centers use one fee schedule for members of churches which provide support for the center and another schedule for people who come from other churches or who have no church affiliation. Members of supporting churches receive a small discount on the cost of weekly sessions and a substantial reduction on the cost of evaluation.

Fee-setting for group therapy involves a decision with regard to whether or not clients should be charged less than they would be if they were being seen in individual or conjoint therapy. One needs to take account of factors such as the reality that groups usually meet for a longer period of time than is provided for individual sessions, that therapy is not diluted but intensified, that the therapist is certainly not working less hard, that there may be more than one therapist, etc.

General practice seems to be to charge a fee for group therapy that is roughly two-thirds of the applicable individual session fee. One fee schedule uses quite broad income categories to establish its group fees so that there is one fee for those with incomes in the lower range, a higher fee for those in the middle range, and a still higher fee for those in the upper range. Where couples are being seen in group therapy the practice of some pastoral counseling centers is to see both spouses for only 60 percent of the fee they would be charged as individuals. For instance, at one income level, individuals are seen in a group for individuals at $13 a session, whereas a couple at the same income level is seen for $16 a session in a group for married couples. Some centers charge the same for group therapy as for individual therapy, although with a lower ceiling.

An issue relevant for individual, conjoint, and group therapy is whether to charge for all sessions scheduled, i.e., whether or not the client is able to be present. With reasonable notice (e.g., twenty-four hours), centers seem not to charge for cancelled individual and conjoint sessions, the assumption being that in short-term practices one can often use the time for consultations or initial sessions. Some do charge for all sessions scheduled in group therapy, the assumption being that no one else can be scheduled to be seen in place of the absentee.

Third-Party Payments

Although there is some difference of opinion concerning whether or not pastoral counselors should be involved in third-party payments, there are situations in which insurance applicability is clear and pastoral counselors need to explore this possibility with their clients. They should be aware that, even if insurance coverage is applicable, their client may elect not to make the necessary claim.

In any case, the counselor needs to make it clear that insurance coverage does not remove the client's responsibility to see that bills are paid. Also, counselors need to keep in mind that it takes time and effort on their part to process insurance claims, even when they lay responsibility for the collection of such claims where it belongs, that is, on their clients.

Insurance applicability is clear where clients are covered for the services of licensed psychologists and the pastoral counselor has sought and obtained such licensing. With regard to the appropriateness of such licensing, one needs to take note of the following statement made by AAPC in 1974:

The Council of the American Association of Pastoral Counselors, representing the membership, takes the position that Pastoral Counselors, who as professional religious leaders are the representatives of the religious bodies which authorize them by ordination or other means, practice their specialized ministry under the authority and oversight of their respective religious bodies. They neither seek nor accept certification or licensure by the state.[4]

During the following year, AAPC's National Research Committee reported that insurance coverage had been provided for the clients of pastoral counselors under several categories other than pastoral counselor or psychologist (viz., marriage counselor, social worker, vocational counselor, mental health worker, and education specialist). At that time and since, coverage has also been provided under the following conditions: where the client is being seen on referral by a medical doctor or a psychologist; where supervision is being provided by a medical doctor, psychologist, or social worker; or where the agency in which the client is being seen is an "approved" agency, which means it has a medical director. A variant of the last category is the situation in which the pastoral counseling center is the outpatient section of a hospital's chaplaincy division and has a psychiatric consultant who takes part in decisions concerning diagnosis and treatment planning. The AAPC National Research Committee Report lists insurance companies known to have paid claims made for counseling by pastoral counselors on their own merits and for counseling done by pastoral counselors with other certification. The report also describes the current situation with regard to state licensing.

Centers can help counselors and clients test the applicability of insurance by developing a set of instructions which detail the most effective way to submit an application. These can be given to a client. A center can also provide a printed description of its operation which will educate insurance carriers by whom claims are being made concerning the kind of therapy which is being provided. Clients can also be provided with a description of their therapist's credentials to send in with their claim.

Further, the pastoral counseling center needs to decide whether the client for whom insurance is applicable will be charged at the rate specified by the fee schedule, or at a standard rate which may be in the upper range of fees charged. Insurance coverage does make it possible for a client to be seen by other mental health professionals than pastoral counselors, and a pastoral counseling center may have an obligation to offer referrals to such clients.

Donations or Grants from Congregations, Judicatories, Individuals, and/or Foundations

It seems to this writer that the critical factor at stake in determining whether or not a pastoral counseling center will seek financial support in the form of donations or grants is the reality that doing so will take some member of the counseling staff away from the primary task of providing counseling. This is the case even if a portion of the work of developing support is being done by a volunteer member of the center's board. This is especially true when one is trying to develop financial support from foundations or governmental agencies. The risk in seeking support from individuals is that doing so will encourage fantasies of power on the part of those individual donors and, perhaps, result in the counseling center's loss of autonomy.

On the other hand, development of financial support from congregations and judicatories can go hand-in-hand with the development of referral sources and with preventive mental health work and, indeed, can enhance both of these aspects of a pastoral counseling center's work. There is a very real sense in which, as congregations and judicatories become partners in ministry with a pastoral counseling center in the economic sense, they also become partners in its service to their own constituencies and the broader community.

Payment for Training and Consultation

Whether or not it runs a training program in pastoral care and/or pastoral counseling, a center will need to take into account the reality that its pastoral counselors will require supervision and/or consultation. From a business standpoint there are several models possible. However, there are three which are basic.

First, the center may maintain a ratio of AAPC Diplomates, Fellows, and Members which allows for adequate supervision or consultation within the staff on an individual and/or group basis. In this situation no fees would be receivable, although the cost of the time spent in supervision or consultation would be part of the general overhead costs of the pastoral counseling center.

Second, the center may use a variety of consultants and/or supervisors from within the center's staff and the community, with payments for outside services borne as part of general overhead.

Third, the center may assume that, apart from initial consultation at the time of the evaluation of each client, the responsibility for providing for supervision according to his or her need will be the financial responsibility of each therapist.

Where a training program is being run, decisions will need to be made concerning the relationship between fees charged for the training and the actual costs of running the program. The extent to which it will be possible to run training programs without charging the full cost to the participants will depend on the amount of money available from other sources. Where subsidy money for educational programs is available, a decision needs to be made on whether to use it to lower the cost across the board or to provide scholarship assistance where it seems to be needed most.

Budgeting for Expenses

Staff Remuneration

Four philosophical questions arise in relation to the provision of a pastoral counselor's remuneration in a center practice:

a. To what extent will remuneration be tied to credentials?
b. To what extent will remuneration be tied to experience and skills?
c. To what extent will remuneration be tied to sharing in the pastoral counseling center's administration?
d. To what extent will remuneration be tied to actual income generated?

Other questions directly related to these four concern the way in which a counselor's remuneration is negotiated. Some counselors may prefer a standardized salary. Some may prefer remuneration based on commission. Others may want an "income package" closely related to the normative parochial model, which includes a proportioned salary, housing and travel allowance, and other considerations.

Where a pastoral counseling center hires nonordained counselors, it will need to sort out equivalencies with AAPC standards for such personnel and will need to make special provision for their inclusion in insurance policies.

One model for determining counselor remuneration is that of *negotiated salaries.* Questions like the following concerning the range of salaries will need to be answered:

1. What is appropriate remuneration for a counselor who has equivalent educational and clinical qualifications? The law of supply and demand requires some equivalence to the counseling professions generally and the field of pastoral counseling and ecclesiastical offices in particular.
2. What is the level of responsibility the counselor will have in the center? How hard does he or she want to work?
3. What is an appropriate division of the income derived from the center's productivity?

There seems to be an assumption, when this model is used, that all counselors are paid at the same level for housing, travel, pensions, income insurance, health and hospital coverage, etc.

With this model, the issue of the extent to which the pastoral counseling center will operate on its fee-generated income is a critical one. Very careful cost analysis is required.

Another model can be characterized by the term *percentage salaries*. In this model, there is no provision for level of experience and skill since income is determined by how hard the counselor works. Of course, experience and skill will affect individual productivity. Neither does formal accreditation have any bearing on salary, although it does on the question of whether or not one is hired. The actual percentage of fees generated by the counselor which he or she receives as salary is determined by the extent to which the counselor participates in the nonfee-generating activities of the center (e.g., administration, task forces, etc.). The range of percentages is determined by the counselor's investment in nonfee-generating activities at his/her center. In some pastoral counseling centers which use this model, the range is 70–90 percent. That is, 5–30 percent is kept by the center to carry nonsalary costs. In this model, the percentage salary is the complete package of remuneration, and the counselor becomes responsible for provision of his or her own pension, health and disability insurance, etc.

One issue when using this model is whether counselors have to wait until their clients pay in order to collect their salaries, or whether they collect their salaries on the basis of their monthly charges. Where, as is the case with at least one pastoral counseling center, counselors are paid according to their charges as long as the client's balance does not exceed $200, the pastoral counseling center needs to make provision for carrying outstanding charges as part of its overhead. Another issue is the need to maintain a balance of income levels so that no one counselor has an overload of low-paying clients.

A variant of the percentage salary model is the *proportional salary* model which is tied to actual productivity and credentials. In a pastoral counseling center where, for example, the average session fee is $25, a Member might receive $18 per client hour, a Fellow might receive $21, and a Diplomate might receive $23, with $7, $4, and $2 per hour, respectively, going to the center to cover other costs. Assuming a weekly client load of thirty hours over forty-five weeks, a Member's annual compensation would approximate $24,000, a Fellow's $28,000, a Diplomate's $31,000.

A more complicated model, which provides somewhat more security for counselors, is the *salary-plus-percentage* model, in which counselors are paid a basic minimum salary for their work as counselors plus a percentage of the actual income which they generate. With such a model as this, adjustments to salary need to be made to compensate counselors for participation in educational and administrative activities.

Another model is one in which counselors are hired at a salary in return for which they are expected to work a specified number of hours for the pastoral counseling center (e.g., 4½ days) and are also given the opportunity to use center facilities for a specified number of hours of private practice counseling (e.g., 4–6 hours). This model is sometimes referred to as a *salary-plus-private-practice.*

In some instances where this model is used, the center refers potential private practice clients to its staff members. Thus, when the center's caseload is such that it cannot take any more clients into therapy, it may provide the client with the names of three private-practice therapists, one of whom will be an agency therapist, with the decision as to whom the client will see being left up to the client. A pastoral counseling center may use this model for public relations purposes. In other words, the center may keep specified salaries at a level which will not cause problems in relationship to ecclesiastical structures, while at the same time giving its therapists an opportunity to earn any income more in keeping with their experience and qualifications.

The question of salary increases can be a difficult one, and the issue at stake is that of whether salary increases should be tied to increased productivity or increased fees. Using the percentage salary model, merit increases are automatically tied to increased productivity of the individual. In a center where the negotiated salary model is used, it is necessary to work out a formula which will relate overall and individual increases in productivity to the salaries of particular counselors. It would seem appropriate that *cost-of-living increases* should be tied to increased fees which may be increased across the board or in a selective way, or to increases in subsidization.

Contracted Services

The cost of "contracted services" is a professional reality. A center may be able to arrange for donation of consultant services from a psychiatrist, specialists in marriage, family, child, or adolescent therapy, and social workers through an institution interested in community mental health services. It is much easier to get an institution to donate the services of its specialists as a token of its commitment to the community's mental health than it is to get private practitioners to give up potentially revenue-producing hours.

Where it is not possible to obtain the donation of such services, it will be necessary to budget for such services out of fees or out of donations. An alternative to outside contracting for consultation in the areas listed above is to ensure that the pastoral counseling center staff includes specialists in a broad range of areas. In my opinion, it is important that there be competent medical consultation, preferably psychiatric, on all clients seen in a pastoral counseling center. An alternative to providing this at the center is to have each client seen for medical evaluation by a physician and/or by a psychiatrist, with whom the counselor then consults.

A center may also arrange for the psychological testing of its clients and, in the view of the present writer, ought to do so. The cost of this may be budgeted for as part of general overhead or billed directly to the client. The AAPC "Code of Professional Ethics" states that:

The use of psychological diagnostic tests by a pastoral counselor is not ordinarily expected nor encouraged. Their use must be related to appropriate supervised training and affiliation with the American

Psychological Association or in conjunction with an adequately trained counseling or clinical psychologist.[5]

This seems to assume that the pastoral counselor will need a consultant in order to make use of psychological testing in diagnosis and treatment planning, and may well be a realistic assessment of the state of the training of some pastoral counselors. However, many pastoral counselors are trained in the use of testing instruments and are able to use either a limited range or a large number of those instruments. Indeed, pastoral counseling centers might do well to include such a specialist among members of the staff. This point will be indirectly underscored in the final chapter on research by Nahrwold, Florell, and Moss.

One way of increasing the availability of counseling services without increasing permanent staff is to provide training for carefully selected pastors and/or seminarians in the art of counseling. This is possible if it has been planned for as permanent staff have been added and as referral sources in the community have been developed. It is difficult to predetermine the point at which the development of a training program will increase the efficiency of operation and availability of services of a pastoral counseling center without increasing costs, so the decision to follow this route in order to increase services is not to be taken lightly. Finally, a center may contract for provision of counseling services to its clients by hiring nonstaff counselors on a part-time basis to do counseling for a specified number of hours, either on a specified salary or on a percentage-of-fee basis, or a combination thereof.

Administrative and Support Services

The various models of administration call for provision of various levels of administrative support and different kinds of budgeting. If counselors are doing their own billing and bookkeeping for their clients, they can be provided with the necessary equipment and it might be possible to get along without a bookkeeper. A volunteer treasurer could handle that portion of accounts receivable which is designated for the center's overhead expenses. Of course, that overhead will need to include the cost of auditing all financial records, regardless of the administrative model in use.

Employment of a bookkeeper may relieve the individual counselors of responsibility for actually handling the billing and money, but they must still notify the bookkeeper concerning the amount which should be billed to each client. Hiring someone to do this kind of work increases the overhead costs, but may increase the productivity of the counseling staff.

It may be necessary to hire someone for receptionist duties and to answer telephone inquiries, but it is possible to do without either of these services. The need for a receptionist will depend on housing arrangements. The need for telephone answering will depend on the style of the pastoral counseling center's operation, including the way in which clients are referred and the way in which they are then assigned to counselors. With the advances in electronic equipment in recent years, it is possible to install a recording machine which will receive all incoming phone calls on a telephone number designated for initial inquiry. Those messages are picked up by the center's intake director or by staff members in rotation. The prospective clients are then called back to obtain the data necessary to determine their place on a waiting list or to make arrangements to send them an application form. This method provides for greater confidentiality than a commercial answering service and is considerably less expensive than hiring someone to answer the telephone. Moreover, it assures twenty-four-hour coverage of the telephone and means that all of the clients' contacts with the center will be handled with some clinical skill.

The costs of maintaining equipment such as typewriters and tape recorders, and of purchasing paper and other office supplies, need to be written into the budget as part of general overhead. Some pastoral counseling centers use donations and contributions from individuals, churches, and organizations to make capital purchases such as furniture and office equipment, rather than budgeting for these items out of counseling fee revenue.

Counseling Facilities

Many, if not most, pastoral counseling centers are housed in churches. As participants in the ministry of those churches, they may receive their housing without being charged rent, although it is certainly important that they budget for responsible participation in the cost of their use of church facilities. Even when no money actually changes hands, it is advisable to include such costs in the budget, showing an amount in the expense column balanced by an item designated as a donation in the receipts column.

In planning for housing of a center, one needs to recognize that use of a church or of several churches may limit the clientele. Feelings about the church or about a particular denomination or congregation may get in the way of the pastoral counseling center's usefulness to some potential clients. This is not necessarily the case where the center is located in a context not normally identified with ecclesiastical structures, although it may still be a problem in relation to the pastoral counselor's "pastoral" identification. In most communities, of course, the "pastoral" identification will enhance the likelihood of pastoral and self-referrals.

Where a pastoral counseling center is the outpatient section of a hospital's chaplaincy division, there is an ethical issue involved in the use of space designated for, and paid for by, inpatients to service outpatient needs. Therefore it becomes necessary to include an overhead charge for use of space in such a center's budget.

As a basic minimum, it would seem to be essential that a center have an office, the use of which is restricted to its own business, in a building which has facilities for regular meetings of the staff. Those meeting facilities could be shared with other groups or organizations using the building. In some cases, center offices are located in rented commercial property, with some counseling done there and the rest done in one or more church buildings. In other instances, pastoral counseling centers have an office and do all counseling in a centrally located church building. In still other cases, the main office is located in a central church building where some counseling is done, but most of the counseling is done on designated days in various church buildings located strategically throughout the community.

Pastoral counseling is usually done in offices designated exclusively for that purpose. However, it is also done in church school rooms, ladies' parlors, and even storage areas. Wherever it is done, care needs to be taken to guarantee the privacy and the comfort of the counselor and his or her clients through installation of locks, double doors, air conditioners, window drapes, etc.

The privacy of clients while waiting for their appointments needs to be taken into account also. It is unwise to have clients wait in an area through which the choir members pass on their way to and from choir practice. Another aspect of the client's need for privacy where counseling is done in several church buildings is the provision of a telephone by which clients may contact their counselor directly without going through volunteers who may happen to pick up the church phone. This may not be necessary in larger church buildings with competent secretarial service, except for night-time appointments for which it may be necessary to hire a part-time receptionist or make use of an electronic secretary.

Where all counseling is to be done in a centralized location, it may be important to differentiate between the provision of "offices" for permanent staff and "counseling rooms" in which counseling is done by others than the permanent staff or to determine that, apart from an administrative office, no room will be designated the particular "property" of a staff member. In the latter case, all staff members, full-time and part-time, will schedule time slots in counseling rooms which are available on a first-come, first-served basis. Where the latter principle is operative, it is necessary to provide a lounge or other space with some desks for counselor relaxation and/or nonclinical work done at the center.

Finally, if psychological testing is used during the diagnosis and treatment planning phase, it will be necessary to make provision for areas which can be used for this purpose, whatever the setting, so that the client can be assured of privacy and quiet.

A list of the kinds of housing models used by pastoral counseling centers follows:

a. an office or suite of offices in a church building, which may be used exclusively by the center or may be shared in part or completely with the congregation;
b. a central office in a church or commercial property, with some counseling being done at that site and also at satellite sites in churches or commercial properties;
c. a range of commercial sites, such as office buildings, shopping centers, storefronts, hotels or motels, with a room being rented one day each week, etc.;
d. diocesan office buildings or equivalent "church head-quarter" buildings, where services are provided for clergy and their families, and to other ecclesiastic staff and/or for the general public;
e. a general or psychiatric hospital, where the center constitutes the outpatient section of the hospital's chaplaincy division;
f. a seminary counseling service which provides counseling for seminarians as a component in the seminary's department of Pastoral Care and Counseling, with services also offered to pastors and parishioners of nearby congregations;
g. the chaplain's office of a college or university;
h. the home and automobile of a counselor employed to provide counseling services to the clergy of a judicatory and their families;

i. an ecclesiastically run social service agency, e.g., Lutheran Welfare Services, which may include an emphasis on reconstructive therapy as well as on societal intervention;

j. the medical department of a university, where a pastoral counseling division is created around two foci:

    i. the need to integrate medical and religious concerns as essential components in dealing with health care problems;

    ii. the kind of understanding of the family which the pastoral counselor who has had parish experience can bring to the training of family practice specialists;

k. career development centers;

l. church information centers founded to propagate a denomination's positions with regard to marriage, abortion, etc.;

m. the guidance and counseling departments of ecclesiastically run secondary schools.

Professional Development

A pastoral counseling center has a responsibility to further the professional development of its counseling staff, not only through individual and peer-group supervision and consultation, but also through the provision of books and periodicals relevant to pastoral counseling, through provision of opportunity to attend conferences, workshops, and conventions of professional organizations, and through its own affiliation with accrediting agencies. All of these cost money, directly, in the sense that one must pay for books and periodicals, for conference fees and travel, and for memberships and accreditation procedures; and indirectly, in the sense that time spent at conferences or in preparing for accreditation procedures does not generate income for the pastoral counseling center.

Whether such expenses are treated as general overhead and paid out of fee revenues or budgeted for out of contributions, they do have a legitimate claim on the center's budget. Where the *percentage salary* model is used, center policy needs to be developed which spells out the extent to which staff members are to invest in continuing professional development through their own affiliations and conference attendance. The cost of institutional affiliations and accreditation needs to be written into the budget as an overhead item, however paid for.

Insurance

Although it is difficult to assess the annual number of "successful" malpractice suits against pastoral counselors, it is important that a pastoral counseling center make provision for such insurance in its budget, including coverage for everyone connected with the center, from volunteer and secretarial personnel to board members and for the center itself. In 1975 the AAPC National Research Committee began a review of the range of costs involved for malpractice insurance and an ongoing compilation of companies who have provided this insurance to pastoral counselors. At the same time, it should be recognized that the provision of malpractice insurance may well have contributed to the increase of malpractice suits against members of other professions, so its use may increase suits against pastoral counselors.

Policies should also be taken to cover liability for accidents and injuries to staff and clients while in the center, including satellite operations or while traveling on center business. There may, of course, be some duplication in this area with individual policies and with the policies of church boards. It is probably better to be overinsured than to be underinsured, although there is a sense in which insurance coverage does increase the likelihood that suits will be filed.

Additionally, insurance coverage should be arranged for the furniture and equipment of the center, and of its employees where these are being used for center purposes.

Miscellaneous

A pastoral counseling center will need to budget for publicity costs, including printed material and the cost of travel and time for staff members to speak to groups and organizations about the center, seeking financial support and developing referral sources. It will need to budget for the cost of auditing its financial records and for the cost of collecting "bad debts"; although when there is a reasonably high level of competence in the center's clinical practice, there should be a minimum of "bad debts." It will also need to budget for attorney fees and, in some cases, will want to have an attorney on an annual retainer. Centers attached to other institutions may be able to contract for legal services from the institution's legal department or from the attorney it has on retainer.

Budgeting for Expansion

Whether expansion involves the addition of a staff member to an existing center or the addition of a satellite center, there are philosophical and practical issues to be resolved if unnecessary emotional stress and financial cost are to be avoided. Most of these issues are also involved when one is in the process of developing a center from the ground up.

Unless there are twenty to thirty clients waiting to see a new pastoral counselor when she arrives on the scene, provision will need to be made for subsidization of her income for an initial period of time. Actually, it is possible to plan for the arrival of a new therapist so that even given the vagaries of the flow of clients into a center, she can be carrying a full load very quickly. One way of planning for this is to have existing staff do intakes at a higher rate than normal during the three to four weeks immediately preceding her arrival so that the new counselor will be able to start doing therapy right away with some clients and not be faced with three to four weeks of doing only intakes.

Even if a new counselor's caseload can be planned for in such a way that he will immediately be earning his salary, there will be other start-up costs for which plans will need to be made. These include the cost of bringing in applicants for interviews, moving expenses, office furniture and equipment, etc. It will need to be determined whether these should be paid for out of a surplus from the existing operation or out of funds raised (in the case of a satellite) by the organization "calling" for the new services.

The models used are variants of familiar ecclesiastical structures. For example, a counselor may respond to a "call" to come to an existing structure just as a pastor is called by a congregation. Another example is a counselor's response to a call to go out and start a center where one's professional competence is self-clarified and one is totally dependent on one's skill as a psychotherapist, just as a missionary goes to a locale were there is no existing church structure and no preexisting salary.

A special case of expansion is the situation where a community with mental health needs, which could be met by a pastoral counseling center, is obviously also a community which will be unable to provide adequate support for such an agency. There are, in actuality, some communities where the socioeconomic level is such that virtually every potential client will be at the lower end of any fee scale which might be used. A pastoral counseling center could be started in such a context using one of the following models:

1. Grants from government, community, charitable, and/or ecclesiastical organizations can be sought to subsidize the entire operation through outright grants or to subsidization of the fees of clients directly.
2. The community can be served through a satellite operation of a pastoral counseling center based in a nearby community which is not only able to support such a center but also able to do so with a surplus which can, in whole or part, subsidize the satellite center's operation. Obviously, this means that the center is started in the

111

higher socioeconomic area and its operations there are stabilized before expansion into the lower socioeconomic area.

3. Where the lower socioeconomic community is in the inner city, the operation of a center serving it could be tied to the servicing of the inner city's commuter population, although with separate housing and different styles of service.

Although there are risks in all three models, it is much more likely that grants from external and/or impersonal sources will dry up than if a center operates on the basis of good clinical and business judgment. In other words, there is likely to be much greater stability in the second and third models.

However desirable the nondependent, autonomous, "missionary" model is, it is also desirable, whether in the case of starting a pastoral counseling center from the ground up or in the case of expansion of an existing center into a new community or population through a satellite operation, to solicit "seed" money which will provide a firmer foundation.

Business-Legal Issues

Where clients ask about deducting their therapy fees on their income tax return, it is not the responsibility of the pastoral counseling center to give them legal advice about the legitimacy of their doing so. Fees paid for pastoral counseling have, however, been successfully claimed as medical expenses in some taxation districts. It should be made clear, however, that fees paid for pastoral counseling are not deductible as charitable donations.

Pastoral counselors working in centers need to be aware that, by waiving self-employment status, they may no longer be eligible for an exemption for their housing costs, an exemption which they would otherwise have as clergypersons (provided they are related to ecclesiastical structures).

112

Centers which offer fellowships or residencies to trainees may need to leave open whether or not trainees are being required to provide counseling services as a condition of their fellowship or grant. If services are required to be performed, such fellowships or grants may not qualify for tax-exempt status.

Clinical decisions need to be made about the kind of *clinical records* which are kept concerning clients. Decisions need to be made concerning whether to keep clinical records and business records separate, and concerning whether or not clients will be identified by name and/or address and telephone number. The bias of the present writer is in the direction of keeping business and clinical records completely separate and obliterating identifying data from the latter if they are kept for research purposes beyond the client's termination from therapy. (A coding system might be used so that identification could be retrieved for purposes of longitudinal study of the effect of therapy.) In any case, both clinical and business records need to be stored in a place assuring security and confidentiality.

The ownership of the records of a clinic is vested in the pastoral counseling center and not in the individual pastoral counselors, so that storage of such records as are kept by counselors becomes the responsibility of the center when the client terminates from therapy, unless special arrangements are made with the client and the center for the therapist to keep his own personal copy. A center may also need to make arrangements for storage and/or derecording of tape recordings in a way that safeguards its clients' confidentiality.

Finally, the pastoral counselor who is starting a center will need to develop forms which meet the particular needs of the center. He or she should be able to obtain copies of forms used in established centers by direct requests to colleagues, particularly members of AAPC. Forms used to obtain legal permission should, of course, be checked by an attorney to make certain that they conform to the legal requirements of the jurisdiction.

Notes

1. *Handbook of the American Association of Pastoral Counselors* (New York: American Association of Pastoral Counselors, 1978), p. 25, II, G.

2. *Ibid.*, p. 36.

3. *Ibid.*, p. 36, II, F.

4. From an unpublished "AAPC Report of National Research Committee," 1974.

5. *Handbook of the American Association of Pastoral Counselors*, AAPC Handbook 2, revised July 25, 1978 (Washington, D.C.: American Association of Pastoral Counselors, 1978), p. 28, II, E.

6

Pastoral Identity and the Fee-for-Service Contract

David M. Moss III

The Judaeo-Christian tradition has never labeled the fee-for-service construct wrong in itself. Presumably Saint Paul was compensated for his tent and leather crafts, and it is probable that Jesus was paid for his carpentry skills (e.g., Acts 18:3, and Mark 6:3). Nevertheless, stewardship literature has consistently cited Jesus' comments about economic concerns as a way of saying that priorities can be measured by one's style of attaining and distributing money (e.g., Matt. 6:21 and Luke 12:34). Such literature reflects a basic attitude of parochial clergy which can spawn adjustment difficulties for ministers who refine their pastoral skills and become professional counselors.

Most parochial ministers choose the position that clergy are to be paid a set income that ought to provide for their basic living expenses. The rationale of this position is the separation of salary (housing, transportation expenses, etc.) from specific duties so that the pastor is available for a wide variety of services at various times and places. In some denominations this financial model traditionally attempts to avoid "simony," the practice of buying or selling ecclesiastical preferment—a so-called "missionary danger."

Obviously, such a model is quite different from the fee-for-service contract that many secular helping professionals have employed, especially when in private practice. Such clinicians (viz., psychiatrists, clinical psychologists, and social workers) have advanced the argument that a fee-for-service model keeps the professional strictly accountable to the clients he or she assists, as well as rewarding competency and industry. Ideally, it avoids waste, since nonproductive professionals do not get paid and incompetent clinicians are forced out of private practice by a lack of referrals.

When these two lines of reasoning are considered, it becomes apparent that a minister's training in psychotherapy will probably include a change and/or adjustment from one financial model to another: a movement from provided living expenses and multifaceted service to a more limited, concentrated professional development accompanied by an expectation of payment for the exercise of specialized pastoral competence.

At the time of AAPC's founding, this distinction was raised as a critical issue. There was a concern that the ministry might return to the abuses of medieval priests who charged inordinate fees from the poor for sacramental functions.[1] Because of the uncrystallized nature of the Association, there seemed to be a fear rooted in an image of the evangelical charlatan exhorting a local congregation with emotional rhetoric. One might even go so far as to recall Johann Tetzel's seductive phrase: "When a coin in the coffer rings, another soul from Purgatory springs."[2] This tenor of caution about what might be labeled "missionary danger" was furthered by other exponents of the movement who were sensitive to possible conflicts between the disciplines of theology and psychotherapy when the two were not adequately related.[3]

A number of years after this debate began, John Houck conducted an extensive investigation of more than six hundred ministers in mainline denominations throughout the United States and Canada.[4] Houck's research focused on the professional identity issues faced by pastoral counselors who were members of AAPC. His findings were extremely important in that he compared the attitudes and professional practices of parochial ministers with those of nearly four hundred AAPC approved pastoral counselors. The graph that follows records his population sample.

Questionnaires Sent Out and Returned from
AAPC Members and Other Clergymen in Selected Denominations

	AAPC			Other Clergy			Total		
	Sent	Ret.	%	Sent	Ret.	%	Sent	Ret.	%
Baptist, Southern	42	23	55	42	8	19	84	31	37
Baptist, American	54	11	20	54	20	37	108	31	29
Christian (Disciples)	27	13	48	27	11	41	54	24	44
Episcopal	73	42	58	73	21	29	146	63	43
Lutheran (LCA, ALC)	46	24	52	46	19	41	92	43	47
Lutheran (Mo. Synod)	15	12	90	15	1	7	30	13	43
Presbyterian (UPUSA)	100	54	54	100	36	36	200	90	45
Presbyterian (US)	34	14	41	34	11	32	68	25	37
Roman Catholic	20	8	40	20	3	15	40	11	27
United Church of Christ	94	46	49	94	34	36	184	80	44
United Church of Canada	16	6	38	16	7	44	32	13	41
United Methodist	179	84	47	179	68	38	358	152	42
Other	92	34	37	—	—	—	92	34	37
Total	792	371	47	700	239	34	1492	610	41

Houck's methodology included a modified version of a lengthy questionnaire designed by William Henry, *et. al.*, for a study of secular psychotherapists.[5] This revised questionnaire yielded valuable data when factor analyzed by several modes. However, Houck's initial description of these findings concentrated on social marginality rather than the fee-for-service contract as a critical point of the pastoral psychotherapist's professional identity.

Then, in 1977, Houck and I reviewed his data from another perspective (including rotated factor matrices of attitudinal responses). When we published this material in the *Journal of Religion and Health*, we underscored what we believe to be the central issue of an AAPC pastoral counselor's sense of professional identity as a minister and psychotherapist—the fee-for-service factor.[6] What also emerged in the course of our research was a profile of the pastoral psychotherapist: an ordained minister, actively committed to a belief system but not invested in normative parochial functions. Attentive to the qualifications and standards Bruehl discussed in chapter 2, these ministers tended to maintain their professional growth by means of personal psychotherapy, health-care organizations, and the study of specific journal articles. For reasons covered in Parts III and, more importantly IV, clinical supervision was also a highly significant factor in the developmental process.

Unlike parochial clergy but similar to secular psychotherapists, these professional pastoral counselors ordinarily charged a fee for their clinical services. More often than not, however, they tailored their fee to fit the income level of the client and his or her (or their) number of dependents. Philosophically, they were very much in accord with the position taken by Hinkle in the next chapter.

Perhaps the most important revelation of this profile is that the fee charged by those AAPC members studied appeared to be directly related to their feelings of competency in ministering via particular modes of psychotherapy and insights gathered from the behavioral sciences. These pursuits, professional practices, and attitudes or variables of self-esteem were quite different from the profile of the parochial clergy sampled.

The pastoral psychotherapist becomes even more distinct when his or her practice of ministry is considered in a particular context. Clear illustrations are three of the models discussed in chapter 1. Carr and Hinkle describe Models C, D, and G as environments which are conducive for the employment of a fee-for-service contract. The reader may recall that the Community-Based Pastoral Counseling Center (Model C), with its broad ecumenical base and its interdisciplinary latitude, utilized a fee-scale contract that included percentage reductions for "sustaining members" or those "member parishes" who donated resources and/or monetary support. The Pastoral Counseling Group Practice (Model D) maintained parochial connections but without a reduction in fees being commonly practiced. This model is the one where the most confidence in ministering by psychotherapy seems evident. It is a locale for the more aggressive professional and, consequently, *may* be viewed—usually, at a marked distance—as a source of the "missionary danger" mentioned earlier. Certainly, such a model is typically inappropriate for geographical areas dominated by lower socioeconomic brackets. Counselors are usually paid a substantial percentage of the fees they charge, the balance going for corporate expenses and housing. The Hospital Outpatient Pastoral Counseling Service (Model G), though it does not provide the independence of the other two models, still offers the counselor an opportunity to use the fee-for-service contract and a percentage of his or her salary may well be determined by the amount charged and/or received. An addition which is in many ways unique to this last model is the revenue engendered by third-party payments, many that are contingent upon supervision by a psychiatrist and/or a registered clinical psychologist.

Returning to Houck's research and my redaction of his data, it seems that Model D, the Pastoral Counseling Group Practice, presents the greatest potential difficulties for the

119

pastoral counselor or psychotherapist moving from a parochial salary structure to a fee-for-service contract. Models C and G are not as independent. Their constitution supplies or governs the counselor's salary in a more pronounced fashion. Thus a subtle but quite rational defense is available for pastoral counselors who want to avoid the unpleasant adjustment reaction that can accompany the movement from salary to a straight fee-for-services arrangement. In other words, payment in the form of salary rather than fees for services, as is made possible in Models C and G, is more consistent with parochial expectations, hence more acceptable to pastors who are beginning to function as professional pastoral counselors.

This issue has several dimensions, as Hinkle points out in chapter 7. Some of the central dimensions are the personality structure of the pastoral counselor; his or her denomination's attitudes about ministers *earning* money clinically rather than being paid by an ecclesiastical institution like a parish church or hospital; the prevailing perspectives of the counselor's belief system and seminary education, especially its views about the pastoral psychology movement, and his or her colleague groups' continued integration of theology and psychotherapy in the service-delivery context.

In some respects the latter is a powerful backdrop that is overlooked all too often in the group model (D). However, theological dialogue with AAPC colleagues can supply the support and understanding which frequently deenergizes an emotional sensitivity rooted in guilt-related inhibitions which were forged in a counselor's early development and subsequently fostered by religious training—especially unexplained viewpoints like "It is easier for a camel to pass through the eye of a needle than for a rich man to enter the kingdom of God" (Matt. 19:24).

By way of concluding this chapter and leading into the next, it is worth reflecting on three issues which ought to be confronted by the pastoral psychotherapist who chooses the fee-for-service contract as an ingredient of ministry. First, the pastoral counselor's professional education ought to include serious study of the psychological values of the fee as a therapeutic agent. Harold Jester in a brief but excellent article entitled "The Pastoral Counseling Center Ministry" summarizes an extensive amount of research related to this dimension of the fee. Jester concludes, as do so many psychologists, that the fee is closely tied to *motivation*. "The client works harder. He appreciates the service more. His dignity is maintained. And he does not become [perpetually] indebted to his counselor."[7]

Second, the clinical ramifications or psychodynamics of negotiation, punctuality, and manner of payment can be meaningful issues for the counselor's supervision. They may well reflect a client's feelings about the counseling process. Those feelings or attitudes may be realistically based or they may be born out of transference *or both*. Consequently, they are potential touchstones of insight for the counselor and his or her colleague, the client.

Third, if the pastoral counselor experiences marked difficulties with the fee-for-service contract—regardless of the amount charged per session—those problems deserve attention in the context of his or her personal psychotherapy for they may mirror intra/interpersonal features of self-doubt, inadequacy, or a false sense of competency.

Facing these three issues can be of great benefit to the professional pastoral counselor who charges a fee for clinical services. As I said, however, the process of adjustment calls for increased awareness in an environment of colleagues who, as a group of fellow practitioners, seek to maintain their identity as *clergy ministering* by means of "psychotherapy," or "the cure of souls."

Notes

1. Readers interested in early position papers pertaining to the fee-for-service model, private practice, and AAPC qualifications will find the following articles of value: Howard Clinebell, "The Challenge of the Specialty of Pastoral Counseling," *Pastoral Psychology*, 15:143 (1964),

17-28, and "The Future of the Specialty of Pastoral Counseling," *Pastoral Psychology*, 16:158 (1965), 18-26; and Seward Hiltner, " 'Credentials' for Pastoral Counseling?" *Pastoral Psychology*, 11:110 (1961), 45 ff.

2. See A. Dickens, *Reformation and Society and Sixteenth-Century Europe* (Norwich: Jarrold and Sons, 1966), p. 61.

3. The following articles clearly reflect this conflict: J. Caldwell, "Issues of Identity, Models, and Methods in Supervision," *Pastoral Counselor*, 5:2 (1967), 16-18; Maurice Clark, "New Trends in Pastoral Care and Counseling," *Journal of Pastoral Care*, 23:2 (1969), 110-12; Carroll Wise, "The Pastor as Counselor," *Pastoral Counselor*, 5:2 (1967), 4-11; David Bennett, "Clinical Pastoral Education, Personal Faith, and Sense of Vocation," *Pastoral Counselor*, 7:1 (1969), 1-2; Armen Jorjorian, "Reflections Upon and Definitions of Pastoral Counseling," *Pastoral Psychology*, 23:224 (1972), 7-15; Heije Faber, "Is the Pastor a Psychotherapist?" *Journal of Pastoral Care*, 27:2 (1973), 100-6; Wayne Oates, "Association of Pastoral Counselors—Its Values and Its Dangers," *Pastoral Psychology*, 15:143 (1964), 5-7; Seward Hiltner, "American Association of Pastoral Counselors—A Critique," *Pastoral Psychology*, 15:143 (1964), 14; and Morris Taggart, "The Professionalization of the Parish Pastoral Counselor," *Journal of Pastoral Care*, 27:3 (1973), 180-88.

4. John B. Houck, "The Professional Identity of Pastoral Counselors," unpublished Ph.D. dissertation (Chicago: Illinois Institute of Technology, 1974).

5. William Henry, *et. al.*, *The Fifth Profession* (San Francisco: Jossey-Bass, 1971).

6. John B. Houck and David M. Moss, "Pastoral Psychotherapy, The Fee-for-Service Model and Professional Identity," *Journal of Religion & Health*, 16:3 (1977), 172-83.

7. Harold Jester, "The Pastoral Counseling Center Ministry," *The Christian Ministry*, 5:3 (1974), 30.

C H A P T E R

7

Central Issues Related to the Use of Fee Scales
John E. Hinkle, Jr.

The commonly held view that pastoral counseling centers have or should have financial policies similar to those maintained in parish settings is inadequate. A major difference concerns the funding of ministry in each situation, especially as this funding relates to charging fees for services. The sliding fee scale is an attempt to reconcile resulting disparities. Sliding fee scale policies have emerged in pastoral counseling centers largely as a result of the commitment to offer counseling services regardless of the ability of clients to pay. Such policies, however, as customarily implemented, appear under close scrutiny to result in serious financial and ethical problems. These difficulties suggest a reevaluation of underlying priorities as well as specific procedures.

Offering services to clients or parishioners regardless of ability to pay has different ramifications in the counseling center than it does in the parish. Pastoral counselors are supported largely through individual fees for services rendered, with occasional supplementation of income from individuals or groups not receiving services.[1] Parish pastors, however, are salaried by the local congregation, and services are not usually rendered on the basis of the ability of individuals to pay for them. The counseling center must either find sources of income in addition to fees for services or cease functioning. (Possible exceptions are centers with a preponderance of wealthy clientele and those who qualify for third-party insurance payments.) Parish ministers, with a regular income from the parish, do not face the same financial problem. For the center director, the issue becomes critical to the ongoing life of the center.

One of the most common methods of providing additional income to offset the cost of the service-without-regard-to-ability-to-pay commitment is the sliding fee scale. In this approach the clients are charged for services according to their ability to pay. As an example, consider an instance where the cost per hour of delivered service is $20. This would include salaries, rents, office expenses, in short, the combined expenses of the counseling center averaged out according to the number of counseling hours. If each client were to pay the cost of delivered services (cds), the counseling center would be financially solvent. Income would then match expenses.

The principle of justice (hence justification) behind the sliding fee scale is that fees are paid in proportion to the income of each client rather than as a specific, fixed (constant) amount. For example, fees would range from $5–$35, depending on a client's income (and possible other factors, i.e., family size, etc.). In this way the center works toward its services-without-regard-to-ability-to-pay commitment (by lowering fees for the lower-income clients) while attempting to remain financially solvent (by raising the fees for those with higher incomes).

Assuming a wide socioeconomic distribution of clients, or one focused on or above the upper middle class level, the center generates fee income which will match the cost of delivered service. If any deficits arise, third-party contributions are needed.[2] Hence, the foregoing fee system seems advantageous in that it appears to satify the ethical commitments of the center while remaining financially workable. If the clientele is not largely upper middle class or higher, the system will not work well apart from the volume of third-party contributions. The use of this system, however, raises several important questions. There would appear to be problems and disadvantages on not only a financial level, but on psychological and ethical levels as well.[3]

From a financial viewpoint, an all too common outcome of the sliding fee scale is a pastoral counseling center that is perpetually on the verge of bankruptcy. There appear to be three main causes for this situation. First, clients who must pay the top fee on the scale often are in the price range of quality therapy from other mental health professionals. Thus the clients on whom the counseling center is depending most to balance things out financially are the very people who can best afford to go elsewhere.

Second, the entire center fails if sufficient third-party contributions cannot be raised to balance the deficit. As a result the center may find itself in the situation where it has, as a matter of policy, offered services it did not have the financial resources to offer, thereby cutting its own financial throat. Instead of offering services without regard to ability to pay, the center may find itself unable to offer services.

Third, the persons or groups who are asked for third-party contributions are often suspicious as to how their money is being used. Are they paying for lights and carpets and paid vacations, or are they paying for an important service? Often these contributions are viewed by the contributor, and sometimes by the center, as being temporary in nature, as though eventually they will not be required. This sets up an inevitable situation of diminishing returns. In other words, it is certainly difficult to raise money from people for something from which they will not directly benefit, but even more importantly, raising such funds gets more difficult as time passes.

From a psychological viewpoint, the sliding fee scale may well tend to devalue the counseling experience for the person who is only being charged $5. This person may know that most forms of psychotherapy presently start around $45 an hour, and thus may well question the quality of service received in the pastoral counseling center. Such an attitude would certainly hinder the commitment of the individual to the therapeutic process. On the other hand, informing the person that the service really costs much more, but since the individual is poor the fee has been lowered, may arouse feelings of dependence and worthlessness which will also hinder the therapeutic process.

The person with a higher income may want religiously oriented therapy, but may not want to subsidize the therapy of others. Since through the sliding fee scale the client is doing exactly that, the individual must, in order to obtain this religiously oriented counseling, subsidize the counseling of others. If the person experiences this as a form of coercion, the resulting anger and resentment will hinder the therapeutic process.

There are also several ethical questions raised by the sliding fee scale. The first concerns the common practice of withholding from the client the information concerning the center's methods of funding. This is the most questionable aspect of the use of the sliding fee scale. Not only does the center use part of the fees of wealthier clients to subsidize lower fees to others, but often it does not inform the wealthier persons about the implication of this practice. Here the "coercion" element is combined with deceit. Often the deceit is in terms of omission. There has been at least one instance in which a client discovered the actual nature of the fee he was being charged and protested quite vigorously. The client maintained that he was unwilling to subsidize the counseling of other persons and resented the fact that such an assumption of his willingness was built into the fee scale. His point is worth considering.

The second question concerns the commitment of pastoral counseling centers not only to giving services regardless of the financial ability of the client to pay but also to the quality of that service. The nature of pastoral counseling demands a specific environment and ethos in order to be effective, and counseling must necessarily be effective in order to be of high quality. Three aspects of the "quality" ethos seem to be undermined by the sliding fee scale system. The first of these is *continuity*. In order for therapy to be effective, the potential for continuity must be present. Because the sliding fee scale often brings counseling centers to an abrupt end for reasons that are largely financial, continuity is threatened, and with it, effectiveness. The second aspect is *commitment*. If a client is not committed to therapy, the therapy can hardly be effective. The client's commitment to therapy is highly related to payment for therapy and may easily be undermined by the negative feelings which often arise as a result of being at either end of the fee scale. The third aspect is *unambiguous circumstances of payment*. If the client is not satisfied with the financial arrangements, the effectiveness of the therapeutic process will suffer as a result. The financial arrangements, as discussed above, are certainly often less than straightforward.

A third ethical question emerges from the financial and psychological viewpoints previously discussed. Can pastoral counselors ethically put themselves in a situation where the *financial method* (the sliding fee scale) of fulfilling one key commitment, i.e., service-without-regard-for-ability-to-pay, *endangers the ability to fulfill a second and equally crucial commitment*, i.e., *quality* of service rendered? One cannot give what one does not have. In offering counseling one must be committed to its effectiveness or else the offer of counseling becomes meaningless. It would seem foolish, therefore, to offer pastoral counseling in such a way that the offer might well become meaningless. One would then be in the situation of offering what one does not have to offer.

In consideration of the entire discussion to this point, it would seem to be appropriate to offer an amendment to the widely held commitment stated earlier. Ability to pay shall not affect availability of service, *so long as the overall effectiveness of the service is not undermined*. This policy revision is recommended, not only to pastoral counseling centers but to the AAPC as well. One practical implication of this revised commitment would be that counseling centers would be expected not to commit financial suicide by offering services at less than the cost of those services if the center did not have the surplus funds to make up the deficit. This would hold true not only for counseling centers which employ the sliding fee scale but also for those which use alternative systems.

One alternative system to the sliding fee scale is based on the cds. The first steps would be to determine the cost per hour of delivered service. Regardless of one's system or intentions, this is a good practice. Include the therapist's fee, the cost for the facilities, for receptionists, for development programs, and for everything that comes under the aegis of the counseling center.[4] If the counseling center is committed to providing services without regard to ability to pay and wishes to dedicate a portion of its income to that end, then this contribution should be *built into the cds*, not added as an afterthought. Then, *charge each client the cds, regardless of ability to pay*. Third, set up a *financial-aid fund*, from third-party as well as the center's own contributions, to make up the difference between cds and the ability of the individual clients to pay.[5] Fourth, offer services regardless of financial situation through financial aid *within the limits of this fund*.

The financial advantages of this system are obvious. First, it comes much closer to guaranteeing financial solvency for the center. The cds is met for each client, either by the client's resources or with the help of the fund. Second, the system does not drive away those who can afford to pay the maximum fee. The cds for most counseling centers is still significantly below the average fee for other mental health professionals. Third, it offers, within the limits of effectiveness as herein defined, services for those who cannot afford the full price.

The psychological advantages are also important. The system offers a much less ambiguous circumstance of payment. It is a straightfoward money-for-services approach, which would tend to minimize feelings of resentment about deception or coercion. Also, the system tends to emphasize the value of the services. Each client, regardless of what each pays, realizes that the service actually costs a specific amount and that any difference is made up by private contributions. Another advantage is that this system offers a much less ambiguous context for third-party contributions. Here, the contribution goes directly to aid persons in need who would otherwise be unable to afford such aid. The third party pays for services.

But what are the ethical considerations? In this most important area the system seems to meet such requirements. It helps fulfill the commitment to quality of service in three ways: continuity through solvency, unambiguous circumstances of payment through a straightforward money-for-service approach, and individual commitment through the financial-aid approach. It helps fulfill the commitment to service-regardless-of-ability-to-pay through the financial-aid fund and increasing third-party contributions because of a more attractive context for giving. The system is set up so that services are offered within the limits of the overall effectiveness of that service. Circumstances which tend to introduce deceit, whether by omission or commission, and coercion into the counseling situation are avoided.

It may be pointed out that the biggest "if" in this system concerns the center's ability to solicit third-party contributions. If sufficient funds are raised, the program works and the commitments are fulfilled. But if *not*, then what? This is certainly a valid criticism, although not of this system alone. Every system which offers counseling services at less than cost must come up with a reciprocal amount of funding or cease to function. *What is different about this system is that, if the funding is not immediately forthcoming, the center will not immediately cease to exist.* With most other systems, and notably with the sliding fee scale, this is a constant danger.

In summary, it should be mentioned that this is not meant to be an attempt to sound the death knell for the sliding-fee-scale approach. The sliding fee scale, properly implemented, is a valid means of fulfilling the commitments of the pastoral counseling center. By contrasting the more conventional approach with an alternative based firmly on the cds, however, certain as yet unrecognized inconsistencies and inefficiencies, as well as strengths, have come to light. Two concerns remain:

(1) that the ethical questions which are raised herein be resolved; and (2) that the ethical commitments on the part of counseling centers be fulfilled as well as possible.

Notes

1. Cf. James C. Hurst, *et al.*, "Current Fee Charging Practices and Perceptions in College and University Counseling Centers," *Student Development Report*, vol. II (Fort Collins: Colorado State University, 1974).

2. *Ibid.*, p. 3.

3. The problems and disadvantages at psychological/ethical levels regarding the sliding fee scale are nicely addressed by Joan Shireman, "Client and Worker Opinions About Fee-Charging in a Child Welfare Agency," *Child Welfare*, 54 (May, 1975), 3.

4. Hurst, p. 7.

5. *Ibid.*, p. 9.

C H A P T E R

8

Legal Concerns of the Pastoral Counselor
Richard E. Augspurger

The United States is increasingly becoming a "legalized" society wherein state and federal laws, and court rulings dictate what is appropriate and what is not appropriate behavior for the professional engaged in psychotherapy. Pastoral counselors need to be aware of the possible legal ramifications of providing professional counseling services in particular states and settings. It is hoped that this chapter will help shed light on the following legal issues of which the pastoral counselor must be aware in today's world: confidentiality, privileged communication, clergy privilege, state licensing and certification laws, tax-exempt status, incorporating, malpractice insurance, and third-party payments.

Confidentiality

The pastoral counselor is accustomed to working in settings in which trust and mutual confidence are of primary importance. The term "confidentiality" is used to describe an often misunderstood and frequently abused concept. What does it mean? To whom is confidentiality extended in a particular professional setting? When is a written, signed "release of information" required to consult with other professionals and yet maintain the confidentiality of the relationship? These are a few of the questions to be explored.

Confidentiality is one of the building blocks upon which effective trust is established in professional and therapeutic settings. According to Webster's, confidentiality is the "quality or state of being confidential, private, or secret."

"Privacy" refers to all that encompasses the individual's thoughts, knowledge, acts including associations, property, and person which he has an inalienable right to hold to himself against encroachment by others, including his government. "Confidentiality" arises when this individual entrusts to another that which is of his privacy—usually because of a vital need to share. It requires the explicit or implicit mutual understanding that this second individual will use it only for the first individual's vital need, and not make it available to a third party without the first party's consent.[1]

Privacy and secrecy are essential in a relationship if maximum potential effectiveness for the client is to be achieved and maintained. The adjective "confidential" is "indicative of intimacy, mutual trust, or willingness to confide." Over time, the relationship between pastoral counselor and client becomes increasingly intimate. It is not unusual for a client to reveal information heretofore not shared with any other person or to express attitudes previously out of conscious awareness. Healing, or resolution of emotional difficulties, takes place within such an atmosphere of mutual trust and intimacy. Even under optimum conditions of confidentiality it is difficult for clients to share thoughts and feelings to another person. Poor professional practice and/or "leaks of confidentiality" can undermine the therapeutic relationship even further.

Confidential communications are those communications which take place between the pastoral counselor and client(s). Persons seeking assistance for emotional difficulties assume the professional counselor treats information shared as "confidential." The certified pastoral counselor, upon agreeing to counsel with a person, agrees to respect, and if necessary, protect the confidentiality of the relationship according to the Code of Professional Ethics of the American Association of Pastoral Counselors. "The pastoral counselor respects the integrity and protects the welfare of the person or group with whom one is working. One has an obligation to safeguard information about an individual that has been obtained in the course of the counseling process."[2]

Foundations of Confidentiality

What is the legal provision upon which the individual's right to confidentiality is based? According to the Constitution of the United States of America, Bill of Rights, Article IV, citizens have a right to be "secure in their persons, houses, papers and effects." Within the context of pastoral counseling, the right to be "secure in their persons, papers and effects" is another way of describing the confidentiality of the pastoral counselor/client relationship. Within that relationship, each has the responsibility to respect the right to confidentiality of the other. Each party exercises discretion in talking about confidential matters with other persons. Public disclosure, or the threat of it, undermines the trustworthiness, and therefore the effectiveness, of the relationship. If to the difficulty of divulging sensitive and intimate information is added the possibility of public disclosure, either in casual conversations or in court proceedings, it can be expected that the client will not speak freely. "At best, the possibility of disclosure will prolong treatment; at worst, it will make thorough exploration of conflicts impossible."[3]

Ordinarily, the scope of professional confidentiality includes peer-professionals, consultants, and secretarial personnel in the pastoral counseling setting on a "need-to-know" basis. Need-to-know criterion is when consultation is needed for clarification, confirmation, discussion, or supervision. A guiding principle in seeking consultation and maintaining confidentiality is that of ensuring delivery of the best possible care to the individual, couple, or group in question. When a professional needs clarification in working with someone, and the care of the client(s) would be improved through consultation, then the need-to-know criterion has been met.

Disclosing confidential information beyond the persons

mentioned above involves securing written permission from the client(s). "Except by written permission, all communication from clients shall be treated in professional confidence."[4] Requesting information from a previous therapist, attending physician, or consulting psychologist, are examples of when a written, signed "release of information" is necessary. Sharing confidential materials with other trained professionals who are capable of interpreting the information is a professional courtesy performed by many professionals when a signed "release of information" accompanies the request.

Privileged Information

"Privilege" is a legislative process which grants immunity-from-disclosure privileges to specified persons, or groups of persons, e.g., clergy, psychiatrists, attorneys.

Under certain circumstances legislatures can determine a "pecking order" of importance and ascribe such an inviolable position to "confidentiality" that even the government (courts) cannot compel disclosure. Such communications are thereby "privileged." Classes of confidentiality so ordained might be "husband-wife privilege," "attorney-client privilege," "physician-patient privilege," "psycho-therapist-patient privilege." Only the attorney-client and clergy-penitent privileges are usually free of exceptions. Do note that "privilege" as a protection, applies against demands made in judicial or quasi-judicial proceedings by bodies having this overriding power to compel disclosure. Legislatures have this power and can delegate it.[5]

The pastoral counselor should not take "privilege" for granted. All persons who are capable of understanding an "oath of office" in the courtroom are considered potentially competent to testify in civil and criminal court cases. Only two classes of potential witnesses are exempt form testifying in court: persons considered mentally incompetent and those who are not required to do so because of "privilege."

"A confidential communication is considered 'privileged' if the courts determine that public policy demands that such evidence be shielded from court disclosure."[6] The late Dean John Wigmore of Northwestern University posited four criteria to be met prior to creating a class of "privileged communications."

1. Does the communication originate in confidence?
2. Is the inviolability of that confidence vital to the achievement of the purpose of the relationship?
3. Is the relationship one that should be fostered?
4. Is the expected injury to the relationship, through the fear of later disclosure, greater than the expected benefit to justice in obtaining the testimony?[7]

Does the pastoral counselor have the right to resist divulging confidential information in a court of law based upon "privilege"? The answer to this question varies from state to state, depending upon the wording of the applicable state laws and the wording of the pastoral counselor's denominational endorsement. Generally, Judge Wigmore's first three critera are met in the case of professional pastoral counseling. The last criterion would have to be determined on a case-by-case basis, although ordinarily it would be met as well.

Laws Protecting Clergy

There are three kinds of laws under which the pastoral counselor might find immunity: constitutional law, common law, and statutory law. According to Article I of the United States Bill of Rights, "Congress shall make no law respecting an establishment of religion, or prohibiting the free exercise thereof." The *AAPC Handbook* states: "In the final analysis, accountability for one's ministry is to the denomination or faith group which ordains a person and continues one's ministerial credentials."[8] If a pastoral counselor is endorsed by a particular denomination to perform a particular pastoral counseling ministry, and if protecting the confidentiality of the pastoral counselor/client relationship is vital to the maintenance of the relationship, then it would seem unconstitutional to establish a precedent which would "prohibit the free exercise thereof" (i.e., the relationship).

Common law is a carryover from England and consists of decisions made by judges, provided they do not contradict constitutional or statutory laws. The case of Binder vs. Ruvel in 1952 in Illinois is considered the precedent for the "common-law privilege" for the psychotherapist-client relationship. A psychiatrist, Roy Grinker, was subpoenaed to divulge confidential information which had been shared with him in the course of psychotherapy. Grinker refused to testify on the grounds that public disclosure of the confidential information in the courtroom would be more injurious to the counseling relationship than would be the benefit gained. The trial judge did not force the testimony, and Grinker was not found in contempt of court. Confidentiality was therefore respected in this case involving the relationship between psychotherapist and client. Although this case has been cited as the precedent in establishing the "common-law privilege" between psychotherapist and client, legal scholars have questioned the strength of this precedent and have speculated that on appeal to a higher court the case might have been reversed.[9] Others have speculated that it was Grinker's stature as a prominent psychiatrist which prevented him from being found in contempt of court.[10]

Statutory law is more fluid and experimental than constitutional law. Statutory law is also more readily repealed. Statutes are laws enacted by Congress or state legislatures provided they are not in conflict with state or federal constitutions.[11] In 1928, New York was the first state to enact a clergy-privilege statute. Its wording is as follows: "No minister of the gospel or priest of any denomination whatsoever, shall be allowed to disclose any confessions made in his professional character, in the course of discipline enjoined by rules of practice of such denomination."[12] Similarly written statutes exempting clergy from disclosure are in effect in a large majority of states.[13]

The pastoral counselor must not be misled into believing that one will be immune from court subpoena in all instances under clergy-privilege statutes. In the final analysis, whether or not confidential information is shared in court depends upon many factors: the philosophy of the pastoral counselor, the wording of the denominational endorsement, the evidence presented in a particular case, the skills of the lawyers involved, and the decision of the judge.

One court ruling in 1949 severely restricted clergy privilege by limiting it to penitential conversations. "Penitence implies sorrow over having sinned or done wrong." In the murder case of Johnson vs. Commonwealth, the Supreme Court of Kentucky ruled that the "confession" made to the minister was not considered privileged communication since it was not "penitential in character," and was not made to the minister "in his professional character."[14] Also, in Arkansas in 1926, immunity was not granted for a written communication made to a clergyman because the "confession of rape" was not made to the pastor "in his professional character."[15]

Denominational endorsement for pastoral counselors is essential if the pastoral counselor expects to be protected under existing clergy-privilege statutes. Denominational endorsement of a specialized pastoral counseling ministry practiced in a particular setting under supervision with a prescribed population may be necessary, but is not necessarily sufficient, to enable a pastoral counselor to successfully resist testifying or divulging confidential information.

In sum, United States constitutional law is clearly in support of religious freedom. Common law provides some support for protection of confidential information between psychotherapist and client, although the strength of this support has been questioned. Statutory law, depending upon the wording of statutes, may or may not provide exemption privileges for clergy functioning as pastoral counselors. It is the responsibility of pastoral counselors to check the wording of the clergy-exemption statute in the state in which they counsel, as well as the wording of the denominational endorsement with which they are affiliated, to ascertain whether or not they are entitled to "privilege."

In 1961, Illinois adopted a "clergy-exemption statute" with broader coverage:

A clergyman, or priest, minister, rabbi, or practitioner of any religious denomination accredited by the religious body to which he belongs, shall not be compelled to disclose in any court, or to any administrative board or agency, or to any public officer, a confession made to him in his professional character or as a spiritual advisor in the course of the discipline enjoined by the rules or practices of such religious body or of the religion which he professes, nor be compelled to divulge any information which has been obtained by him in such professional character or as such spiritual advisor. [16]

Although broader in scope, this statute still emphasizes the importance of confession and professional role function as important prerequisites to being protected.

The following proposed model statute provides good privilege protection for a wide variety of professionals doing psychotherapy with individuals, families, or groups:

A client, or his authorized representative, has a privilege to prevent a witness from disclosing, in any judicial, administrative, or legislative proceeding, communications pertaining to the diagnosis or treatment of the client's mental or emotional disorder, or difficulty in personal or social adjustment, between the client and any of the following: a member of a mental health profession, any other professional or lay person who participates with such a member of a mental health profession in the diagnosis or treatment, or members of the client's family, or between any of these persons as concerns diagnosis or treatment. [17]

Examples have been given of constitutional-law, common-law, and statutory-law exemptions under which the professional counselor might find "privilege." In addition, some faith groups have established guidelines protecting the confidentiality of the communications between clergy and persons they counsel. The pastoral counselor should check with denominational head-quarters to see if guidelines or policies protecting confidentiality have been established within his or her faith group.

Denominational endorsement is a requirement if the pastoral counselor wants to work within the parameters of Article I of the United States Bill of Rights. If the pastoral counselor wants to practice independently, then state licensing may be required. Fulfilling any one of the following conditions constitutes "private practice" and is opposed by the AAPC: "Working in isolation without professional and interprofessional consultation; working apart from administrative responsibility to any organization; or working apart from responsibility to a faith group."[18]

State Licensing and Certification

State licensing is a screening process whereby state examining boards acknowledge that certain persons are qualified to provide stated professional services, e.g., pastoral counseling, marriage and family counseling. "Certification" is a legal regulation by a state which restricts the "use of a title," e.g., pastoral counselor, psychologist, social worker, psychiatrist. If a state passes a "certification law" no one may use the restricted title unless he or she has met the requirements set forth in the statute and obtained a certificate from the designated state board or office.

Another form of state regulation is "licensure laws." A licensure law restricts the function of the professional, which is more restrictive than just restricting the title the professional uses. A professional may not engage in the practice as defined in the law unless he or she meets the requirements set forth in the law and obtains a license. Practicing the regulated function without a license opens one to the possibility of fine or imprisonment, or both. As a matter of practical importance, licensure laws which regulate function generally have sections in them on certification which protects the use of the title as well as the function.

Certification limits the use of a specific title to those who are officially declared qualified to provide service. In states where there are certification laws, persons not certified may continue to render the service if they can find the clients.[19] Licensure is more restrictive than certification because it makes it illegal to practice the defined activities, e.g. marriage and family counseling, without a license. Here is an example of restriction of title found in the New Hampshire Act to license pastoral counselors:

Any person not a licensed pastoral counselor who shall represent himself as a licensed pastoral counselor as defined in this chapter, or having had his certificate of licensure suspended or revoked who shall continue to represent himself as a licensed pastoral counselor by means of any sign, letterhead or written or verbal advertisement or notice, shall be guilty of a violation.[20]

The proposed "marriage and family counseling licensing act" in Georgia could severely restrict the functioning of the pastoral counselor if it were not for the following exemption clause in the law:

Nothing in this Act shall be construed to prevent qualified members of other professional groups such as social workers, psychiatric nurse specialists, psychologists, physicians, attorneys-at-law, members of the clergy or guidance counselors from doing the work of a marriage and family counseling nature consistent with the accepted standards of their respective professions.[21]

Included in this proposed licensing act is the section on "certification" which restricts the use of the title:

. . . no person who is not licensed under this Act shall advertise the performance of marriage and family counseling services or represent himself to be a licensed practicing marriage and family counselor, or use a title or description such as "marriage counselor, advisor or consultant," or "family counselor, advisor or consultant."[22]

Pastoral counselors who wish to perform marital counseling in states where they are not "licensed pastoral counselors," and where marriage and family counseling is restricted by similar laws without the exemption clauses, need to become "licensed marriage and family counselors."

In states where psychologists, marriage and family counselors, social workers, and other professional groups are writing restrictive legislation, it is important for pastoral counselors to organize and create appropriate exemption clauses. The Legislative Committee of the AAPC can be of assistance.[23]

The following are examples of exemption clauses taken from the Code of Virginia. Title 54, which regulates professions and occupations, states under chapter 5.1, Virginia Board of Psychologists Examiners, section 54-102.14: "Nothing in this chapter shall be construed to regulate or limit: activities of rabbis, priests, ministers or clergymen of any religious denomination or sect when such activities are within the scope of performing their regular ministerial duties"; chapter 12, Medicine and Other Healing Arts, states the following exemption clause in section 54:276.2: "Nothing in this chapter shall be construed to prohibit or require the licensing of the practice of the religious tenets of any church in the ministration to the sick and suffering by mental or spiritual means without the use of any drug or material remedy, whether gratuitously or for compensation."[24] And finally, under the Virginia Board of Behavioral Science, Department of Professional and Occupational Regulation, the 1975 revision of the exemption clause states, "The requirements for licensure or certification provided for in this chapter shall not be applicable to:

The activities of rabbis, priests, ministers or clergymen of any religious denomination or sect when such activities are within the scope of the performance of their regular or specialized duties, and for which no separate charge is made or when such activities are performed, whether with or without charge, for or under auspices or sponsorship, individually or in conjunction with others, of an established and legally cognizable church, denomination or sect, and when the person rendering service remains accountable to the established authority thereof."[25]

141

This last exemption clause allows Virginia clergy to decide whether or not they want to become licensed. Licensing usually involves successfully completing a written examination, payment of an annual fee for renewal of the license, and submission of annual data regarding professional practices.

It is the responsibility of each professional organization to set the standards for excellence within the profession and monitor the professional and ethical practices of its member constituency. One of the goals of licensure laws is to protect the public from exploitation and/or damage. The laws are designed to limit, as much as possible, those persons who either intentionally or unintentionally provide useless or harmful services. Another goal of licensure laws is to establish minimum standards of training and experience in order to assure the consuming public a reasonable degree of professional competency. Laws alone cannot guarantee competency or eliminate fraud and that is why professional organizations like the AAPC must take seriously these responsibilities.

Pastoral Counseling Centers and Tax Exempt Status

Up to this point in the discussion the focus has been on the individual pastoral counselor. At this juncture, the focus will shift from the individual to the pastoral counseling center. What steps must a pastoral counseling center go through in order to attain "tax-exempt status" from federal income tax? "An organization may qualify for exemption from federal income tax if it is organized and operated exclusively for one or more of the following purposes: charitable, religious, scientific, testing for public safety, literary, educational."[26]

Procedures for obtaining recognition of tax exemption can be found in Internal Revenue Service Publication 557, "How to Apply for Recognition of Exemption for an Organization." Materials required to accompany the application for recognition of exemption include: (a) articles of incorporation, constitution or articles of association; (b) a copy of the organization's by-laws or other rules for its operation; (c) statement of financial support; (d) statement of fund-raising activities; and (e) a narrative description of the activities carried on by the organization.

An activity code number will also be necessary on the application. This code number identifies the purposes, activities, or operations of the particular organization requesting exemption. Activity code numbers of exempt organizations which might apply to pastoral counseling centers include: 166, mental health care; 653, marriage counseling; 569, referral service; 004, church auxiliary; and 029, other religious activities. Activity code numbers and other information can be obtained from Internal Revenue Service Publication, Package 1023, "Application for Recognition of Exemption."

Form 1023, the "Application for Recognition of Exemption," should be used to apply for a "ruling" or "determination" of an organization's tax-exempt status from federal income tax. The official "ruling" could be a useful document when it comes to claiming certain tax benefits or third-party insurance coverage. If a pastoral counseling center qualifies for federal income tax exemption, the "ruling" would recognize the organization's tax-exempt status under Section 501(c) (3) of the Internal Revenue Service Code which was quoted above.

Organizations formed after October 9, 1969 have fifteen months from the time of organization in which to file Application Form 1023 in order to qualify as a tax-exempt organization. Failure to meet the deadline could result in an Internal Revenue Service classification as a "private foundation," an entity which is taxed at the rate of 4 percent per year.

Some organizations created after October 9, 1969, are not required to file Form 1023. These are churches, their integrated auxiliaries, and conventions or associations of churches; and organizations having annual gross receipts normally no more than $5,000.00, and which are not private foundations. . . . However, if such an

143

organization wants to establish its exemption with Internal Revenue Service and receive a ruling or determination letter recognizing its exempt status, it should file Form 1023 with the (IRS) District Director.[27]

Incorporation

Incorporation is a legal process regulated by state laws to formalize an organization or a business into a legal "entity." State laws are designed to protect the corporation, the state, and the consuming public. Guidelines for incorporating can be obtained by writing the secretary of state's office in the state in which the pastoral counseling center exists and/or by securing the services of a competent lawyer. The "Articles of Incorporation Under the General Not-for-Profit Corporation Act," which is the application for incorporation in Illinois, requires that the following information accompany the application: (a) names and addresses of three incorporators; (b) the name of the corporation; (c) the period of duration of the corporation; (d) the address of the corporation; (e) the names and addresses of the first board of directors; (f) the purposes of the corporation; and (h) the seal of a notary public. An application fee of $25.00 is also required in Illinois.

There are two practical reasons for incorporating as a not-for-profit corporation. First, incorporation provides the corporation with a "life of its own," including assets apart from the private lives of the individuals employed by the corporation. This could be important in the event of a lawsuit against the corporation. With incorporation, only the assets of the corporation could be liable, whereas without incorporation, personal property and individual assets could also be liable. That is, incorporation serves to protect the personal lives of the individuals employed by the corporation apart from the corporate entity.

A second practical reason for incorporating is the enjoyment of certain tax benefits. In the event of high income, above $50,000, the corporation is taxed at a lower level than is an individual.

144

Malpractice Insurance

It seems appropriate that pastoral counselors and pastoral counseling centers be covered by malpractice insurance. Otherwise one lawsuit could sufficiently occupy staff time and/or finances so as to cripple the organization. In a recent survey, 62 percent of the pastoral counselors who responded indicated that they were covered by some form of malpractice insurance. The annual fees ranged from $15–$100, with the median being $40.[28] As with other kinds of insurance coverage, group plans offer more reasonable rates than do individual policies. Professional organizations like the National Alliance for Family Life, Inc.,[29] the American Association of Pastoral Counselors, Inc.,[30] and the American Association of Marriage and Family Therapists, Inc.,[31] offer members and other interested professionals the opportunity to join group malpractice plans at reasonable rates.

National Health Insurance

It appears likely that by 1990 national health insurance of one form or another will be a reality in the United States. Whether or not pastoral counselors will be eligible for third-party reimbursements is, as yet, an unanswered question. Many professional organizations are taking steps which increase the likelihood of eligibility. NAFL, Inc., is a broadly based, interprofessional organization attempting to influence national health insurance legislation so that it will provide reimbursement for mental health services rendered by all "clinical counselors," whether they be psychiatrists, pastoral counselors, social workers, psychologists, or marriage and family counselors. It is conceivable that pastoral counseling centers could become qualified "comprehensive community mental health centers" as defined under proposed national health insurance plans and therefore be eligible to receive reimbursement for services rendered. The Association of Clinical Pastoral Education, Inc., is attempting to become

145

so qualified. However, with increasing governmental involvement in and regulation for national health insurance, in order for pastoral counseling centers to receive third-party reimbursements, increasingly stringent and complex standards and specifications must be met. The AAMFT legal struggle with CHAMPUS[32] is a case in point. AAPC joined AAMFT in a costly and strenuous legal struggle to restore reimbursements to pastoral and marriage and family counselors from the Department of Defense for counseling services rendered.

There seems to be anxiety, not only in Virginia, but around the country, that we will all go out of business if we can't dip into the insurance till. I doubt if this anxiety is grounded in much reality. . . . My concern is that the pressure of economics related to third-party payments not force the pastoral care and counseling management into an increasing insistence on the mental health practitioner stance.[33]

In some respects clergy potentially have unique protective qualities under principles of separation of church and state in the United States Constitution. On the other hand, clergy are maximally vulnerable because historically they have not been well organized. The latter point is an ever-increasing necessity in order to propose protective legislation in our more and more legalistic society. Professional organizations like the AAPC can be helpful in these matters.

It is hoped that this chapter serves to shed some light on a few of the legal issues facing the pastoral counselor and the pastoral counseling center. A few of the topics discussed, like national health insurance and third-party payments, are broad and complex enough to warrant separate chapters; those chapters will be saved for another book.

Notes

1. Walter E. Barton and Charlotte J. Sanborn, *Law and the Mental Health Professions: Friction at the Interface* (International Universities Press, 1978), p. 139.

2. *American Association of Pastoral Counselors Handbook*, AAPC

Handbook 2, revised July 25, 1978, p. 28. Address: 3000 Connecticut Avenue, N.W., Suite 300, Washington, D.C. 10008.

3. Goldstein and Katz, "Psychiatrist-Patient Privilege: the GAP Proposal and the Connecticut Statute," *American Journal of Psychiatry*, 118 (1962), 734.

4. *AAPC Handbook*, p. 29.

5. Walter Barton and Charlotte Sanborn, p. 139.

6. Leila M. Foster, "Do you want to share your therapy tapes with the court?" *Professional Psychology* (November, 1974), 369.

7. J. H. Wigmore, *Evidence in Trials at Common Law*, rev. ed., vol. 8, Section 2285 (Boston: Little, Brown, 1961), p. 527.

8. *AAPC Handbook*, p. 24.

9. Binder vs. Ruvel, No. 52C2535, Circuit Court of Cook County, Illinois, 1952, reported in the *Journal of the American Medical Association*, 150.

10. Ralph Slovenko, *Psychotherapy, Confidentiality, and Privileged Communication* (Illinois: Charles C. Thomas Press, 1966), p. 105.

11. Morris L. Ernst and Alan U. Schwartz, *Privacy: The Right to Be Let Alone* (New York: Macmillan Company, 1962), p. 150.

12. Herbert J. Johnson, "Don't Confide in Me," *Christian Advocate* (January 27, 1966), 9.

13. *Ibid.*

14. *Ibid.*, p. 10.

15. *Ibid.*, p. 9.

16. Illinois Revised Statutes, chapter 51, section 48.1, *Communications to Clergymen*, approved August 17, 1961.

17. Leila M. Foster, "Privileged Communications: When Psychiatrists Envy the Clergy," *Journal of Pastoral Care*, 30:2 (June, 1976), 118.

18. *AAPC Handbook*, p. 26.

19. William C. Nichols, "Marriage and Family Counseling: A Legislative Handbook," American Association of Marriage and Family Therapists, Inc., 924 W. Ninth Street, Upland, California 91786.

20. Secretary of State's Office, State House, Concord, New Hampshire 03301, *Licensed Pastoral Counselors Act*, chapter 330-B.

21. James Kilgore, personal correspondence, Nov., 1973, p. 2. 275 Carpenter Drive, Atlanta, Georgia 30328. 22. *Ibid.*

23. Contact the Executive Director, American Association of Pastoral Counselors, Inc., see note 2.

24. *Virginia Code*, The Virginia Code Commission, vol. 7A, 1950.

25. Robert L. Myers, "State Licensing and Pastoral Identity," *Journal of Pastoral Care*, 30:2 (June, 1976), 80.

26. Internal Revenue Service, Code Section 501 (c) (3) in "How to Apply

for an Exemption for an Organization" (Washington, D.C.: U.S. Government Printing Office, 1968), Publication 557, p. 3.

27. *Ibid.*, p. 5.

28. John L. Florell, "Results of AAPC Research Relative to Insurance Payments and Internal Revenue Questions," February, 1975, The Health Center, 702 North East Street, Bloomington, Illinois 61701.

29. National Alliance for Family Life, Inc., 1801 K Street, N.W., Suite 220, Washington, D.C. 20006.

30. See note 2.

31. American Association of Marriage and Family Therapy, Inc., 924 W. Ninth Street, Upland, California 91786.

32. Civilian Health and Medical Program for the Uniformed Services.

33. Robert Myers, 80-81.

P A R T

THREE

CLINICAL AND CONSULTING FACTORS

9

Issues of Clinical Practice
in Pastoral Counseling Centers
Emily Demme Haight

The concept of clinical practice encompasses all aspects of a pastoral counseling center which directly affect the kind and quality of treatment provided by the center. Whenever an aspect of the pastoral counseling center (e.g., policy, procedures, personnel, theoretical orientation, etc.) interacts with a given counseling session, there is a need for careful evaluation of the situation from a clinical perspective. Therefore, issues of clinical practice overlap considerably with concerns for business practice, center development, training, administration, and legal integrity. Of particular interest for discussion here are: (1) the psychological orientation and theology of the pastoral counseling center, (2) personnel job satisfaction, (3) clinical procedures, and (4) quality control.

The reader is referred to the *AAPC Handbook* and particularly to the "Code of Professional Practice and Standards for Membership" for guidelines regarding the issues treated in this chapter.

The Psychological Orientation and Theology of a Pastoral Counseling Center

With the current proliferation of psychological theories and concomitant treatment methodologies, pastoral counseling centers may vary considerably in their approaches to the treatment of emotional distress. The complexity of choosing a treatment philosophy can be simplified into two basic issues: (1) the choice between a single or multiple approach, and (2) the selection of a general model of human personality which will be used to determine appropriate clinical procedures.

A pastoral counseling center may provide a single-treatment approach in which all the counselors adhere to the same general theory of treatment, e.g., psychoanalytically oriented psychotherapy, Rogerian methods, transactional analysis, etc. All of the clinical procedures (initial contacts, client assignments, staffing reports) are somewhat standardized to enhance that one treatment modality. A client may know fairly accurately what to expect from knowing the center's reputation for offering a particular style of counseling. The advantages of such a unified, single-approach center are: (1) the staff will tend to have less trouble communicating with each other by using the same technical vocabulary and theoretical presuppositions, and (2) training and supervision resources can be more universally applied for the entire staff.

Other pastoral counseling centers have a multiple-treatment approach in which each counselor practices his or her own particular specialty or preferred style of counseling. Clients may choose from the diversity of treatments offered or may be assigned to a particular counselor who specializes in a particular type of problem. The advantages of the multiple approach include the possibility of serving a wider variety of client populations and clinical problems, and the possibility for mutual dialogue across theoretical lines. In multiple-approach centers, counselors usually arrange individually for their training and supervision with professionals outside the center.

The choice of a single- or multiple-approach center is usually made by the founding organization at the inception of the center or at the time the center grows from being a single- to a multiple-member staff. If the center director is given the authority to hire future staff members, there should be a clear understanding from the governing board as to whether the center is to be a single- or multiple-approach center.

The second basic issue in deciding a center's orientation is whether its procedures will reflect a particular theoretical view of human behavior, e.g., deterministic, nondeterministic, or modified deterministic. Some centers, such as those using a group-practice model, might not embrace one particular viewpoint. A highly organized center in which counselors are interdependent through staffings or group supervision of each other's work will operate more smoothly if it does not try to combine opposing theoretical orientations, such as deterministic and nondeterministic viewpoints.

Pastoral counseling centers also differ in relation to how they understand their "pastoral identity." For some centers, it is sufficient that the founding organization has a religious affiliation. The pastoral counseling center is simply a ministry performed by a religious body which provides professional counseling services to the community (e.g., community-based, group-practice, or satellite-center models). In this case, the religious affiliation of staff members is not an issue. Other centers are very conscious of their pastoral identity. They seek ordained or theologically trained personnel who are skilled in bringing the resources of Scripture, sacramental understanding, and religious ideation, as well as psychological expertise, into the treatment situation. Some centers retain a theological consultant. Nonclergy personnel might be asked to seek AAPC affiliation as Professional Affiliates, for example. Wherever a center stands on the continuum from minimal to strong religious commitment, careful thought should be given to the theological rationale and purpose for the center's existence. Such an understanding might emerge from a dialogue including the founding organization, the board of directors, the advisory board, cooperating parishes, staff members, and local theologians.

Personnel

"The best counselor is a happy counselor." This statement, made at an AAPC workshop for directors of pastoral counseling centers, does not mean that good counselors are never sad. The speaker was referring to the necessity for personnel satisfaction with the job situation to ensure optimal performance. Issues involved in personnel satisfaction are the determination of an amount of remuneration and fringe benefits provided; center organization; expectations regarding administrative, public relations, training, or supervisory responsibilities over and above counseling hours; facilities; opportunities for growth and/or advancement; caseload; case assignments; and peer relationships and morale. To the extent that these personnel issues intersect with the counselor's proficiency in the therapy session, they are clinical issues.

Remuneration. For a discussion of the variety of ways in which staff salaries or fees may be calculated, see chapter 5 on business practices. Whatever system is utilized should be clearly and concisely understood by all staff members. If an administrator has decision-making power regarding increases or advancement, periodic review of a counselor's performance should be guaranteed.

Job descriptions. Due to the variety of functions to be cared for in the operation of a pastoral counseling center (e.g., administration, public relations, training, screening of applicants) and the current demand for counseling services, clear job descriptions are indispensable. (Sample job descriptions are given in Appendix B.) Time estimates for each assigned responsibility should be included and kept realistic within the time commitments of the staff member to the center.

Caseload. Counseling, unlike many other types of work, requires that the counselor invest a considerable amount of his or her emotional energy into an intimate two-way relationship with clients in distress. For this reason, care must be taken to safeguard the counselor's effectiveness and to prevent over-loading. A counselor spending six hours a day (thirty hours per week) in one-to-one or group therapy (and/or supervision of trainees or other professionals) is operating at maximum capacity. Additional working hours may include staffings (case conferences), personal supervision, and administrative, public relations, or training responsibilities. At best, the noncounseling hours can be interspersed among the counseling hours so as to provide some relief from the intensity of the therapeutic situation.

Peer relationships and morale. Pastoral counseling centers vary in their methods of organization from hierarchical, delegative structures to democratic, group-process decision-making for the assignment of responsibilities. Whatever system is adopted should be clearly understood by all. Grievance channels should be included. Prompt attention to problems of staff morale or job dissatisfaction will benefit the center's clients by upholding the quality of counseling provided by the center.

Some larger centers have found it helpful to provide a coffee lounge for "staff only" so that staff members who work in isolation much of the day can congregate for informal discussion, or unwinding.

Clinical Procedures

Although pastoral counseling centers vary in the clinical procedures utilized, five general stages of treatment can be identified for purposes of comparison and discussion: (1) initial contact; (2) intake procedures; (3) staff consultation; (4) treatment or referral; and (5) termination of treatment. In some centers there are clear delineations between these stages, while in others they are less distinguishable.

Initial contact. Several options for handling initial contacts are listed below:

1) When the prospective client calls the center, a secretary takes the name and address and mails the person an application which can either be mailed or brought back to the center. Completed applications are distributed to staff counselors (or trainees) and when a counselor is available for an intake session, he or she makes an appointment with the applicant.

2) When the prospective client calls the center, a secretary

trained in interviewing asks the client questions regarding the problems for which he or she is seeking help. An application for counseling is completed by the secretary on the basis of the interview. If a counselor has time open which is designated for intake interviews, the secretary will arrange the initial session for the next available time.

3) One staff member (sometimes the center director) is assigned the administrative responsibility of returning calls of prospective clients and, on the basis of a short telephone interview, assigns the client to a particular counselor for treatment. The decision is based on which counselor the prospective client is likely to "buy" and what fees the person can afford. This system is usually used in group practice centers when the fees charged are determined by the expertise of the particular counselor, and/or when there is no intake procedure before treatment begins.

Other alternatives are obviously possible by combining facets of these three options in different ways. In any case, the importance of the initial contact should not be underestimated. The effectiveness of whatever treatment is to follow may depend upon the sensitivity and concern as well as the professional competence the client perceives in his or her first experience with the center.

If there are particular client populations who cannot be served by the resources of the center or particular types of referrals which are not accepted, these limitations should be clearly explained and an appropriate referral made. Appendix B gives a suggestive list of client populations and types of referring agencies.

Intake procedures. The initial issue regarding intake procedures is whether or not a formal evaluation of the client's history and functioning is called for by the center's psychological orientation. Some centers provide a circumscribed intake evaluation which is contracted and paid for as a single entity apart from counseling. Other centers have no distinguishable intake process. The two examples below indicate the range of possible procedures:

1) Center X, a hospital outpatient pastoral counseling center, operates largely on a medical model of mental illness and highly values a thorough diagnostic intake procedure. Clients agree to a three-to-five-session intake process for a designated fee and understand that the staff person doing the intake may or may not be the counselor assigned for treatment. The initial session is used to establish a contract for the intake procedure, to probe into the nature, etiology, and development of the presenting complaints, and to ascertain the expectations the client brings into the treatment situation. One or two fifty-minute sessions are devoted to obtaining a thorough history. Additional history sessions may be required for a couple or family intake process. The Taylor-Johnson Temperament Analysis is administered in order to obtain the person's perceptions of him- or herself and of significant others. Records of any previous psychological treatment are requested after the client authorizes the release of that information. If there has been no recent medical examination, clients are advised or required to obtain one. If there are signs of possible neurological lesion or damage, the hospital facilities are utilized for a complete examination and consultation. The counselor writes a comprehensive summary report for presentation to a full-staff consultation before a psychiatric consultant. The final session of the intake period is used for feedback and treatment recommendations to the client.

A university-seminary pastoral counseling center uses a similar approach but relies on available psychometric resources, including the Minnesota Multiphasic Personality Inventory (MMPI) and the Wechsler Adult Intelligence Scale (WAIS).

2) Center Y assigns clients to counselors on the basis of the initial telephone or walk-in interview. Treatment begins immediately with only the developmental material the client chooses to offer and regards as significant. The client "buys" or does not "buy" the particular counselor and the relationship they establish as being helpful to him or her. After four to six

156

weeks of therapy, a staff consultation evaluates the progress they have made toward establishing a working therapeutic alliance and may recommend a different course of treatment (group, referral, change of counselor, etc.)

These two examples illustrate polar points on a continuum of intake procedures. Many possibilities lie in between. In my opinion, some exploratory intake procedure is highly valuable before any particular treatment is undertaken. Too often several months of treatment can be wasted before a client mentions or recognizes a key aspect of the problem, which is often brought out in a routine history or testing situation. Physical or neurological symptoms may be overlooked without a comprehensive historical perspective of the problem. Many clients find the history-taking process to be a novel and integrating experience which instigates much initial self-evaluation and enhances counseling readiness.

The usefulness of psychological testing as an intake procedure is widely debated. If psychological instruments are to be used, care must be taken to ensure the proper administration, scoring, interpretation, use, and storage of test materials within professional and legal guidelines. Persons with proper licensing and expertise should be members of the staff or consultants. One danger of using tests is that the client sometimes feels that "the therapist knows more about me than I do" and a highly dependent attitude toward the therapist may be engendered. Clients should understand what tests can and cannot do.

Whether or not there is value in clinical diagnosis is another contested issue. If pathology is labeled, such information must be handled carefully. Diagnostic categories are for the convenience of the therapist in establishing and carrying out a treatment plan. It is rarely helpful for clients to know their diagnostic labels. In any case, if in doubt, choose the category with the less severe prognosis and communicate it only to persons who know the technical meanings and proper use of such labels.

Staff consultations (see conferences). In larger centers, staff consultations are usually a built-in professional service for the therapist and, indirectly, for clients. For one-person or small pastoral counseling centers, obtaining adequate case consultation is more problematic and may entail liaison with larger centers, cooperation among several small centers, or contracting with nonpastoral professionals or groups. In hospital settings, staffings before a psychiatric consultant are often mandatory by hospital policy or state law. Case consultations may also include the client's parish pastor or previous mental health worker, and in at least one center, the client has the option of sitting in on the conference (for a higher fee). The case staffing, or restaffing, in the case of a change in recommendations for treatment, is one of the basic tools for quality control of the counseling provided by the center, internal staff development, and trainee exposure to case material.

Treatment and referral. Usually case consultation results in a recommendation for a particular type of counseling within the center, for referral to an outside therapist or agency, or for no treatment at all. For accurate judgments to be made, it must be clear what services the center can provide. Limitations of staff, lack of expertise, and considerations related to the efficient use of center resources may dictate referral.

Referral is itself an important form of treatment—the application of the center's resources to the client's problem. The *art* of referring clients in such a way that the referral is completed with a smooth transition is discussed in chapter 12. Additional resources treating the issue of referrals made by pastoral counselors are (1) William B. Oglesby, Jr., *Referral in Pastoral Counseling* (Philadelphia: Fortress Press, 1968) and (2) Ronald R. Lee, "Referral as an Example of Pastoral Care," *Journal of Pastoral Care*, 30:3 (1976), 186-97. Also, see chapter 12 on referral in this *Handbook*.

If referral is done properly, the client does not feel rejected and does not "fall through the cracks" because of faulty communication. A comprehensive, up-to-date, annotated list of local referral resources, or a library of information, is extremely valuable. Local United Fund or similar agencies may have lists of community referral resources. Establishing and maintaining personal contacts with local private-practice professionals is an important aspect of a center's development and ongoing operation.

Termination. In some centers, a client who has terminated or is about to terminate therapy is again presented to the staff consultation for evaluation and possible recommendations for future therapy or personal growth. Most centers require that a termination report be filed.

Quality Control of the Product

The concept of quality control is no less applicable to pastoral counseling centers than to a pharmaceutical company—and no less essential. Periodic review is a mandatory professional responsibility; ongoing evaluative research on therapeutic effectiveness is a desirable luxury. The major tools for evaluating and maintaining the quality of the center's product are: (1) personnel standards, (2) supervision, (3) case conferences, (4) job reviews, (5) adequate record keeping, and (6) access to statistical and demographic data about the center's performance.

The most important single factor in quality control is *personnel standards,* the basic tools and skills with which a staff member comes to the center. Training programs should be carefully studied for the amount of clinical and academic experience required of their graduates. A clinical social worker may have better qualifications than a Ph.D. in pastoral psychology if the doctorate required little or no direct clinical experience or supervision! AAPC membership categories provide excellent guidelines for personnel standards.

Supervision, either individual or group, is the responsibility of every mental health professional, whether it is provided by the pastoral counseling center or contracted for individually.

The number of hours of recommended supervision varies from one hour of supervision for every one hour of counseling for the beginning trainee, to one hour for every three to four of counseling after two years of training, to one hour for every seven to eight or more for experienced therapists. Supervision may include listening to taped sessions, analyzing verbatims, role playing, or other methods which help therapists evaluate both their personal style and effectiveness, and their feelings about developments in therapy. In some centers a psychiatric consultant oversees staff supervision and any supervision of supervisor-trainees. Group-practice pastoral counseling centers often use a system of peer supervision.

As mentioned above, the *case conference* (staff consultation) is a valuable check on the quality of treatment provided by the pastoral counseling center.

A period *job review*, whether conducted by a superior in a hierarchical structure or by a peer group in a colleagial structure, is another step toward maintaining quality service. Besides a review of how well the job description is being fulfilled and a discussion of significant cases, other more subtle indications of effectiveness may be evaluated—how tardy are the therapist's clients in paying their bills, what is the average length of time the therapist's clients stay in therapy, how many appointments are cancelled or broken, how many referrals are carried through to completion, how much overtime is the therapist using to complete the assigned job, how complete are his or her clinical records, and what is the current status of the therapist's own use of personal psychotherapy?

Adequate record keeping. This topic is discussed here because quality control is one of the major reasons for keeping records in a pastoral counseling center. It is important for anyone evaluating a staff member or the center as a whole to be able to ascertain from records (1) what services were provided (kinds of counseling, style, and modality), (2) to what kinds of clients (diagnosis if used, age, sex, income level), (3) for what fees, (4) with what results (satisfactory or unsatisfactory terminations, effective or ineffective referrals, client complaints, etc.). Obviously, billing records and information for referrals need to be readily available. Some centers may require a summary of the intake evaluation, weekly or monthly process notes with a record of supervisory or consultant comment, and a termination report on file in case of legal action against the center. Other centers do not keep such records. Any records beyond those required by the basic necessities of the center's operations are for the convenience of the therapist and may be flexible for his or her own use. Records which are essential for the operation of the center should be clearly understood as such by the staff. In any case, forms should be as simple as possible and kept to a minimum. The confidentiality of all records should be carefully safeguarded with clear guidelines as to how information is disbursed. Chapter 8 discusses confidentiality and other legal issues related to record keeping in more detail.

Other Clinical Practice Issues

Taping of sessions. Some centers encourage the taping of all sessions for potential use in supervision, case presentations, training programs, or research projects. Clients should be aware that sessions are being taped, for what reason, and who has access to the tapes.

Facilities. Chapter 5 on business practices contains a listing of types of facilities used by pastoral counseling centers. The clinicial issue involved is the image which various facilities convey to clients. The clinical setting (e.g., in a church building, hospital setting, private office, etc.) affects the expectations clients bring with them into treatment. The decor should be tasteful, appropriate for the comfort of the particular client population, and should communicate professional competence and pride in its maintenance. Offices should be soundproof if possible, well marked, easy to locate, and well away from other activities in the building.

Public relations. The image which a pastoral counseling center presents to the public is a clinical issue because it affects both the expectations which clients bring with them to the center and what types of clients will be referred to the center by other professionals. Good taste and professional quality are important ingredients of any public relations display, brochure, or presentation. The goal of public relations efforts for a pastoral counseling center is not only to raise funds but also to present a simple and accurate description of what the center is and is not, what it can and cannot do. If the public relations task is done properly, many initial obstacles to clinical effectiveness can be avoided.

Crisis intervention. Some pastoral counseling centers provide additional services designed to help persons in need of immediate, short-term crisis intervention, usually supportive in nature. Examples are walk-in appointments during office hours or a twenty-four-hour telephone service with a counselor "on call" at all times. Such services are often a much needed form of community mental health care, and they also provide the center with many long-term client referrals. However, crisis intervention services also require a large investment of staff time and energy, often without any return of fees to the budget. Additional nonfee funding may be required to support such services, or special funding might be more effectively used in training local pastors and laypersons to carry on this ministry. If crisis intervention is provided as a service of the center, there should be a clear limitation on the length of time a person may use the short-term services.

Relationship to parish pastors. Some pastoral counseling centers are designed to be extensions of the pastoral care provided by local parish pastors. To fulfill this function, particular attention is focused on establishing and maintaining close working relationships with clergy. Priority is given to referrals from pastors. Persons terminating therapy are referred back to their local pastor for continuing follow-up pastoral care and to their local congregations as a source of future support and religious growth. Pastors are encouraged to remain informed about the progress their parishioners are making in therapy and to play an active, supportive role. Special efforts are made to provide educational and training opportunities for pastors in pastoral care.

Female staff members. With the growing numbers of women graduating from accredited pastoral counseling and other mental health programs, it is becoming possible to offer clients a choice of having either a male or female counselor, or both. Much very recent theorizing and research is appearing regarding previously neglected, poorly interpreted, or currently emerging problems faced by women in modern society. Male-female therapist teams have reported new treatment possibilities. Any center which fails to evaluate itself in light of these recent developments is in danger of providing less than adequate care for both women and men.

In concluding this chapter an overview seems appropriate. Five issues have been addressed, each one central to the clinical practices conducted in pastoral counseling centers. Like other contributors to this volume, I believe these to be vital components of the pastoral counseling movement. A pastoral counseling center, regardless of its model, must have: (1) a psychological orientation and a theological thrust which complement each other holistically; (2) its personnel need to be consistently aware of the far-reaching effects of clinical proficiency; (3) advocates of the pastoral psychology movement need to be attentive to the different clinical procedures utilized in different centers by other ministers; (4) quality control in areas such as staff certification in the clinical categories of AAPC (especially at the Fellow and Diplomate - levels), supervision, and consultation as well as record keeping practices are but a few practices which should be the subject of evaluation; and (5) selected rather than routine taping of sessions, public relations, and ongoing interdisciplinary

163

dialogues must be maintained. Collectively, each of these issues blends, supports, and continually effects the basic ideal of the pastoral counselor—the best and most appropriate service for those who seek assistance from clergy who have specialized in psychotherapeutic ministry.

C H A P T E R

10

The Psychiatric Consultation in Pastoral Counseling Centers

Carl W. Christensen

Not all pastoral counseling centers need or want a psychiatric consultant as part of their organization. Frequently, such centers perform a useful but limited service in their community. However, depending upon the goals of the center, a psychiatric consultant can be an asset in many respects. His or her presence as an active participant in the functioning of the center can increase the scope of its services, add prestige to its functioning, and augment its credibility in the community. If a psychiatric consultant is utilized, there are a number of factors to be considered in order to employ this expertise in a manner which can eminently fulfill the aims of the counseling center. These factors are not intended to spawn what might be considered "medical imperialism." They are issues that foster interdisciplinary support, legal assistance, and quality care in pastoral service.

To begin with, the function of a consultant is to consult. A psychiatric consultant to a pastoral counseling center consults on matters within the scope of the medical aspects of the center. This will depend on the goals of the center, its aims, orientation, affiliation, procedures, service, client population, income, sponsorship, and similar matters. Participation of the psychiatric consultant in the center can vary from expressing a medical opinion to involvement in basic programs. If a psychiatric consultant is going to be a part of a counseling center, care in selection, with specific delineation of the consultant's function, is essential. While some of the sources of concern are obvious, early attention to them during the process of selection will ensure the establishment of a workable relationship. The problem is relatively simple in the case of an established counseling center seeking to hire a psychiatric consultant. All that is necessary is to determine if the psychiatrist can adapt to existing practices. It is more complicated if the counseling center is in the process of being organized. I would think it a good idea to hire the psychiatric consultant early in the planning stages and seek his or her advice as indicated. This can save time and money, which often repays the initial expense.

Most of the factors important in the selection of a psychiatric consultant to a pastoral counseling center can be epitomized by the word "compatibility." This word has the dual meaning of "coexisting in harmony" and "compassion." Both qualities are essential if the psychiatric consultant is to fulfill the function of a physician in the center. Essentially, it is imperative that this person be compatible with other personalities, differing theoretical orientations and techniques, varied philosophies, and diverse motivations.

It is not redundant to emphasize that the psychiatrist must be capable of working harmoniously with other professionals. This person needs to be able to subordinate his or her authority, except in those areas where a medical opinion or judgment is indicated. In other words, the consultant must remember that a pastoral counseling center is not a psychiatric outpatient clinic. Pronouncements, recommendations, advice, counsel, and opinions are merely that and will be considered but not necessarily accepted. The exception, which involves making a medical diagnosis and prescribing treatment—legally the psychiatrist is a physician—has some interesting ramifications. But more about this later, especially relating to third party payment of fees and staffing.

In addition to personality compatibility, there must be accord regarding the theoretical orientations of the consultant and the center. While we understand that these factors are primarily of concern to the therapists and not to the clients, congruence is essential for purposes of understanding people, communicating that knowledge, and prescribing treatment. Psychiatrists favoring a medicophysiological approach to the treatment of mental disorders, for example, might find it difficult to accept a dynamic formulation of behavior as presented by a psychoanalytically oriented pastoral therapist.

Associated with the theoretical orientation is the basic philosophy of the consultant which needs to be in harmony with the aims and goals of the center. While the consultant does not necessarily have to be a member of an organized church, it is essential that this person be able to accept the historical involvement of the church with the sickness of people, and the establishment of hospitals for their care and treatment.

The conscious and unconscious motivations of the psychiatrist selected to act as a consultant must reflect interests and concerns compatible with the rationale for establishing a pastoral counseling center in the first place. An empathic, sympathetic awareness and understanding that people may prefer to consult a pastor rather than a physician in times of emotional turmoil is essential. The consultant must be able to accept the fact that there may be an "overlapping" of function in the treatment of mental disorders. Such treatment is not necessarily the sole province of the physician—others can and do learn these skills and apply them. Once it has been established that there can be a congenial relationship between the psychiatric consultant and the pastoral counseling center, then the more pragmatic functions of the psychiatric consultant can be delineated.

Practically, the psychiatric consultant has no voice in the administration of a pastoral counseling center. He or she is hired by, and subject to, the administrative authority of the center. However, a consultant can expect to be utilized in accordance with professional competence, not just as a signer of insurance forms or a sharpener of pencils. The specific nature of the consultant's functions will vary from center to center, but there are some practices which might have a general application.

In our complex society the keeping of adequate records is important. A filing system must be established which protects the anonymity of the patient while allowing adequate access to records of payment, number of sessions, diagnosis, type of treatment, consultation and supervision notes, and other mundane information useful for statistical purposes, insurance claims, and legal matters. These records are a part of the privileged communication between therapist and client, and are not to be available for casual perusal.

I think a two-file system is preferable. The second file would contain progress notes and other data useful for therapy. This is kept in the therapist's office and is not available to *anyone* except the supervisor. When therapy is terminated, a summary of the treatment with major areas covered, type of counseling, and an estimation of prognosis is filed in the first file as a termination report, and kept there along with administrative records. The second file is destroyed.

The psychiatric consultant can be of assistance in suggesting the type and form of records. For example, information essential to include on intake forms, staffing forms, and termination forms can be submitted to the consultant for suggestions and commentary. The psychiatric consultant can advise about procedures for keeping adequate progress notes and records of consultation and supervision. In obtaining information about previous medical treatment, sometimes a letter from the consulting psychiatrist will be honored when one from a pastoral therapist has been ignored.

An important function of the psychiatric consultant is to advise the administration whenever any of its practices or policies may be contrary to the best interest of the clients. This is one reason why compatibility between the administration and the consultant is so important. A consistent orientation tends to eliminate differences of opinion as to treatment modalities. In addition, knowledge of the therapeutic practices of the staff counselors is invaluable in determining their effectiveness as therapists. This knowledge is also useful during "staffing" procedures when the consultant can advise as to medical problems to be considered as part of the evaluation of the patient. But more about this in detail later.

Most pastoral counseling centers will probably operate on a fee-for-service basis. Because they may be partly sponsored by a church organization, many pastoral counseling centers will charge on a sliding scale. The psychiatric consultant can be of assistance in acquainting the center with local practice and advising concerning such factors as interpretation of nonpayment of fees, collection of delinquent accounts, and the like.

The salary paid to the psychiatric consultant is a matter of some concern. Practices will differ depending on local custom. In some instances, a yearly salary or retainer fee is indicated. More often the psychiatric consultant will be hired on an hourly basis, in which case the usual fee is that which he generally charges for psychotherapy. Rarely, a fee schedule is determined in which there is a charge for each specific service. Occasionally, the psychiatric consultant will function for a reduced fee if there are ancillary benefits.

Educationally, the psychiatric consultant can perform a valuable work, depending upon the structure of the pastoral counseling center. Case presentations during staffings may be utilized to illustrate specific problems and the rationale for prescribing treatment. In-service lectures and seminars can be a source of continual education. This is easier to arrange when the counseling center has education and community participation as part of its aims.

Since most of the community related projects are probably church sponsored, the psychiatrist's participation is, properly, limited. Of course, his or her own personal needs and interests might indicate that he or she take a more active part in this outreach. If the counseling center is affiliated with a university, seminary, or hospital, it may be actively involved in their teaching program. Didactic seminars can be held at the center in which the consulting psychiatrist can participate. The center can provide a source for clinical experience under the supervision of the staff. In such circumstances, a multiple approach will often prove effective where medical students, clinical psychologists, pastoral therapists, and social workers can meet together for matters of mutual interest. The psychiatric consultant can actively teach in such a program if interested.

As in all situations where multiple disciplines are involved, care must be given to clarify the scope of the program before it is implemented. Where clinical instruction, at the undergraduate level, is part of the program, experience would indicate this be done by members of each specific profession. It would seem reasonable that pastoral counselors be taught by pastoral counselors and so forth. Taped recordings of intake and therapeutic sessions by the students can be an important learning experience for them. Interpretation of therapeutic interaction and process by the psychiatric consultant may greatly influence the maturation of students as counselors. In this area there is often an "overlapping" of function; the consultant can effectively teach counseling techniques, not to make quasi psychiatrists but to improve counseling skills.

The research functions of the psychiatric consultation are only limited by motivation and the case material. Publishing research should be encouraged, giving credit to the center and sponsoring institutions when indicated. In my experience, most Ph.D. candidates have had more training in the interpretation of research than the average psychiatric consultant. However, the consultant can be a resource person in the research activities of the center.

One of the more prepotent functions of the psychiatric consultant is active participation in staffings, provided such a procedure is part of the center's organization. The psychiatric consultant has a dual responsibility.

First, from the data presented by the pastoral therapist, the psychiatrist makes a working diagnosis. This is generally a multiple diagnosis which includes any psychoneurotic or psychotic process and a diagnosis of the characterological structure (e.g. depressive reaction with a passive-aggressive personality trait disorder). Ancillary diagnoses may also be made such as: marital maladjustment, psychophysiological gastro-intestinal reaction, history of duodenal ulcer, and the like.

Although practices will differ, generally the psychiatric consultant does not interview the patient, so the working diagnosis is an expression of an opinion based upon the presentation of the staff counselor. It is, therefore, imperative that the consultant have knowledge of the counselor in order to interpret the data. Quite often, it is this working diagnosis made by the consultant which is the accepted one for payment of insurance claims and which is the only diagnosis that has legal validity. Thus, if the counseling center is going to use staffing procedures, it is necessary that the psychiatric consultant have adequate data which can substantiate the diagnosis, since this may be a legal responsibility.

Second, it is a responsibility of the psychiatric consultant to collaborate with the staff counselors about the preferred mode of psychotherapy. Most of the people who come to a pastoral counseling center have the expectation of being treated at the center. Thus, the consultant must understand the different modalities of treatment utilized at the center and indications for their use. Knowledge of the technical skills of the staff is helpful in assigning therapists. Disposition will be made on the basis of these factors and the dynamic formulation as presented by the intake counselor. While disposition is usually the result of staff discussion and concurrence, if there is disagreement, the psychiatrist's recommendation should be reconsidered. This is because it is on the basis of his "prescription" that most insurance companies pay for counseling done by nonpsychiatrists.

Questions as to whether counseling is psychotherapy, whether marital therapy is medical treatment, and whether group therapy is valid treatment are actively being discussed. So far there are no answers based upon standard practices, but as more and more therapy is being done outside the medical profession, decisions will be made.

In the course of counseling, various factors impinge upon the process, positively or negatively, which might call for a modification of treatment. Under such circumstances, restaffing could well be indicated. Depending upon the practice of the center, the psychiatric consultant may advise and/or prescribe treatment. If the consultant's counsel is not sought and he or she believes the anticipated change is contrary to the best interests of the client, the consultant has the obligation to express this opinion, which is recorded as part of the restaffing progress note. Rarely is the consultant's opinion disregarded by the staff.

Ultimately, therapy terminates for a variety of reasons. Termination staffing can be a valuable learning experience for the entire staff. In this respect, a positive conclusion to counseling is as important to share as a negative one. Premature terminations must always be staffed so that all may benefit from the experience. The psychiatric consultant can function as a teacher. Compassion will help to keep instructing from becoming lecturing.

In the course of time there will be people seeking help at the center who can better be treated elsewhere. It is one of the functions of the staffing to make such referrals. The psychiatric consultant can be a source of counsel in these matters. Particular knowledge of community resources can aid in the referral process. It is clearly understood that the psychiatric consultant does no treatment at the center. He or she does not offer psychotherapy or prescribe medication. The psychiatric consultant does not accept referrals from the staffings. If psychiatric treatment is indicated, the client is referred to his or her own physician, to a mental health resource, or to a psychiatrist in the client's community. Concentrating as it does on the briefer individual therapies, group therapy, conjoint marital therapy, and the like, the center has limited therapeutic goals. If long-term treatment is indicated, the individual staff counselor may include the psychiatric consultant as one of several resources available to the client.

As previously mentioned, an important responsibility of the psychiatric consultant is the supervision of psychotherapy by the staff counselors. Coming as they do from a variety of training programs, there are differences in their practice of therapy. Supervision by the psychiatric consultant serves to crystallize a relatively uniform technique at the center. For this reason, it is essential that there be compatibility between the theory and practice of the pastoral therapists and the psychiatric consultant. Supervision is a complicated process with which we are not concerned at this time. Nevertheless, there are aspects of supervision which influence the effectiveness of the counseling center. One of the more obvious concerns is whether a pastoral counselor should be supervised by a psychiatrist at all. Of course, the question has a broader application relating to those professions presuming to do psychotherapy.

I think supervision of psychotherapy needs to be done by those qualified to do supervision. In the years that I have supervised the psychotherapy of medical students, interns, psychiatric residents, ministers, and pastoral therapists, I have found them anxious to learn what I had to teach them. However, there are those who cannot be supervised because of their own fears, resistance, ignorance, and the like. This needs to be recognized early and dealt with administratively. Certainly, the extent of supervision will be determined by the philosophy of the center. Whether supervision is therapist oriented, patient concerned, or process directed, will depend upon actual circumstances. A psychiatric consultant as supervisor has the responsibility of meeting these needs.

The mechanics of supervision will differ considerably in practice. Ideally, one hour of supervision for every three hours of therapy, by an experienced therapist, is preferred for a beginning therapist. I believe that the psychiatric consultant should have autonomy regarding the techniques employed. Where supervision is a standard part of the operation of the center, tape recordings of therapeutic sessions are an invaluable adjunct to the supervisory process. Indeed, some counseling centers make it mandatory, as center policy, to tape record all patient-therapist interactions, except telephone conversations. The use of this material is left to the judgment of the psychiatric consultant. I prefer to focus on the therapeutic process as revealed through patient-therapist communication. A "microscopic" analysis of vocabulary, associations, silences, expletives, body movements, is preferred to the more "macroscopic" analysis of the interaction of the total hour, especially with the less experienced therapists. Supervision of therapy gives the psychiatric consultant the information needed to evaluate the data at staffings and prescribe treatment.

A significant responsibility of the psychiatric consultant is implied in the advisory function with the center. For the most part center policy, determined by the administration, will be representative of the highest ethical standards. If they are not, the psychiatric consultant has the duty to engage the administration in conversation about their practice. This can be a source of some concern when, as a result of this supervisory function, the consultant determines that in his or her best judgment a minister is, in fact, incompetent and untrainable as a pastoral psychotherapist. In the interest of maintaining quality control, when the counselor's own psychopathology interferes in the treatment process, adequate remedial action must be taken. In some instances the supervisor might recommend to the administration that certain types of personalities not be assigned to the therapist, temporarily, pending resolution of an impasse, a blindspot, or other countertransference phenomenon.

Periodically, it is good practice for the counseling center to review its administrative policies, examine its treatment modalities, assess its service record, and evaluate the performance of its staff. The psychiatric consultant needs to participate in these activities as they pertain to his or her own work at the center. In addition, the consultant can often profit by an appraisal of personal performance from those of the staff

174

with whom the psychiatrist interacts. Such mutual evaluation helps maintain high standards of performance and ensures continuance of quality control.

In this day, the importance of third-party interference in treatment relationships, be it pastoral counseling or psychiatric therapy, is increasing. The old adage that "he who controls the purse strings calls the tune" is still true. More and more, as government becomes involved in the financial aspects of mental health care, it will exercise regulation of treatment centers. The same is true of private insurance companies. Given the attitudes and convictions regarding confidentiality expressed by more than one contributor to this volume, this growing tendency has a negative look, to say the least.

Insurance company policies differ and are a source of concern. In increasing numbers they are refusing to pay claims for any therapy other than that done by a physician. Some will pay for treatment under the supervision of a psychiatrist or if it is prescribed by a psychiatrist. In the latter instances, they want assurance of the physician's participation and will accept only limited types of therapy as valid. With the active involvement of the psychiatric consultant in the function of the clinic, his or her signature on the insurance form assures some insurance companies that the claimant is receiving the service they are paying for. Others are demanding additional evidence that such is, indeed, the case. United States federal law requires that the Internal Revenue Service be notified of all such insurance payments.

It is acceptable practice for the psychiatric consultant to be paid by the center. Any monies paid by insurance companies to the consultant are returned to them for correction and repayment to the center. For this reason, the employer identification number of the center, not the psychiatric consultant's social security number, is used on the insurance claim form and all correspondence—which is often voluminous. Legal opinion has also held that the psychiatric consultant can endorse insurance checks over to the center, not counting them as personal income. Prudence would indicate that records (xerox copies, etc) of all transactions be included in the client's file and in the consultant's personal income tax file, where they will be available for future reference. Needless to say, the psychiatric consultant will only sign the insurance forms of clients of whom he or she is cognizant.

Finally, the psychiatric consultant can act in the service of public relations. A psychiatrist's name on the center's brochure is assurance to many that the center is an ethical organization devoted to quality care and interdisciplinary support. This person symbolizes its dedication to those spiritual and humanistic values which are such an integral part of a pastoral counseling center. Thus, a psychiatric consultant can be an asset in direct porportion to the compatible utilization of his or her expertise by the pastoral counseling center.

C H A P T E R

11

Social Work and Psychological Consultation in Pastoral Counseling Centers

George Siskind and Jan Lindemann

B efore starting our discussion of the social worker and the psychologist as consultants, we will present our basic position in relation to consultants. All too often consultants are seen as awesome experts who come to impart their wisdom to the unenlightened. Unfortunately, this view is very often supported by the holders and beholders of advanced degrees. Our purpose in writing this chapter is to present what a pastoral counseling center would look for in selecting consultants whose expertise merits respect and with whom a center can establish egalitarian working relationships. We realize that this type of professional relationship, like so many others, if established on the basis of awe, leads to authoritarian dictation rather than *mutual* health care commitments. This we consider undesirable, however benevolent and well-intentioned the consultants may be. Carefully selected, with good working relationships established in the very beginning, consultants can be a dependable and appropriately changing source of help and stimulation for professional growth. They can provide the pastoral counselor with an opportunity to relate to other professionals in a way that can enhance the counselor's own self-evaluation as a competent professional. On the other hand, poorly chosen consultants will be, at the very best, a bore, and at the worst, obstructive and disruptive.

In this first section we will share the task of presenting the general considerations and specific criteria that serve as a basis for a sound choice of a social work or psychological consultant.

Many of these considerations and criteria also serve as guides in establishing productive, mutually beneficial working relationships. As we present the relevant ideas and information, it will become apparent that they apply to consultants regardless of profession. They also apply regardless of the basis on which the consultant is working with you, paid or volunteer. After having jointly presented the general considerations and criteria, each of us will discuss the process of applying these considerations and criteria to our respective professions of psychology and social work. Unavoidably, there will be some duplication or overlap, hopefully a minimum.

The choice of a consultant who will fit the general model we propose involves several areas of decision: first, the center's expectations of a consultant; second, the returns that a center is prepared to offer a potential consultant (any potential consultant who does not recognize and admit that he or she wants something in return, however vaguely stated, should automatically be dropped from consideration); and finally, the type of working relationship that you desire to have with a consultant. The center staff should clearly recognize that these areas of decision are always involved but that the decisions themselves are temporary in that they should be regularly reviewed and evaluated. Such regular review and evaluation should both reflect continued professional growth and development, and provide stimulation for healthy organizational growth and continuing productive relationships with consultants.

The center staff's expectations of a consultant will develop from two sources, an evaluation of the center's own professional service and growth needs and the legitimate expectations that a center may have of a consultant. These expectations are easily organized by first considering three general categories of consultant characteristics—credentials, competence, and attitudes. (In our separate sections, each of us will discuss the specifics of credentials and competence as they apply to our professions.) Credentials are admittedly not always the most dependable of indicators. Two common errors are: accepting at face value a consultant who is highly "credentialed" but minimally or not competent to meet your particular training and service needs, or rejecting someone who is not highly "credentialed" but is competent to meet your needs. Sound judgments of competency rest upon many of the considerations and criteria that we will discuss further along.

Attitudes

Inasmuch as there is a theological basis for a pastoral care and counseling center, religious values and theology are part of the working content and of the efforts of the counselors. A frequently made mistake is to assume that a potential consultant has attitudes toward religion and the ministry that are conducive to good working relationships with pastoral counselors. One has only to consider such issues as pregnancy and abortion or living together unmarried to realize that evaluation of the religious values of the potential consultant is not an academic exercise.

Having indicated the importance of the issue of religious feelings and attitudes in relation to choice of consultants, we think a discussion is unnecessary for pastoral counselors. All we shall do is present a checklist of questions:

1. Is the consultant aware of his or her own religious values and theology?
2. Does this person know something of yours?
3. Are there several denominations in the center?
4. If differences exist among you and between the consultant and the center staff, is this person aware of them?
5. Does this person appreciate and understand the implications of such differences?
6. Does the consultant have unresolved religious conflicts?

Having obtained answers to these questions, there is one more decision. The center needs to decide whether or not it will consider a potential consultant with less than desirable attitudes and/or knowledge because of good credentials and competence, and under what circumstances.

Returns for the Consultant

A desirable consultant is well aware of the quid pro quo nature of the consultant role. Returns to the consultant can be thought of as professional, monetary, personal, or any combination of these. Professional returns could include sharpening of skills and knowledge through work in a setting reflecting a breadth of professional capabilities. The contacts formed may enhance the consultant's professional image in the community and be a source of referrals (if in private practice). Some formalized returns a center may want to consider giving to consultants are certificates of service, letters of appreciation, letters to agency directors commending consultants' work.

Monetary returns, needless to say, can be a strong motivational factor to a consultant. An experienced practitioner is more likely to require financial reimbursement than is a beginning professional who desires the experience. Whether salaried or unsalaried, the expectations and contracting procedures discussed in this chapter should be applied. A center may be tempted to set up few, if any, expectations for the nonpaid consultant, thinking that this person is doing a favor. This only makes for a vague, noncommittal-type relationship which will not lead to productive consultation arrangements. It should, however, be pointed out that the paid consultant is more likely to be flexible in scheduling, due to the monetary incentive, than is the nonpaid consultant. For example, the nonpaid consultant might be willing to come for an hour case conference over lunch but be unwilling to give up time in the evening. Another consideration is whether the consultant can take time from regular employment to consult or must use personal time to consult. A center might also keep in mind that if a potential consultant has the choice of two equally desired consulting positions, the monetary reward may be the deciding factor. Consultant fees naturally vary based on qualifications, geographical location, etc.

Personal rewards for the consultants are, of course, very individualized. They may have a religious and/or moral commitment to assist the clergy in expanding their knowledge and skills or a humanistic interest in the growth of others, a quality that often attracts social workers and psychologists to their chosen profession. Stimulation by interactions with persons with value systems that differ from their own can be rewarding. Whether or not a consultant is reimbursed, it is still appropriate to ask a consultant what is expected as a return for consultant services.

Working Relationships

Several components to be considered in formulating a working relationship are: (1) the basic nature of the relationship; (2) the role assigned the consultant; (3) the style used; and (4) the people for whom consultant services are being made available. Preferably the nature of the relationship will be an egalitarian one as mentioned in the introduction. That is to say that the consultant and center staff are in a joint venture which is intended to be a productive, mutually beneficial working relationship. The assessment of a consultant's potential for egalitarian relationships is not an easy or well-defined task. There are, however, some questions that may be raised with the consultant or with those already in a working relationship with the consultant that will provide some ideas as to this potential:

1. Can this person respond to questioning of ideas without becoming defensive?
2. Is the consultant willing to give supporting explanations or information regarding his or her conclusions?
3. Is this person respectful of other professions and their areas of expertise?

A consultant relationship established to make available some particular knowledge or skill with express purpose of answering a specific question or set of questions does not require significant amounts of personal interaction and involvement to successfully complete the task. An example of a limited function would be having a psychological consultant to answer questions as to whether particular persons are too emotionally disturbed to benefit from the services a center offers. Another similar example would be asking a social work consultant for information about agencies or facilities to which such a person could appropriately be referred and how to accomplish this. The more frequent and the closer interactions required in the consultant's designated role, the more crucial the egalitarian relationship.

A consultant's role may be that of an information giver, teacher, facilitator, leader, model, or a combination of these. As an information giver, the consultant may present lectures, conduct workshops, or any variation of these which may or may not actively involve the center staff. The teaching role implies imparting knowledge and exchanging information; there is more interactional potential in this role. Consultants may function as facilitators with the expectation that they will primarily deal with interactional flow, keeping discussions moving in a productive direction. Consultants may act as group leaders who focus attention on interpersonal and intrapsychic processes in cases presented by staff members and/or trainees. They can participate in activities involving interpersonal growth and dynamics of the center's staff. Implicit in all of these roles is a modeling function, but it is also appropriate to specifically ask consultants to serve as models, for example, by presenting one of their own cases.

Within each of these legitimate consultant roles, the style of working relationships develops. In some instances, a structured style is desirable whereas in other functions a less structured approach is preferable. The consultant's style in terms of comfort in structured, unstructured, or both types of settings should be considered in selecting consultants and asking them to fill a particular role. Another aspect of style is whether a consultant largely imparts information and expects under-standing or works primarily to elicit ideas and conclusions. In some consultant functions, one particular style may be more suitable than another to produce the desired outcome. The final consideration in forming working relationships is the people to whom consultant services are being provided. Will the consultant be working with only one person at a time, a small group, or a large group of people? A center may want to give some thought to such variables as age, sex, and level of experience which can influence the working relationship. For example, if a counseling center has all male staff members, a female consultant might bring a different perspective into discussions.

The elements in forming working relationships that have been discussed in this section provide a basis for formulating a clear, explicit contract. Concise ideas of what one can expect from the consultant and what the consultant expects in return will make the negotiating of a contract much easier and more rewarding. Contracting should be an ongoing process because the center's needs and the needs of the consultant will change. In addition to the above, proper contracting will afford an opportunity to set specific goals and directions which can be evaluated as to outcome.

The Social Worker as a Consultant

Credentials

What qualifies a person to be a professional social worker is a beginning question a counseling center must ask in formulating their expectations of a social work consultant. The title "social worker" has unfortunately been used in a random fashion to apply to almost any helping person including the well-meaning volunteer and other individuals without specified training from an accredited social work school. The term "social worker" can be clarified by reviewing the classification of the four professional levels set forth by the National Association of

Social Workers. Information regarding the training requirements and the functions assigned to these respective levels will assist a center in the selection of a qualified social work consultant. The four levels of professional social work include: (1) social worker, (2) graduate social worker, (3) certified social worker, (4) social work fellow. The social work level requires that the person has a baccalaureate degree (BSW) from a social work program approved by the Council on Social Work Education (CSWE). A social worker at this level must be under direct supervision and is not trained to work totally independently in any of the tasks carried out. As a general rule, this level of practitioner would not be used in a consultant position.

The second level of classification is the graduate social worker who must have completed a master's of social work (MSW) program in an institution accredited by the Council on Social Work Education. This level worker is under professional supervision, but a large portion of this person's work activity involves independent judgment and initiative. Workers at this level are trained to do psychosocial assessments, interventions or treatment, and evaluation of the outcomes of these interventions. They have training in the theory of human behavior and development to assist them in the above tasks. In addition, they have a knowledge of organizational structure and social service systems which would enable them to make critical appraisals of these systems. Their knowledge of community resources in terms of referral procedures and appropriate referrals could be beneficially put to use in a consultant capacity. In most cases a recent graduate will not have the level of skill or knowledge that a more seasoned worker would have in any of these areas. Therefore, with only credentials being considered, before looking at specific competencies, the next level practitioner would be the more appropriate choice for a consultant.

The certified social worker is the third category and entry into this level requires certification by the Academy of Certified Social Workers (ACSW). In order to become an ACSW, a worker must be a member of the National Association of Social Workers, graduated from an accredited master's of social work program, have worked two years after receiving the masters degree, pass a professional test, and submit three professional references who will attest to the applicant's ability. This level of worker is considered capable of autonomous, self-directed practice which would involve matured skill in psychosocial assessments, interventions, and evaluation outcomes. Consultation with major social services or community action programs is an appropriate task for this practitioner. A certified social worker could work with your center in an ongoing intake conference to assist in teaching what information is needed in a psychosocial evaluation and how to obtain such information. Supervision of center staff or trainees involved in intensive ongoing casework with individuals or groups is yet another possible function of the consultant with certification. It should be noted that not all persons who have several years postgraduate school experience and have the training and knowledge of this level practitioner become members of NASW or take the ACSW test, for a variety of reasons. Therefore, be careful not to overlook qualified persons just because they do not have the ACSW certification.

The final level of professional social work is the social work fellow. Qualifications required are completion of a doctoral program at an accredited school of social work, or in a related discipline, with two years of specialization in an area of social work, or certification by ACSW and two years of social work experience in the field of specialization. Persons in this level of classification would, of course, be able to function in any of the . capacities noted within the other levels. In addition, they can conduct independent research and evaluation, and work as independent consultants in private practice. If a center is looking for someone to set up a research project, this level would be advisable. A social work fellow can develop and direct research programs for a consultant agency specializing in social problems. They may be employed as professors on faculties of schools of social work where a center might go to locate this level consultant.

As noted, each of these levels requires the completion of educational training at a school accredited by the Council of Social Work Education. A listing of undergraduate, graduate, and doctoral programs approved by the Council of Social Work Education (CSWE) can be found in pamphlets available by writing: Council of Social Work Education, 345 E. 46th Street, New York, New York 10017. There are local chapters of the National Association of Social Workers (NASW) which should be able to provide you with a listing of members within these various levels. If you do not know the name of your local NASW chapter, you can inquire by writing: National Association of Social Workers, Inc., 1425 H Street, N.W., Suite 600, Washington, D.C. 20005. A directory of NASW members published in 1972 lists members as of that date, along with addresses and ACSW credentials. Unfortunately, this book is somewhat outdated and available only in special libraries, such as school of social work libraries. Since there is no complete directory of social workers available, a more reliable source would be to write NASW or to check with licensing boards or state registries (if applicable).

Competency

Awareness of areas of competency will help counseling centers decide not only what can be expected from the consultant but also to decide in what part of your center's program a social work consultant could be used. A social work consultant's competency or specialized skills can be viewed in light of the following: (1) setting in which he or she works, (2) social work method used, (3) theoretical orientation, and (4) continuing professional growth.

Professional social workers can be found in a variety of settings which may reflect their particular area of competency. Mental health facilities, medical settings, correctional institutions, family and children's agencies, and welfare services are some of the major settings. There are various age groups such as children, adolescents, young adults, adults, and aging persons served within each of these settings. Some of these age groups require that the workers have a particular skill—play therapy, for example, which is unique to working with children. Although a consideration of skills with certain age groups is not extremely significant, it may be useful if the consultant services are to be focused primarily on a specific client age group.

A social worker within a mental health setting would be expected to have particular competency in evaluating emotional disturbances and treatment of psychiatric illness. Family dynamics and environmental factors leading to mental illness as well as ways to work with families of the mentally ill are functions of this worker. In a consultant capacity, the psychiatric social worker could be used to supervise special cases, such as a family of a suicidal person. Assisting pastors in formulating criteria by which to decide on interventions with emotionally disturbed patients and families would be another use of a social work consultant. A consultant knowledgeable of the wide range of mental health resources could teach center staff how to evaluate clients for referral purposes and how to make referrals to appropriate agencies. As a brief aside, it is worth noting that a competent psychiatric social worker should be able to identify strengths as well as pathology or weaknesses in clients. Community mental health clinics are required to have a consultation and educational service as part of their program so that may be a useful resource for locating a social work consultant.

Social workers working in medical facilities usually have a specialty according to the unit within which they work (e.g., spinal cord injuries, respiratory unit, terminally ill patients, etc.). They can provide information on dealing with the social adjustments of various illnesses and with families of patients. You may consider them to work with individual cases that arise, to lecture on the social adjustment of specific illness, or to work with issues of death and dying to name just a few areas.

Social workers within correctional institutions could be used in a consultant capacity to help staff understand the societal conditions that lead to crime as well as gain insight into human behavior and development that leads to social isolation and aberrations.

Family service social workers have particular competency in marital and family counseling. In addition, they are knowledgeable of community resources for families. Some family services have family life education programs conducted by social workers which may provide a consultation service to your center. Consultants skilled in marital and family counseling could provide supervision to those on your staff who are involved in this type of counseling. They might also give presentations on topics such as the family life cycle, communication exercises, establishing contracts with couples, and when to use individual or conjoint sessions.

Children's service agencies provide foster home placements and adoption services, in addition to counseling for children and parents. They would be good sources of information and expertise for topics such as how to counsel the unwed mother or how to help parents cope with a runaway child.

Many people readily identify social workers with the welfare system and a knowledge of resources for lower income families and disabled persons served by welfare programs. Social workers in welfare settings will be able to contribute valuable information about resources and an understanding of the welfare client. This is not an exhaustive list nor is the service provided within each category as clearly defined as may seem indicated. Hopefully this will give pastoral counseling centers some broad categories of social work service in which they may wish to examine competency or areas of expertise.

Most communities have a community service directory which could be used to locate various social service settings; it would be advisable to contact the director of social services in the agency selected to get information about the credentials and competencies of staff members. Another place to get information on settings and potential consultants would be a school of social work if there is one in your community.

A second consideration when assessing competency and your center's needs is the social work method in which the consultant has experience and expertise. The three social work methods are work with individuals, groups, or communities. Most social workers are primarily involved in individual casework and do the greatest portion of practice in this area. These workers would be competent to consult in areas of your program related directly or indirectly to working with individual clients. There are social workers who specialize in group work and have concentrated their training in group theory and practice. Consultants' assignments dealing with group process, whether it be working with staff persons leading client groups or direct leadership in growth groups for center staff, would be appropriate for a group worker. Frequently a social worker will have a combination of experience in working with groups and individuals. The third social work method is work with communities which may include competency in planning, organizing, management, and/or administration. An example of a consultant function for a worker specializing in this method would be assisting in organizational tasks (e.g., how and where to get referrals, how many staff members are needed, etc.). A formulation of how to use a consultant may be made clearer by considering these methods and how they might be applied in your center.

The social worker's theoretical orientation is a dimension to consider in deciding on expectations and evaluating competency. Professional social workers are expected to have a knowledge of some theories of human behavior and social environment such as theories of personality, development, socialization, motivation, learning, etc. If in-depth knowledge of one of the above areas is desired, a counseling center may then want to consider a consultant who has particular expertise in the chosen area. If your center staff operates primarily out of one theoretical framework, it will need to decide whether it wants a consultant who has an orientation similar to that of the center or one who will bring a different orientation.

The major practical approach used by social workers is the psychosocial model which is built on research in a number of the above areas. The psychosocial approach takes into consideration the person-in-gestalt. The person or group being helped is seen in the context of their interactions with the external world. The social system as well as the individual system, seen in terms of any of the areas mentioned, must be understood. A social work consultant with this orientation could assist staff and/or trainees to see more than just the intrapsychic or interpersonal elements in cases and focus on the interplay between persons and external social systems.

The final criteria to be discussed in evaluating competency is the potential consultant's continuing professional growth. It would be appropriate to ask a potential consultant about his or her own continuing education. A competent professional should be able to respond to this question with some specificity. Professional growth or education can be evidenced to some extent by attendance and/or presentations at workshops and professional conferences. The nature of workshops and other formalized training experiences sought out by the worker will give you indications as to areas of interest and possible competency. For example, if a social worker was trained to be a teacher of Parent Effectiveness Training, it would be expected that he or she has some competency in parent-child interactional patterns. Membership in professional organizations such as the American Association of Marriage & Family Therapists can also be indicative of areas of competency or interest. Publications in professional journals, such as *Social Casework*, *Family Coordinator*, and *Journal of Marriage & Family*, would be still another measure of professional competency.

The Psychologist as a Consultant

On the basis of the preceding section, one could readily and correctly conclude that credentials are not of the utmost importance. They are, however, an excellent beginning for a discussion of the specifics of selecting a good consultant and establishing productive working relationships. All of which leads us to a very necessary caveat, necessary because the term "psychologist" is essentially a generic and often misused term. It is used to describe people who have degrees ranging from the baccalaureate to the doctorate in the major field of psychology; it is used as a job title with a very wide variation of job requirements; and it is used to describe people who specialize in a variety of content areas of psychology, some of which may not be directly relevant to a center's efforts. The potential confusion of such wide usage can be avoided by looking in the *Biographical Directory of the American Psychological Association*. Unfortunately, the information about a particular member may not be complete. The data is gathered through the use of a voluntary questionnaire, but it is the best source of the following information:

1. Degrees and year granted
2. School from which obtained
3. Positions held
4. Present major field
5. Areas of specialization
6. Licensure and certification
7. American Board of Professional Psychologists and American Board of Professional Hypnotists

An additional source of information that is helpful in evaluating credentials is the *National Register of Health Service Providers in Psychology*. The criteria used represent a combination of training and experience:

1. Currently licensed or certified by the State Board of Examiners in Psychology for the independent practice of psychology.
2. A doctorate degree from a regionally accredited university.

3. Two years of supervised experience in health services, of which at least one year is postdoctoral and one year (may be the postdoctoral year) is in an organized health service training program.

Using the information from the APA *Biographical Directory* and the criteria from the Register, it is possible to evaluate a group of possible consultants without having to meet with them. At this point, you do not have knowledge of specialty areas, nor of competence, but it would be possible to legitimately decide that some psychologists are not potential candidates for your center. The next step is to acquire more detailed information as to the content of an area of specialization. This is most quickly done through the use of *Psychological Abstracts*. Under every specialty area heading there are summaries of the materials published in the area, providing specific information as to the content of the specialty. Becoming acquainted with the *Psychological Abstracts* in this way has an advantage for the future. As the center changes, the needs of its staff will change. If a psychological consultant is sought to work with your center because of changed professional needs, use of the *Psychological Abstracts* will readily allow determination of whether or not your center's identified needs fall within a particular specialty of psychologists. More immediate reasons for being familiar with and using the resources described above are: (1) quicker preselection of possible candidates; and (2) the information will be part of the basis that you develop for making judgments about the competence of particular psychologists.

In the first section we discussed the relationship between what a consultant is asked to do, and the degree of personal interaction and involvement that is required to successfully complete the task. The relationship between these two factors needs more detailed discussion because a good understanding

192

of it is fundamental to formulating realistic expectations of a consultant. Realistic expectations, in turn, will serve as a basis for establishing productive working relationships with consultants. Inasmuch as the goal of the chapter is to provide as much practical information as possible, the discussion of the working relationship will be organized by considering possible consultant functions in relation to the services a client will receive as part of successful participation in the counseling process. In addition, the professional growth needs of counselors as they participate in the process will be discussed in relation to the possible contributions of a consultant.

Starting with the task of establishing diagnostic intake procedures, one might legitimately ask a psychological consultant any or all of the following questions:

1. Should we use psychological tests and/or inventories as part of our intake procedures?
2. If we should, what techniques are appropriate?
3. What kinds of information would we obtain?
4. Would the information be valid?
5. How would we use the information in the initial evaluative effort?
6. Can we use the information obtained in the counseling process? How?
7. In order to use tests and/or inventories, are there additional skills that we would need to acquire in order to properly and productively use these techniques?
8. What would it cost us in time, money, and effort to acquire these skills?

A thorough discussion of these questions would require several hours or more spent with a competent psychologist. The job of supplying a great deal of usable information could be done very well, to everyone's satisfaction, yet the amount of personal interaction and involvement necessary would be relatively minimal. In a very different role, as part of the intake process, a psychological consultant could be asked to participate in an intake evaluation conference on a regular, continuing basis. Rather than have a primary function of supplying information, the consultant would be part of the decision-making process. Inasmuch as a decision-making process always has a potential for conflict, the issue of awe versus respect as reflected in authoritarian versus egalitarian relationships becomes highly relevant. If a consultant is disposed to assume an authoritarian position, let us say on the basis of actually having greater clinical experience and skill, and the other members of the conference want an egalitarian relationship, the potential for disruptive, unproductive relationships are obvious. If both want an authoritarian relationship, there will be little conflict, but the consultant's contribution will be that of supporting dependency rather than contributing to professional growth. It is most important that the initial invitation to the consultant contain a clear, explicit statement of what is expected of the consultant as a participant in the conference: supplying evaluative judgments based on professional knowledge; making recommendations for the counseling process; participating in making the necessary decisions, but not attempting to make them for the group. Participating in the intake process as just described obviously involves a very different level of interaction than when the psychologist only provides information in response to questions the center asks. A third type of participation in the intake process could be for the purpose of developing in-service training for the conference participants. In this situation, the consultant would be present as an observer in order to make use of the data of personal observation as a basis for designing and/or conducting a training program. The goal of the program would be to facilitate the efforts of the members of the intake evaluation conference to increase their knowledge and skills. With this type of consultant function, the degree of personal interaction falls between the first and second functions discussed, with the quality of the interaction being important but not crucial.

The next stage in which a psychological consultant can function is in relation to actual counseling of the client. A limited function, in terms of the relationship with center staff, would be to have the consultant work directly with the client. Personal interaction with the center staff would increase and become more complex if the consultant were to record (audio or video, if available) sessions with the client for the purpose of presenting the material of the session and discussing it. Here again, there are several ways in which the discussion of the materials can occur, each having different degrees of interaction. A formal didactic presentation with questions from the others to be answered by the consultant would be a less complex form of interaction, having a high potential for an authoritarian relationship. A presentation of the materials with discussion ranging from questions to comments and ideas of alternative methods or techniques would become much more complex in relation to the interactions among the members of the conference, including the consultant. A very relevant issue at this point is that of defensiveness, or self-protection. It would not be unusual for a consultant in such a situation to show some degree of defensiveness. The more competent consultants are, the less likely they are to be defensive. Now, for a moment, let us apparently digress. It has long since been obvious that the need for competence in a consultant has been stressed but not the means by which to evaluate it. We have just discussed one criterion, the willingness to perform for critical public scrutiny. If the center has a one-way mirror, one could appropriately ask a consultant to conduct counseling sessions with center staff members and/or trainees having the opportunity to observe the session with discussion following. This, of course, is a form of public scrutiny. Properly conducted discussion after the session, focusing on techniques, methods, understanding the client's behavior, and the nature of the interaction between counselor and client would be a most productive format. If it is to be productive, this particular activity is also one that requires the greatest attention to the quality of the personal interaction among the members of the conference, including the consultation.

During the intake process or during the counseling, the staff and consultant may realize that a particular problem presented by a client calls for specific techniques or methods. If the appropriate techniques or methods are not part of the skills of the counselor or counselors, a consultant can provide a training program for the center staff. Much of the methodology of behavior modification would fit this kind of situation. A center might have a consultant or consultants whose expertise does not include behavioral modification techniques or only some of them. If such a training program is beyond the consultant's range of knowledge, he or she should be willing and able to identify people who are capable of doing a good job of the desired program. Here is another important indicator of competence: Can the consultant comfortably acknowledge limitations? During the initial process of evaluating a psychologist as a possible consultant, it would be appropriate to ask if he or she can train the counselors to use assertiveness training techniques or to help a client establish a self-controlled behavior modification schedule. If these are not techniques that the consultant uses regularly and therefore does not have sufficient experience with the techniques to train someone else in their use, the person should be able to say just that and be willing to attempt to enlist the aid of someone who can.

Another function for the consultant during the counseling process is as a supervisor for a particular counselor or counselors, or working with the staff members who are acting as supervisors. In evaluating a consultant for possible use in either or both of these capacities, the crucial issue is the consultant's ideas as to what constitutes good supervision. The consultant should be able to make a fairly explicit statement of the goals and process of supervision as he or she understands and uses them. This statement may not necessarily be one with which you agree, but it ought to be explicit enough to allow you to evaluate its potential usefulness for your staff and/or trainees. The explicit statement has another value; it is, in fact, the statement of terms of a contract that is acceptable to a consultant. As such, it provides a basis for a later evaluation of the functioning of the consultant and the relationships with the center staff.

There is one consultant contribution that can be made anywhere in the counseling process, participation in a case review. A case review may be made for a variety of reasons, but whatever the reason, it can be a legitimate function of consultants to participate in case reviews even when their areas of competence do not specifically include counseling. Therefore, the contribution would not always be that of a skilled clinician, but of an observer who has a different point of view.

The last topic of this section is the most difficult task, evaluating competence. It is appropriately the last task because many of the ideas we have discussed form a basis for making judgments. There are, however, two criteria of competence that do not require a judgment by the center staff; the consultant either meets the criteria or not. As discussed earlier, inclusion in the *National Register of Health Service Providers in Psychology* or meeting the criteria for inclusion indicates that a psychologist has offered evidence of education, training, and experience that are considered sufficient for at least acceptable competence. The Diplomate status mentioned earlier is an indication of a higher level of competence than that indicated by the criteria of the *National Register*. Diplomate status is awarded on the basis of more qualifying experience and thorough examination over work samples submitted by the candidate for the Diplomate.

Generally, the crucial issue in evaluating potential consultants whose areas of specialization will be relevant for your efforts will be that of candor and lack of defensiveness. As you proceed through the points we have discussed in this chapter, the potential consultants will have many opportunities to be candid or defensive, acknowledge limitations or try to hide them, be explicit about a particular topic or admit that they had not given thought to it. In addition to all this, a prospective consultant should recognize from the fact that your center has done its "homework" very carefully that you consider the choice of consultants an important matter. If your center has any doubts about conducting such a searching and thorough evaluation of a potential consultant, remember that in the final analysis such efforts do indicate the importance attached to the consultant role and are a genuine compliment.

Summary: A Checklist

The heading indicates what we believe to be the most useful form of summary:

1. Has your center identified its present and foreseeable professional needs? How explicitly and specifically can they be stated?
2. Have you formulated the possible returns that your center can offer to a consultant?
3. Is your center prepared to evaluate credentials? Do you have sources of information such as the APA *Directory* available? Have you thought of your needs in terms of the areas of competence that a consultant might have?
4. If all of the above have been done, your center is now ready to list the social workers and psychologists that might be available to it. Select the most likely candidates.
5. Ask them to meet with you for the purpose of mutual evaluation and possible offer of a consultantship.
6. Meet with your candidates prepared to evaluate their attitudes toward religion and ministry, style of working, and areas of competence they are prepared to offer. Be prepared to state what you have to offer them.

7. Select your consultant or consultants and offer a "contract" to them.
8. Have you tried to apply the ideas and information in the chapter to the selection of other kinds of consultants, not just social workers and psychologists?

And a last reminder—one that is not reinforced enough—*better no consultant than a poor one.*

12

Dynamics of the Referral Process
G. Edward Alley and David M. Moss III

Generally speaking, the health care professions have given a great deal of attention to issues that surround referral resources, processes, and their dynamics.[1] Even to review the literature recently published by the psychiatric community— let alone the realm of social work or psychoanalysis—would be an unusually demanding project. Certainly such a task is beyond the scope of this chapter. However, we mention the quantity of publications in these fields because of the comparative dirth of referral literature produced thus far in the pastoral psychology movement.

Granted, a few referral resource books have been published for pastors. William Oglesby's text *Referral in Pastoral Counseling* is one good example.[2] Another is *Where to Go for Help* by Wayne Oates.[3] These two books are notable exceptions. Most books on pastoral referral are basically directories of health care agencies with a brief commentary in the introduction about the need for clergy to be acquainted with community resources. These lists are frequently compiled by people who evaluate such resources at a distance (e.g., a questionnaire), and it is not uncommon that an agency listed will be inactive within a short period after publication of the book. To our knowledge, the only referral list that is annually reviewed for ministers is the American Association of Pastoral Counselors' *Directory*.[4]

While book length publications on referral dynamics are rare, journal articles are not. *The Journal of Pastoral Care*,

Pastoral Psychology, and the *Journal of Religion and Health* have published several excellent papers on the subject. Of these, two articles by Ronald Lee are exceptional.[5] In "Referral as an Act of Pastoral Care," Dr. Lee cites an important study conducted by Gurin, Veroff, and Feld.[6] He then goes on to point up some disturbing facts.

Since the Gurin, Veroff and Feld study established the oft-quoted figure that 42 percent of people interviewed said they sought a minister as their first source of help, it has been assumed that clergymen are in a position to make more referrals than any other professional. Actually, only 9 percent of this number ever get referred to another professional. While ministers take evident pride in the fact that so many people come to them initially, other professionals have wondered what has happened to the other 91 percent. By far the largest group out of the 42–66 percent are generally nonreferrable and have sought out the minister to request help in maintaining their present life-style. They have no thought of changing their basic personality structure and a referral in their case would constitute an inappropriate response to their call for help. I will focus briefly on this group, but I wish to spend the greater part of the paper on the referrals that the pastor has an opportunity to make, some of which are made successfully—the 9 percent in the Gurin study, and some of which fail to be made—25 percent that might be referred if ministers would improve their techniques and recognize their own resistances.[7]

Dr. Lee's concluding comment is quite significant. There is a definite need for ministers to improve their referral techniques as well as recognize their own internal resistances to making workable referrals, defenses often characterized by grandiosity, rigidity, or guilt. If a parish minister is able to recognize his or her limitations as a professional in a multifaceted position, referral is not a "threat" or an abdication of responsibility.

Lee outlines the dynamics of referral phases. He believes that a referral from a minister has three phases, an initial, middle, and terminating phase. The middle phase is perhaps the most crucial in that resistance to rejection must be confronted and explored. It must be clarified to the counselee that referral is an expression of empathic concern, not rejection.

One avenue that Dr. Lee suggests which we have found helpful is the use of the relay technique. "The chances of a successful referral are enhanced by the use of the 'relay' technique. As you know from athletics, in a relay race sprinters run parallel until a baton is transferred. In a similar fashion the person referred may see both the referring and referred-to professionals concurrently for a brief period of time."[8] He also adds three other points which heighten the probability of an effective referral:

1. The chance of a successful referral is enhanced if the professional to whom the referral is made is personally known to the one making the referral;
2. The chance of a successful referral is enhanced when a positive transference is present;
3. The chance of a successful referral is enhanced when the client or parishioner is given an honest, straightforward evaluation which neither exaggerates nor minimizes the situation.[9]

What Dr. Lee sets forth in his first referral article is worth considering also from the vantage of the professional pastoral counselor or psychotherapist. The pastoral counselor's assessment of the interpersonal dynamics affecting the referral process may need immediate attention, because some "undoing" or some "reinforcing" may be critical before therapy can take place.

In Dr. Lee's papers, in the books by Oglesby and Oates, and in other articles that created the framework of this chapter, case reports are the springboard for speculation and dialogue. The examples that follow are likewise intended to evoke (or provoke) reflection. Our focus, however, is not exclusive. We are concerned with the dynamics of referral to a pastoral counseling center as well as the referral of a parochial minister to a psychotherapist who may or may not be practicing in one of the models described by Drs. Carr and Hinkle in Part I.

Examples

1. A clergyman referred a couple to a pastoral counseling center because both parties had been previously married and wanted some professional aid in determining whether or not they could avoid repeating interactional patterns that destroyed their first and second marriages. Their parish minister remarked, "It's a good group. They'll know how to assist you."

2. A family physician referred one of his patients to a counseling center with the hunch that a religious problem was at the core of some psychosomatic symptoms. Thus, the doctor selected a pastoral counselor rather than a psychologist.

3. A member of a counseling center's board of directors referred her son and daughter-in-law to that center for marital counseling.

4. A couple has been seen at a center by one counselor, ostensibly to work through some divorce related problems. The husband in this terminal marriage concurrently referred his girlfriend to another counselor on the same staff because she had grown tired of waiting for him to finish his property settlement struggles with his ex-wife.

5. A parochial priest who just moved into the area referred three or four of his parishioners to a center because he assumed that a pastoral counseling center would charge low fees or none at all.

These brief descriptions indicate the influence of the person who makes the referral on the counseling process. As we said, it is very important for a pastoral counseling center to assess the effect of the referral. In fact, we believe it is more elementary to raise the issue regarding referral dynamics than it is to posit the so-called pragmatic questions of: How are referrals encouraged? How does a pastoral counseling center keep referral resources active? While both questions are important, and we will discuss them in this chapter, they are secondary.

The five examples indicate that how a referral has been made, and by whom, may have a lot to do with the counseling process. The person who comes into therapy expecting to pay a very low fee may resent getting help when the fees range up to $45 per hour. One would want to closely examine the client's motivation for change. The manner in which the referral was made will be reflected in the success or lack of success that will be enjoyed in the therapeutic process.

When the referral source is highly influential and capable of bringing power to bear on the individual counselor or the center, there may be potential problems. When counseling is done, even unconsciously, for someone who is not present in the room, the process is contaminated and the therapeutic alliance is threatened. The counselor and the center may get locked into trying to help more than the client wants to be helped, and the results will be minimal.

The question arises as to what would motivate a client to refer his girlfriend for counseling when divorce counseling seems to be at a stalemate. Could the client be getting anxious about the pressure from two women and want the counselor to take one off his hands? Or does he want to maintain a process wherein no one is talking to anyone else about the situation and thereby block further work? Or could he be wanting help in getting his therapy moving? These and other important questions, all stemming from and relating to the nature and meaning of the referral dynamics, would have to be considered.

A referral source whose assumption about people is that they need to be taken care of or looked after in a paternalistic way may hinder the therapeutic process. Individuals referred in this manner become accustomed to being treated as though they were helpless. One man came for an initial interview on referral from a trusted pastoral colleague. The man seemed to need to spill out a long list of problems; however, no specific help was asked for. The counselor noted that the man did not ask for help and also that the pastor who had sent the man had referred him to several agencies and counselors over a period of years.

Whenever the man got in trouble in his work or his marriage over a period of ten years, he had gone to see the pastor who had married him. He would dutifully go wherever the pastor referred him but get no help. The man made a second appointment with the pastoral counselor, which he did not keep.

A sense of urgency may hamper the client's ability to get help. In the case above the client had called saying he had a real emergency and needed to be seen as soon as possible, in fact, sooner than possible. When he was seen, he was not clear about what he wanted. The pain had subsided somewhat. The referral source was known to be a man who went about everything he did with a great sense of urgency. One wonders if the client picked up that sense of urgency, added it to his own, and had too much to handle when he finally got to the counselor for help.

It is often the case that the first time a counselor gets a referral from a suicide prevention agency there is a kind of anxiety to do well and a lot of it. One counselor found that he got hooked on helping the potential suicide, that is, preventing possible suicide. The result was that he pushed too hard when the client began to move and scared the client away. The counselor's own feelings and expectations about certain kinds of clients and certain kinds of problems affect the successful negotiation of the referral process.

In our experience, pastoral counselors sometimes have difficulty dealing with persons in other helping professions. We have seen this, for instance, when some pastoral counselors relate to physicians and others in the medical field. If one's sense of the importance and meaning of being a pastoral counselor is not secure, a referral by a physician might arouse resistance in the counselor to the referral source, which may in turn affect the counseling process. What has been said so far indicates the importance of knowing who the referral source is and how the referral was made. The therapeutic process can be enhanced or hindered by these factors.

Having reviewed the dangers of poorly handled referrals, let us look at what the function of a referral is. The process of referral obviously can go in at least three directions: in, out, and in-house (i.e., to the center, from the center, and within the center). Each of these deserves some attention of its own. There are some principles which apply to any referral, but the direction of the referral has a lot to do with the problems that may be encountered.

Whatever the direction of the referral, it is important to let clients know that they are being taken seriously. Clients need to know that they are not just being passed from one professional person to another. They need to have the feeling that they have been heard, that referral is a humane process in which their needs are the most important factor in determining where they are sent when they ask for help.

The Process of Referral

At this point the process of referral can be examined so there is a framework for further understanding. If a center has difficulty establishing itself, referrals may look like fresh meat to a starving man. One may then see referrals primarily from the standpoint of "how to get 'em" and build up a practice or agency from that premise, but the persons who are referred and the purposes for which they came may inadvertently get swallowed up. It must not be the main concern of the referring pastor that he or she be seen by the person requesting help as the sole means of assistance. This, as well as a number of other factors, may seriously hinder the establishment of a good referral. Poor diagnosis, pride in one's ability to help *everyone*, jealousy of other professions' ability or status, may all get in the way of treating referrals properly. Let us look first at the process of receiving referrals from outside the center.

The point of first contact is likely to be the telephone. The referring person may call to inquire about the possibility of help for a client. This is an important contact, not only for good public relations, but more importantly for the referral process.

What is the referral source asking from you? Can you provide what is being asked? Are you being asked to be an extension of work already being done with the person? Occasionally a referral source will suggest a certain form of treatment, such as group or family therapy. The recipient of the referral needs to recognize the needs and desires of the referral source while maintaining the pastoral counseling center's prerogative to do its own diagnosis and treatment recommendation. Sometimes, a referral is seen by a professional as a way to get rid of a difficult client. Or, it also may be that the person on the other end of the line may have no real idea of what your center can do and may be fishing. A person's understanding or expectations of pastoral counseling may be influenced by a variety of things; the caller may have known a kindly pastor who seemed a good shoulder to cry on or may have experienced someone with dubious qualifications whose work was also suspect.

Clearly, what the referring person expects or wants is central in that opening call. If you can and are willing to give what is expected or wanted, your initial contact will be constructive. However, if expectations and desires cannot be meshed with your abilities and intentions, the potential client will probably get little help even if a referral is made. The professional whose services are sought must be treated with respect and consideration for that person's professional ability. A written note of gratitude for the referral including an offer of future assistance can frequently underscore this professional respect.

A problem that may arise is language. Persons from other disciplines may not be conversant with the vocabulary used in your center. Likewise, you may not be familiar with the terms belonging to their discipline. It is important to try to bridge that gap if possible. One way to do that is to talk in terms of the behavior being exhibited by the client that causes the referring person first to suggest the referral. Then you can talk about what the person does, not what the person has or what diagnostic category the person may fit. It should go without saying that acquaintance with and use of commonly used psychological vocabulary may be useful at this point, although this may lead to labeling someone before he or she is actually seen.

Contact with the individual making the referral should establish what is desired from the center; what kind of problem it appears the potential client has; and whether the agency is willing and able to do what is being asked. This should be done by professional staff where possible, so that contact is made professional to professional. The referring person may need some reassurance that the client will be dealt with in an understanding and professional manner, and also want to know what kind of feedback to expect from the pastoral counseling center in regard to the progress of the client. If there is to be a continuing, cooperative working relationship between the center and referral source, that needs clarifying. As an illustration, suppose a pastoral counseling center has a contract with a local parish to do pastoral counseling with members of a certain parish on referral from the ministerial staff or on self-referral by parishioners themselves. In the case of referrals from members of the staff, it is clear that the staff can and should expect more feedback than when parishioners come on self-referral. Some agreement needs to be reached in a situation like that which would include how and to what extent one considers the pastoral counselor a part of the ministry of that local church.

When it is established that the center can or will do what the referral source wants or needs, it is time to firm up the referral. It is then advisable that the next contact be made by the person being referred. This gets the individual involved in the referral process in a responsible manner. To some extent it avoids the problems that may arise if the referral source takes too much responsibility, thereby making the need for help that person's problem, not the client's. Having the individual referred call for the first interview also gets him or her tied into the center as a helping place and makes the referral his or her own.

When a potential client calls, telephone contact becomes extremely important. Empathic, open, helpful contact with the initial call can do much to help the person bridge the anxious chasm that most clients feel when calling a strange agency for help. Questions should be answered as clearly and precisely as possible. If the first telephone contact is with a secretary, as it will be in most agencies, the secretary should deal with questions as well as possible, but should not try to work with the client if problems arise. Questions relating to treatment available and other matters should be deferred to the counselor who will be seeing the person(s). Working with psychological and human problems is an infectious disease, and those working amidst the counseling setting may feel that they know how to do it. It's a kind of qualification by association. This may lead well-meaning secretarial staff to try to talk on the phone like a professional staff person. Such activity must be avoided since that person's credentials for doing so are lacking; there is little possibility of supervising what is said during such phone conversations which further complicates the situation. The telephone answering personnel should restrict the conversation to answering questions about the mechanics of getting into a counseling situation. All other questions should be referred to the counselor who will be seeing the client. If the telephone receptionist gives information to the counselor about the nature of the telephone interview, it should be restricted to the facts: what happened, what was said, what questions were asked, and avoid describing the seriousness of such happenings or making other interpretations.

By the tenor of the preceding paragraphs, it can be noted that it is of utmost importance that entry into an agency's processes be as clear and uncontaminated as possible. The conversation with the referral source, when it occurs, should clarify procedures without getting into things that will be harmful to the client. The call may also test the center's need to "take care of" certain interest groups for the center's own good. Doing a favor for someone by accepting or making a referral may corrupt the counseling process. Such referrals may not leave the counselor free to work with the needs of the client only.

Additionally, the telephone receptionist should steer as clear of clinical material or involvement as possible, so that the client and counselor can work together with as little influence from extraneous forces as possible.

If the telephone receptionist does not have responsibility for making counselors' appointments (and there is good reason this should be the case), the next step is a call from the counselor to the prospective client. The basic reason the telephone receptionist should probably not make the initial interview appointment is that there may be significant therapeutic issues that need to be dealt with before the client actually comes to the center for counseling. The telephone receptionist is not in a position to deal with these issues. The counselor can and must. If these issues are not dealt with, a significant number of persons will not make the first interview. Persons who are phoning on referral from one professional to an unknown person or agency may have some anxiety about the move. They may ask a lot of questions about the center, the qualifications of the counselors, etc., which is their right. But behind those questions lurk other fears and questions: "Can I trust these people with these important things about me?" "Am I ready to make the changes that getting into counseling assumes I will make?" "Will this person really understand me?"

The initial phone contact should help persons deal with those fears and anxieties, as well as their need to know that they are dealing with reputable and capable professionals. Clients-to-be need to feel that the person to whom they talk is open to hear what they are saying, and that they will not be treated as just another case.

The potential client may have very different expectations of what will happen than the counselor. There may be questions as to who is to show up for the initial session. One woman told a counselor over the phone that she had a marital problem, but she didn't want her husband to know it. Similarly, when parents call for family counseling, they may want to bring only the child who is "causing the trouble," who is identified as the patient, or symptom-bearer. A majority of family therapists will want to have something to say about who shows up for the first session, and most people will respond favorably to a simple explanation of the reason for wanting everybody who lives in the house to come for family therapy, or both partners in a marital situation, at least for the initial interview. Others may need to have some help in deciding that everybody involved in the problem needs to show up, or that it is "OK" to broach the subject of strengthening a relationship with one's partner.

At this point, the clients-to-be have invested considerable time and energy in the agency to which they have been referred, and they are just getting an appointment! They have talked with their pastor, physician, attorney, or school authority and have decided there is a need to seek help in an unfamiliar place. They have gotten up the courage to talk with others who may need to be involved with them, and secured their consent or lack of same. The potential client has called and talked to the secretary, getting whatever information can legitimately be supplied about the center, its costs, professional backing, and so on. A counselor has called back and talked about the time and setting for an initial appointment. Now the appointment has been made! One wonders, if the process were made more complex even than that described above, would anyone make it for the initial session?

Once the client appears for the initial interview, there is more work regarding the referral. Inquiry into the source of the referral could lead to the counselor sending a letter. The illustration of the referral by the family physician used at the beginning of this chapter is a case in point. What are the doctor's opinions about the psychological factors of this patient's illness? Such a written request assures the client that the reasons for the referral are being taken seriously, as are the opinions of the source of the referral. It also provides a link between the familiar and the strange. Again, by writing the source of referral, the counselor is establishing a link with the referral source, so that the client feels he or she is not on completely unfamiliar territory.

211

A reason for writing this letter, in addition to keeping the referral source alive, is to let that person or agency know that the referral and his or her judgment about the need for it are being taken seriously. In a sense, a bond is formed on behalf of the client that supports the therapy just beginning. More than that, the pastor or physician who has referred the client may be expected to have continuing contacts with the client in another setting. Contact between the center and referral source enables both agencies to continue to serve the client in ways that are appropriate to the ongoing situation.

It may be useful to the center and to the referral source to include the referral source further in the counseling process. If it is a pastor who has sent a parishioner for help, the pastor may be able to give valuable adjunctive help and support to the person being treated. Similarly, a physician, attorney, or school authority may give valuable support and input. Having said this, one must remember that it is important to keep the counseling situation confidential and sealed off from interference from outside sources. This is particularly important in the case of adolescents or others referred because they are in some kind of trouble.

It might be instructive to some pastors to sit in on the staffing of the case they have referred. One couple went from helping agent to helping agent, managing to get no help from anyone. Finally, they went to see their pastor. Overwhelmed by the complexity of what they presented, the pastor referred them to a nearby pastoral counseling center. The pastor was invited to sit in on the staffing and gained considerable insight into how a minister could support the difficult long-term therapy this couple and their relationship required. He also became aware of how they might subtly draw him back into the therapy, or discussion of same, and thus contaminate and cripple it, as they had other therapies along the way.

Obviously, persons who have referred others to your pastoral counseling center have given you a vote of confidence and are asking you to join with them in helping persons who may be important to them. Information and support can and should flow both ways in an effort to help those referred. It needs to be clear that the process of dealing with a referral from outside the center is not finished until some contact has been made with the party who was the referring source. If you have referred someone for much needed help, not knowing if they ever made contact or what disposition was made when they did, you may have serious cause for concern. Referral is a responsible part of professional function, and an important part of that process is saying, "I hear you."

Another aspect of referral is in-house referral. If the person who does the initial interview is not to continue with the client for some good reason, the client will need help in dealing with that reality.

Consider the person who has gone through the process just described in order to use the facilities and staff of an agency. On meeting the intake counselor, the person may spill out some of the most painful aspects of his or her life, telling this stranger things never told to anyone before. If he or she is able to do that, a strong positive transference may be started with the intake counselor. That is, of course, the stuff of which good counseling comes. But, if having established such a relationship, the client is expected to see someone else and have to tell the same story over, there could be problems. Some persons may feel betrayed. Others will feel abandoned. Still others may not be able to imagine that they could be so candid and open with anyone else. Added to this may be an unexpected recommendation: the disposition and "treatment-of-choice" may be group counseling, family counseling, or some other mode of therapy to which the client has given no thought.

The client's fears and feelings around in-house referral must be taken seriously and dealt with. Does the person understand what is being recommended or have any idea why it is being recommended? No referral will stick very well if the client hasn't made a firm commitment to the diagnosis and recommendations the counselor presents.

This is part of the reason for what might be called an interpretation interview. In an interpretive interview, the counselor can help the client see the parameters of the problem. Clients can begin to see fairly clearly what they will have to do to turn things the way they want them. Clients must commit themselves to the change in setting, mode, or personnel required for the therapy being recommended. If clients fail to make that commitment, but go along with the recommendation because it comes from someone with whom they feel they cannot argue, they may get little from the therapy. The client needs to make a commitment to change and to working with the recommendation suggested. Otherwise, further counseling may flounder, no matter who the therapist is or what the setting is.

Transferring the counselee to someone else within the center, to another setting or mode of therapy, is an in-house referral. The new therapist might come to the last part of the interpretation interview to begin the process of identification between new counselor and client. The intake counselor may need to do some grief work with the client to make sure both the counselor and the client have put the relationship aside in such a way that the new counselor or setting may have a chance. The counselor may have feelings of loss after having personally invested in this human being. To share those feelings can help the process of leave-taking and be useful to the client, particularly if this person does not see himself or herself as one who has an impact on others.

If the referral is to another setting, as to a group of which the intake counselor is not part, or to a counselor who cannot be part of the interpretation interview, the referral needs to be made firm, including a setting up of the next appointment for an interview in the new setting. To leave the relationship between the center and the client up in the air by saying, "We'll call you when we decide which staff member will be seeing you," is to guarantee a certain number of losses of clients. The client needs to feel that the referral is a caring decision, not a rejecting or cold one. If the counselors and the center are

214

making an effort to cement the referral through relationships, it will probably adhere well. If it is done simply through procedures, the client may get lost. An apt analogy is that of sending a patient from one department to another in a large city hospital through strange corridors marked by colored arrows on the floor. The patient may find small comfort in the little slip of paper in his hand that tells the next person in a somewhat impersonal process what to do with him. In-house referrals that work are relationship to relationship, not office to office.

Even with attention to the relationship matters suggested above, someone will occasionally get lost in the process of referral. A client who agrees to enter a strange group the next week may lose courage as the hour grows closer. Probably the person most able to help, should the client fail to appear for the new groups, will *not* be the new and as yet strange counselor. A policy that makes the client the responsibility of the intake counselor until after at least one interview in the new setting makes sense. If the intake counselor calls to inquire about the difficulty, the caller is known to the client. Further, that counselor should know the dynamics of the case well enough to understand how the person's failure to show up for the referral may fit the case. Sometimes a telephone conversation or an additional intake interview can help the client work through whatever has kept the referral from being completed. The intake counselor needs to avoid being manipulated into giving the client treatment the counselor believes is not indicated in the process. "No one can help me the way you do!" may sound good to a weary counselor, but narcissistic gratification has never been sufficient reason for practicing pastoral psycho-therapy. In fact, such a statement would probably preclude the possibility of the person getting authentic assistance.

One aid to the successful care of a client as he or she moves from one counselor to another or one setting to another would be notes on the interpretation-referral interview. These should be put into the client's file for the information of the persons responsible for continued treatment. A note that the person had difficulty accepting the referral would alert the new counselor to possible issues early in the treatment process.

An important step in the in-house referral process is the staffing of new cases, sometimes called an intake conference. Here the staff of the center, with perhaps consultation from other professionals, takes a hard look at the recommendations made by the intake counselor. Someone will need to have a sense of the kind of quantity of cases being handled at any one time. That person, who might carry the title of clinical or intake director, will want to keep records as cases are presented. This person will know, and may have much to say about, the disposition of any case. Facilitating the referrals that are made from setting to setting is this person's responsibility.

In addition to the rather formal tracking process, communication is necessary between the person making the referral and the person receiving it. Times and conditions of future interviews with the referred client need to be cleared. After the referral has been made, further communication may be necessary between giver and receiver, especially if there was any difficulty in the referral.

A third kind of referral is a referral to someone outside the center. This is out-of-house referral. Referrals outside the center are not for the purpose of ridding oneself of unwanted persons or cases. Out-of-house referrals are made for a number of reasons: The caseload of the center might be overloaded. A client may need a service the center cannot provide, such as social service work, like housing, clothing, and so on. The individual may present problems ordinarily not seen in a pastoral counseling center, such as those in active psychotic processes. The person may need medication which the center cannot prescribe. Psychiatric or psychological evaluation may be needed as part of the diagnostic or ongoing treatment of a case, or, in some cases, hospitalization of a seriously disturbed patient may be indicated.

Referral out-of-house may be to turn further treatment over to someone else. Or it may be to get adjunctive services that cannot be provided in the pastoral counseling center. An example of the former would be referral to another professional who is more suited to carry out the whole therapy or hospitalization. Referral to a psychiatrist for prescription of medication, while the psychotherapy is carried on in the pastoral counseling center, is an example of the latter.

Nearly every profession is subject to parochialism and territorialism. In discussing the services of a proposed pastoral counseling center in one community, a physician indicated that he was not sure such services were needed. The doctor went on to say that most physicians do a certain amount of counseling in their practice. And further, what physicians want to know, the doctor indicated, is some other physicians they can refer a patient to if they run into something they do not want to treat, not information about a bunch of quack pastoral counselors!

The physician exhibited the kind of suspicion and protectiveness of one's territory that every profession has. Most of us are trained in facilities that are similar to the area that will be ours, whether church, hospital, or courtroom. We are trained with others with similar goals and skills. There may be little knowledge about the skills or desires of persons in other fields. Grandiosity has reared its ugly head in every profession. Jealousy over preferred approaches to treating persons may also make one reluctant to refer. A pastor was heard to utter thanks for the opening of new pastoral counseling services in his community, for now he would have somewhere to refer people who needed help. He had completely ignored the medical, psychiatric, and psychological services already available to him in that community. When out-of-house referrals occur, it is for the good of the client. Cultivation of good relations between pastoral counselors and other professionals and agencies in the community is important to this process. So is awareness of what your own and other agencies can and cannot do.

Out-of-house referrals are subject to the same kind of care discussed in relation to referrals into a center. First of all, the client must have a good idea why the referral is being made. He or she must be committed to doing what is suggested. An off-hand remark that a person needs to go somewhere else for treatment will not do it. That could be interpreted as rejection by a client who is already upset, otherwise the person wouldn't be in your office in the first place. Clients' needs and feelings must be given high priority, in order that they will feel free to carry out the referral.

Secondly, the referring person must be clear about the reason for the referral. Good diagnostic work is necessary to refer properly. It is often useful to talk to the person who will receive the referral about the reasons for the referral and what you want that person to do for the client. In the case of clients who will not be seen by you again, this is important so that the new setting may provide what the client wants. If you will be continuing to see the client, it is important that the recipient of the referral be clear about what you want. If the referral is for medication, evaluation, or other services, it is important the person receiving the client know that, so that further consultation may occur smoothly. Confusion may result when this sort of thing is not clear. A client who is going for evaluation may end up having to decide which of two professionals to see on a continuing basis.

Though it seems so obvious as not to need stating, pastoral counseling centers need to be aware of the services available in the community for possible referral. Nearly every community has a listing of helping agencies provided by the Mental Health Association. The pastoral counseling center will want to be listed there. Also, someone from the center could well spend some time becoming personally acquainted with some of the major agencies and their personnel, as well as letting them get to know a pastoral counselor. One would want to know the feel of other agencies so that people are not being sent to get help in a place that is foreign even to one's knowledge.

Another thing is that the referral is not completed until the person has made the transition and gone for the help. You will want to know from the other agency or person that the client has made the transition. You will also want to give, on written permission from the client, a summary of what you saw in the client that prompted the referral and what you have done in treatment with this person. If you intend to continue to see the client, you may want to spell out that fact and indicate the direction you plan to go. It is possible the person you make the referral to will not see things the way you do. If so, you may or may not want to revise your ideas about the client and what you plan to do. The consultation you get from the other professionals in this manner should be taken seriously.

Finally, the client needs, in our opinion, to have a hand in the referral process. Clients need to call for their own appointments. Taking that initiative will get them involved in moving from one person to another. They will have made some emotional investment and have taken an important step in furthering their own growth. Until they take that important step, it may still seem like your idea, not theirs. Even then some people have trouble accepting this step as their own.

Problems in Referral

A number of things may interfere with a referral being made smoothly. Many of these have been mentioned in the text above and need not be repeated. Some other items that merit consideration follow.

When handling privileged information, getting and giving information in the referral process should be done with the client's knowledge and written permission. Such procedures keep the trust issues out front, where they need to be. A release of information form may be useful in this regard.

One who has done pastoral counseling in a center setting will realize that the client's expectations of a *pastoral* counselor are an important part of the referral process. One woman asked for help in enduring a marriage that had given her little real satisfaction and a lot of pain for twenty years. It seems that she expected pastoral types to be good handholders. When confronted about whether she wanted to do anything about her life, she felt it unfair. The pastoral counselor involved was not able to help her move past her expectations of pastors.

All of us have to answer to some extent for the well-meaning, or simply inept, work of others who are called pastoral counselors, in parishes and other settings. In some cases, we may find ourselves dealing with transference issues not resolved with the last therapist or with the referring source's concerns. Their views of what a pastor is and how a pastor may be expected to relate to persons and to problems may cloud at least the initial sessions. It is important to work this out with clients and others when it arises or the therapy may be blocked.

Pastoral counselors' own mental health, financial condition, or need to prove personal competence may also provide difficulties in relation to referrals. If counselors are too hungry, they may take on clients beyond their capabilities or make contracts that are not in the best interest of clients. Mature counselors are able to establish limits regarding how much and what kinds of work they can and will do. If a counselor is flattered by receiving referrals, a close look at what he or she can do realistically is in order. The grandiosity of one's own ego may cost clients more than they should be expected to pay for the therapy.

Similarly, a pastoral counseling center just getting started or having trouble financially may try too hard to take on too much. Adequate financing and support systems will help to insure that a person or agency is not accepting or seeking referrals out of desperation.

The foregoing two paragraphs illustrate reasons for leaving the question of how to get referrals for last in this chapter. The soundest and most likely way to get referrals is to do good professional work with those you work with. Some things that will help that good work to continue include the following:

1. On opening a new agency or service, letters to prospective sources of referral will get your work before people. An

open house will give people an opportunity to look you
and your facilities over.

2. Visits to other professionals or agencies will allow them to
experience you and acquaint them with your center. This
will also give you a chance to know the resources of the
community.

3. News releases about significant events in the life of the
center will get your name before the public. The
appointment of new staff, election of officers of the board,
opening of new services, all merit telling the public about
your work.

4. Public relations appearances will usually garner some
new referrals. Appearing on television programs, when
you can get invited, preaching, speaking, teaching classes
in the community, any kind of exposure that allows
persons to experience you as a helping, understanding
person will result in referrals. This is multiplied if more
than one staff member works in the name of the pastoral
counseling center.

5. Letters to sources of referral on referral of new clients or
on termination will keep your professional function clear
and fresh in their minds.

6. Offering services to persons and groups will acquaint
them with your center's services. Training pastors in how
and when to refer is an example. Offering continuing
education for pastors and other professionals is another.
Doing consultation with other groups in the community
will get you involved where others feel the need. Offering
classes, seminars, and retreats for local churches at the
point where they feel the need will result in goodwill and
referrals.

7. Sending publications and annual reports to other
professionals and former clients will keep the center alive
for them.

8. Yellow pages listing—not an advertisement—is a way to
get your name before a lot of people.

9. A policy of doing good public relations with the public media and specialized groups will undergird the work of the whole center.

In conclusion, we want to restate what was implied at the outset of this chapter: Research and clinical reflection on referral dynamics is needed in the field of pastoral psychology. A better understanding of dynamic issues will build more efficient referral networks. Consequently, more people in need can be aided by pastoral counseling centers. Referral resources are invaluable to such growth. While centers are difficult to establish, their maintenance is a considerable responsibility, as well as a serious obligation for the pastoral counseling movement.

Notes

1. With very few exceptions, psychological associations which accredit various branches of the health care professions publish annual directories. For example, contributors to this volume are listed in such directories as the *Register of the American Association of Marriage and Family Therapy*, the *Directory of the Association of Family Conciliation Courts*, and various division publications of the American Psychological Association. Each of the journals published by these organizations either features articles on referral or lists persons and agencies which are respectable resources.

2. This small book was first published as a twenty-four volume set entitled "Successful Pastoral Counseling Series": William Oglesby, *Referral in Pastoral Counseling* (Englewood Cliffs, N.J.: Prentice-Hall, 1968). While a revised edition of this well-known book was published by Abingdon in 1978, it is still rather dated. One might even say that the earlier edition is more valuable than the later one. The first, for example, acknowledged the need for specific referral sources for women, whereas the latter sidesteps such a need altogether. The first edition discussed extramarital pregnancy. This was noticeably absent in the second, as were wife-beating and rape counseling. Nevertheless, Oglesby can continue to claim that his work is the only how-to *book* for pastors devoted entirely to referral counseling. For an excellent comparison of these two editions see Dr. John R. Johnson's critique in *The Saint Luke's Journal of Theology*, 22:4 (1979), 329-31.

3. The several resources listed in this book are no longer active, but Dr. Oates raises a number of important issues in the selection of health care

services. His book also reviews a small sample of the literature published by various psychological disciplines. Wayne E. Oates, *Where to Go for Help* (Philadelphia: The Westminster Press, 1967).

4. AAPC also maintains current offset listings entitled *Directory of Pastoral Counseling Centers* and *Registry of Training Programs in Pastoral Counseling.* These are available upon professional request. Address: 3000 Connecticut Ave., N.W., Suite 300, Washington, D.C. 20008.

5. Ronald Lee, "Referral as an Act of Pastoral Care," *The Journal of Pastoral Care,* 33:3 (1976), 186-97; and "Totemic Therapy," *Journal of Religion and Health,* 18:1 (1979), 21-28.

6. Gerald Gurin, *et al., Americans View Their Mental Health* (New York: Basic Books, 1960).

7. Lee, "Referral as an Act of Pastoral Care," 187.

8. *Ibid.,* p. 192.

9. *Ibid.,* p. 191.

P A R T

FOUR

SUPERVISION AND COUNSELOR
TRAINING PHILOSOPHY

C H A P T E R

13

Supervision of Pastoral Psychotherapy

Blaine B. Rader

The aim of this brief chapter is to describe the supervision of pastoral psychotherapy as it is found in a pastoral counseling center which is broadly ecumenical and operates within a dynamic ego psychology framework. While not all pastoral counseling centers operate within this orientation, a large number of those in the United States currently do. The process of supervision of pastoral psychotherapy is assumed by the writer to be much the same even in widely different theoretical perspectives. The nonanalytic worker will need to make his or her translations.

Definition

An operational definition of pastoral counseling supervision includes two fundamental processes.

1. *The maintenance of the center's standards of clinical performance via review and correction of clinical performance and service.* In this regard supervision functions like a quality control process. Both the patient and the therapist are protected from that which would be less than what the center holds to be minimal service. Supervision urges patient and therapist toward excellence in the experience of therapy.

2. *The assistance of the therapist in acquiring greater skill in provision of clinical service.* The functions of supervision may be identified by the words: training, education, growth, facilitation, and stimulation. Unlike conventional classroom teaching or

didactic instruction, supervision attends to the affective as well as the cognitive. It is the major methodology through which the person who has learned about pastoral psychotherapy comes to know how to do pastoral psychotherapy.

Sources

In regard to its goals, ideals, and methods, pastoral psychotherapy supervision has developed from two primary sources: the helping professions' practice and theory, and the church's experience with discipline, education, and organization.

Of the helping professions, medicine (clinical medicine as a whole and not just psychiatry), psychology, social work, and professional education have most clearly set forth procedures for the socialization or professionalization of the practitioner. There is also a broad tradition in the church for conscious discipline of the practice of ministry which has included a diverse set of practices to ensure that the professional's help will be appropriate. I believe this may have developed due to the church's awareness of sin and finitude in corporate life and the necessity of institutional provisions for dealing with human evil. Polity and organization may well reflect a sober view of the controls which people usually require to help others lovingly.

In the pastoral counseling movement this limitation is well represented in the stance of the American Association of Pastoral Counselors that there are no autonomous practitioners of pastoral psychotherapy, and there is no private practice of pastoral psychotherapy. Pastoral psychotherapy is guided and limited by the church. If it is not, then it is not *pastoral* psychotherapy. Any person who is not in supervision may consider himself or herself outside of pastoral psychotherapy.

Group Practice

The practice of pastoral psychotherapy supervision in a counseling center presupposes a group of persons interacting to carry out numerous functions. Some functions may be carried out by more than one individual in the center's system of interactions. At a minimum, the following persons and functions involved are:

1. the community at large,
2. patients,
3. therapists,
4. supervisor(s),
5. nonsupervisory facilitators (therapist peers; personal therapists of therapists; didactic teachers; consultants in medicine, psychiatry, psychology, social work, theology, etc.),
6. administrator(s) of clinical and organizational activity of the center,
7. church (parishioners, churches, denominations, parish pastors, ecclesiastical officers, etc.).

Supervision involves interaction of all the above. Optimal operation of supervision requires sensitivity and responsiveness to the totality of these functions and persons who do them. In a basic way, then, pastoral psychotherapy supervision is a group activity. In my opinion anything less than this is poor psychotherapy supervision of pastors and is not fully responsible to the community, the patient, or the supervisee.

Supervision's Operations

Who should be designated as the pastoral psychotherapy supervisor? In its infancy, pastoral psychotherapy often turned to helping professionals or nonclinically trained ecclesiastical officers. While this may have been necessary during the formation of the discipline of pastoral psychotherapy, it is no longer the desired practice. A psychiatrist is not a better supervisor than a pastoral counselor. In fact, the only persons who ordinarily would be fully aware of the seven elements of pastoral psychotherapy practice as outlined above are those who are pastoral psychotherapists. Usually "pastoral" is identified via ordination and "psychotherapist" by accreditation by professional, state, or other agencies regulating psychological treatment. We all know of those rare psychiatrists who function as pastors or those gifted helpers who would not be recognized as psychological workers, but these are the exceptions.

Increasingly, it is clear that the capacity to function as a pastoral psychotherapist at a high level of skill is *not* a guarantee of competence as a supervisor. Additional administrative and instructional capacities and skills are required. These added elements are identified most effectively via experience in doing supervision under an able pastoral psychotherapy supervisor. In AAPC's history it has been the practice to designate supervisors as Fellows and Diplomates. Membership requirements of AAPC for Fellow and Diplomate status include training in supervision skills and review of abilities through the membership evaluation process.

The experience of pastoral psychotherapy supervision is multifaceted. It requires the therapist to report what he or she has done with patients. While this may involve presentation of audio or video tapes, the reporting of the therapist to the supervisor requires a capacity to select from the vastness of his or her encounter with a patient that which will enable the therapy to be understood and changed. Much of this information will be *post facto*, yet it is the present reporting which enables the therapist and supervisor to work together. Complete reporting gives attention not only to the patient and the therapist but also to all the other participants in the center as noted above in the discussion of group practice. The therapist or supervisor who cannot fully report his or her own experience is blocked in learning and helping.

It follows from this that the work of supervision is the mutual anticipation, diagnosis, avoiding, and correcting of impasses in therapeutic work or in the therapist's learning. Supervision is not directed primarily toward the healing of the therapist or the supervisor but toward the patient. The goal of supervision is not smooth functioning of the center but the therapist's overcoming of impasses and learning problems that arise in the course of doing therapy. The therapist's personal growth and effective management of cases usually accompany sound supervision of pastoral psychotherapy, however.

The techniques of pastoral psychotherapy supervision are not greatly different from those of the other helping professions. They do add to those of the other disciplines such things as theological reflection and religious practice. A typical listing of the major techniques includes the following activities of the supervisor directed to the therapist: clarifying, confronting, demonstrating, and prescribing or telling. Listed in order of frequency, it would be preferable that these functions also occur in the order listed here, since it is the more autonomous (within the guidance of the center, community, and church) functioning of the pastoral psychotherapist which permits the full gifts of the therapist to be utilized. While this work may be done in a dyad of therapist and supervisor, it has been found that a peer group of several therapists may also be highly instructive. Some therapists can overcome their learning difficulties more easily in group settings with their peers. In no case is it thought that group supervision can supersede individual supervision.

Who should be the supervisees? In one sense, supervisees include all professional pastors, but in regard to the pastoral counseling center's specialization the following characteristics could be considered minimal attributes of the beginning therapist in training.

1. *Pastoral identity.* Usually this is operationally defined by ordination and good standing in one's faith community, yet some may have credentials of this sort and still not experience themselves or permit others to experience them as pastoral helpers. There are also those in the churches who are set apart to minister by their parishioners or by the larger community rather than by the churches (e.g., some Protestant women, Roman Catholic sisters and brothers, some lay therapists, and some formerly ordained clergy).

2. *Sensitivity to self and others.* One way in which sensitivity

to self and others is demonstrated is the capacity to establish an alliance with other people that is helpful and enduring. An insensitive person may be able to help a limited few, but the sensitive person who also possesses objectivity can be of help to a greater number.

3. *Personal experience of growth and change.* While not limited to the experience of therapy, many pastoral counselors have been most aware of growth and change as patients in psychotherapy.

4. *Report skill.* Sensitivity to self and others is of no avail to others unless one is able to communicate. Most often this includes ability to empathize, introspect, and interpret. As one mental health worker noted: "To know what one knows and how one knows is part of learning."[1]

5. *Knowledge of theories of therapeutic dynamics.* Some basic theory of change underlies all psychotherapeutic work. Therapist and supervisor work best if they have somewhat similar understandings.

6. *Theological and psychological understanding.* To work together with sophistication, therapist and supervisor should possess a common grasp of personality structure and dynamics, personality development, and psychological diagnosis as well as a theoretical grasp of the faith in terms which they can share. The mature practitioner should have an awareness of many approaches but the new practitioner often functions more effectively at first and emerges eventually with his or her own perspective if he or she works with one psychological and one theological orientation.

Typical Supervisory Issues

In order to convey something of the nature of the experience of supervision, the following representative supervisory issues are set forth.

1. *Sensitivity of therapist and supervisor.* Problems in doing effective therapy may be traced to characterological difficulties

in the therapist, supervisor, or patient. Mueller and Kell[2] identify this typical supervisory difficulty as anxiety binding whereas Fleming[3] writes of personality defects. In evaluation of therapy or supervision this concern is fundamental.

2. *Knowledge of theories of therapeutic dynamics, development, or change.* While the separation of the cognitive instruction of the therapist from his or her affective training may be done in theory, this is not operative in practice. Often impasses and learning problems are traceable to the fact that therapists have not read what they should to understand what they are encountering in their work. When the supervisor can facilitate examination of pertinent professional literature so the therapist can use it with a patient, the learning is enduring. Students can be led back to what they have been taught earlier with great meaning by effective supervisors.

3. *Transference and countertransference.* Very frequently with the less experienced but also with the more experienced therapist, difficulties in doing therapy are to be traced to the inappropriate, unrealistic, and defensive repetition of earlier significant conflicted relationships. Those distortions of the patient are termed transference, whereas those of the therapist are described as countertransference. Supervision, then, clarifies and occasionally eliminates problems through uncovering the distortions of transference and countertransference.

4. *Identification with the patient.* The therapist or supervisor who is unable to get "into the shoes" of the patient will not be able to have a helpful relationship, whereas the therapist who "becomes one" with the patient also is not of help. Both over- and insufficient identification can be a problem. The therapist needs to be able to understand the patient without losing a necessary distance from which he or she may bring new and appropriate understandings to the patient. Some of us have come to label the ideal as "objective concern."

5. *Capacity to nurture and confront.* The therapist or supervisor who cannot be tender and giving to others loses the capacity to help, but the one who cannot be firm and denying

loses that capacity also. Primary modeling for nurture and confrontation are offered the therapist in supervisory training.

6. *Regression with the patient by the therapist and supervisor.* There is a sense in which the therapist or supervisor must regress with the patient to be with him or her in the therapeutic struggle and quest, but there is a danger of losing the stance of objective concern which often prevents the help from being of assistance. The therapeutic experience of the therapist as a patient often assists here, as does modeling by the supervisor.

7. *Formulation of the therapeutic plan.* Both therapy and supervision operate effectively when there is an anticipation of next steps. Without this both therapy and supervision are superficial, contradictory, unnecessarily repetitive, and potentially destructive. While the whole series of steps may be missing to the therapist or supervisor, as in the analogy of the middle steps in a chess game, the next several steps should always be anticipated by the professional pastoral psychotherapist.

8. *Evaluation of clinical services of therapist or supervisor.* Without the ability to evaluate and assess, change is difficult to guide. At times, growth in depth, particularly that growth which focuses on unconscious processes, may be seen only "through a glass darkly," yet not all participants in the work of the professional should be in darkness. Stanley Weiss and Joan Fleming's brief article could serve well as a model for those who wish to be more uniform and thorough in their evaluation of supervision and therapy.[4]

Inadequate Supervision

That there are many deliverers of pastoral psychotherapy supervision is not to suggest that the quality of supervision is what it should be. In fact, few persons do pastoral supervision well. In part, this is due to inadequate provision of training in supervision by pastoral psychotherapy teachers. Most formal counselor training programs are only able to provide trainees with certain fundamentals of counseling by the program's completion, and have no time to teach supervision. Few are those who actively seek formal training years later when they are ready to learn supervision.

However, the inadequate state of present supervision of pastoral psychotherapists is also due to misunderstandings or distortions of pastoral psychotherapy supervision. Ten of these *misconceptions* in widespread evidence are noted below.

1. *Pastoral psychotherapy supervision is didactic instruction.* Having learned about therapy in an academic setting, some therapists attempt to do therapy in like manner. This is occurring less with more rigorous professional standards. Supervision by the book and through lectures is still in widespread practice. By itself such instruction is deficient since it only deals with the cognitive and is not fully experiential. The therapist at best learns *about* other's, not how to do his or her own therapy.

2. *Pastoral psychotherapy supervision is directed primarily to the patient's experience.* This misconception may make perfect sense at first glance. On reflection we find that it does not lead to effective practice. The practical consequence that results from this conceptualization is that the supervisor tries to do therapy with the patient, using the therapist as the middle man. In this "over-the-shoulder" supervision, the therapist/trainee becomes an extension of the supervisor's personality and tends to become mechanical and noncreative. Many a potentially creative therapist has been led to do therapy as a technician by supervisors who mistakenly operate on the basis of this misconception.

3. *Pastoral psychotherapy supervision is a form of psychoanalytic therapy.* In this instance supervision becomes an analysis of transference and countertransference phenomena and the like. While some learning difficulties are due to these factors, many are not. Not every therapist who is having difficulty doing therapy can be said to have a case of countertransference. Sometimes the therapist who works under supervision so conceived is not allowed to move beyond the patient role. The

popularity of these psychoanalytic labels is shown by the frequent requests of therapists to be done with supervision and to be in consultation. In short, it is because the "sick" role is inappropriate for the therapist.

4. *Supervision of pastoral psychotherapy is a skill which is synonymous with therapeutic skill.* While there are many similarities between supervision and therapy, the two are distinct. Managing cases, understanding learning difficulties, resolving impasses, etc., are in many ways separate from the practice of psychotherapy. Supervision requires professional training in the same way that therapy requires it. I believe that supervision of one's supervision is the best way to learn how to do supervision. This fundamental understanding has been held by pastoral psychotherapy's "cousin," clinical pastoral education, for several decades. One is taught in supervision to become a CPE supervisor and so it should be for pastoral psychotherapy supervisors. It is apparent, however, that to have been a supervisee is no guarantee that one can function as a supervisor any more than a well-analyzed patient can declare himself or herself a psychoanalyst.

5. *Supervision of pastoral psychotherapy does not deal with the personal identity or inner issues of the therapist.* The remark: "That is something which is inappropriate for supervision, you should deal with that in your personal therapy" has been heard by many supervisees. It is true that supervision is not personal therapy for the supervisee, yet in a basic way supervision cannot operate if issues of the therapist are removed from supervision's attention and resolution. The supervisory experience enables revelation of behavior and dynamics of the therapist which are often not observed in the therapist's own therapy. Professional identity and operation is not fully separable from personal identity and operation. It can be the understanding of the supervisor and the therapist that those issues of the therapist which are addressed must pertain to the psychotherapy of the patient and that no lengthy investment in the therapist's issues is appropriate for supervision. Significant changes in a therapist's

personality structure have been known to occur in brief periods of attention to a therapist's core issues in supervision.

6. *Supervision of pastoral psychotherapy is not for the mature practitioner.* As noted in the basic definition of pastoral psychotherapy at the beginning of the chapter, this misunderstanding is in effect a denial of pastoral psychotherapy. There are still those who consider the possibility of the practitioner attaining a state of excellence wherein he or she is able to function outside the guidance of others. It is noteworthy that AAPC now is requesting reports of supervisory experience from all pastoral psychotherapy practitioners, regardless of level of skill. I believe that this is a move to eliminate the category of consultation used in place of supervision by those who think themselves beyond supervision. All pastoral psychotherapists require supervision. It is noteworthy that the helping professions have come to a similar understanding: "We believe that none of us is ever so wise, or learns so much that discussion and dependence on colleagues becomes unnecessary."[5] Theologically, there may be no clearer demonstration of hubris than the claim that one no longer requires supervision, even though one acknowledges a need for consultation. I believe consultation alone is not enough for a pastoral psychotherapist.

7. *Supervision may be done with any therapist and supervisor.* Just as some teachers and students do not work well together and some therapists and patients do not work well together, so some supervisory styles and personality combinations of supervisor and therapist do not work well together. Often this can be discerned by either of the participants, i.e., the supervisor or therapist, but it seems to me that another person, such as an educational coordinator or administrative officer of the center, should be involved in the matching of supervisor and therapist. Self-selection sometimes results in a mismatch in which therapist and supervisor feel resistive to growth and learning.

8. *Supervisors of pastoral psychotherapy have the final word in the therapist's clinical practice or education.* While the

supervisor generally will have knowledge that the therapist does not, it is also true that the patient is in direct relationship with the therapist and not with the supervisor. Also, impasses in work can be brought on by the supervisor's errors or blindspots. Therefore a source of appeal or a reconciler of differences is needed from time to time. This role is generally taken by an administrator of the center such as a clinical director or educational coordinator. Both supervisor and therapist need to trust this arbitrator and not experience this person as siding unfairly with either supervisor or therapist. This person may represent other vital participants such as the patients, the community, or the church.

9. *Supervision of pastoral psychotherapy is best done in one-to-one weekly sessions.* The models of operation used in supervision have been carried over from psychotherapy and need to be seen apart from that procedure. Frequent review of work is necessary if modification of therapy is to take place. Generally the new therapist requires no less than one hour of supervision for three hours of clinical work. Movement beyond a ratio of eight therapists to one supervisor makes supervision coverage spotty and learning slow. Since there is transfer of learning from one case to another and persons learn by observing others and identifying with their learning too, group supervision could well be the way to extend supervision ratios if that is mandatory. However, it can only supplement individual supervision of a frequent nature.

10. *A smooth flow of supervision is to be considered the ideal.* Just as physical and emotional growth is noted by its spurts and lags, its turbulence and steadiness, so is the process of supervision. Always to avoid impasses and difficulties may not be desirable. An impasse may be an indispensable prelude to a significant change in a relationship or to a new learning. Those who wish for total order, optimum efficiency, and conflict-free relating should stay out of pastoral psychotherapy, and supervision in particular. After all, it is in the struggle and pain

and in the hassles with each other that God has shown us that our healing is to be found.

Notes

1. Joan Fleming and Theresa Benedek, *Psychoanalytic Supervision: A Method of Clinical Teaching* (New York: Grune and Stratton, 1966), p. 27.

2. William Mueller and Bill L. Kell, *Coping with Conflict: Supervising Counseling and Psychotherapists* (New York: Appleton-Century-Crofts, 1972).

3. Fleming and Benedek, p. 32.

4. Stanley Weiss and Joan Fleming, "Evaluation of Progress in Supervision," *Psychoanalytic Quarterly*, 44 (1975), 191-205.

5. Mueller and Kell, p. 48.

C H A P T E R

14

A Training Philosophy and Its Implementation
Brian W. Grant and David M. Moss III

It used to be said that the basic question about pastoral counseling is: "What, if anything, makes pastoral counseling different from the other therapeutic disciplines?" Answering that essential question has been necessary in order to justify our continued existence as a professional specialty. Since we have now developed a professional identity as effective clinicians, that battle is no longer necessary. However, it does remain an important question to consider in the development of a training philosophy and strategy for pastoral counselors.

There are things that we bring to our work that other mental health professionals, on the whole, do not. These can be summarized in a twofold distinction grounded in a theological worldview. The first is our prior training and/or predilection to think in terms of real and clear-cut turning points for people, a clear breaking away from a given way of life or a given condition. That mindset pervades the pastoral counseling field in several ways. It does not endorse a view of therapy geared simply to symptom management or the maintenance of a half-sick but stable status quo. The kind of therapy that is exciting and ultimately worthwhile aims for a clear-cut personality change, or at least a clear-cut behavior change, which sets in motion a continuing process leading to greater mental health. One difference between pastoral counseling and the secular mental health professions is that we have accepted this view of human possibilities along with our religious training. To a mature religious consciousness, the notion of people making peace comfortably with their "sinfulness" and continuing to live in it sounds abhorrent.

Built into the religious tradition that we share, however distantly and through whatever symbols, is the belief that God makes all things new and that Providence is a reality. If we were to secularize that, as some pastoral counselors attempt to do, we would say that all things and persons are in principle renewable and that whatever force we are allied with as agents of healing can produce positive change in anyone. In other words, any attempt to deny the possibility of growth for a person, or to fail to offer a person treatment that believes growth to be a possibility, is to sell short the tradition from which we come. This is not meant as a normative statement; it is a descriptive one. Pastoral counseling, as a movement, tends to take this position, and such convictions are shared by the other contributors to this volume.

Another perspective pastoral counselors bring to their professional services, one that secular mental health practitioners ordinarily do not, can be traced to an appropriate historical accident rather than anything that has been clearly analyzed. Most of us came through a training experience, either in Clinical Pastoral Education (CPE) or some comparable training agency in pastoral counseling, that has substantially affected the way we practice psychotherapy. What has happened in those experiences seems different than what has happened in the training experiences of every other kind of mental health professional.

The analogy that describes these experiences best is that training is like being tossed into a vat along with a group of other trainees. At the very edge of this vat, though not in it, are a small pack of ambivalently loved and hated supervisors who periodically raise questions like, "How does it feel to be sinking and drowning in that mess?" and hopefully, "Isn't it great that you've learned to swim?" The focus of supervision has been on helping candidates, who are struggling to avoid being swept away, overwhelmed, or submerged in the training experience, to consciously articulate what is happening to them as a way of becoming more agile in coping with their confusion. They are becoming aware of their own processes and learning to conceptualize them while under substantial environmental stress.

Most of us who have reached this perplexing but necessary transition point have learned to swim, and have even achieved a certain comfort swimming around in that mixture of feelings that once felt so life-threatening to us. Moreover, we recognize it as the very essence of living. Those of us who learned to become conscious of our own processes, to learn what it was that was happening to us as we struggled for survival in that mess, learned enough about the mess itself—the environment or the institution or the relationships we were in—to be able to cooperate with it and eventually achieve mastery of it. As a result, we have figured out how to get out of the vat. We got up on the edge of the vat to become one of the supervisors who invited other people to dive in and occasionally help the best ones out—those who typically feel no longer a need to escape in order to survive.

Moving from analogy and talking more directly about the process, we need to be sensitive to students who choose to enter CPE or a good training program in pastoral counseling. Making such a choice confronts students with a form of cultural shock, a form so radical that it deprives them of many of the traditional role supports that have kept them from needing to think about who they are and how they feel in all their experiences. They are cast upon their own relational resources to bring them through and, in the process, begin to see in bold relief what those relational resources are. They begin to examine what they do with other people and to see what works, or what does not. Those who make it out achieve the necessary alterations in their basic interrelational skills so they can sustain their movement with increasing health, regardless of environment. That is to say, a central factor in the effectiveness of both CPE and the kind of training we do comes precisely from the sort of confusion it produces in students. They are deprived of the supports that would otherwise keep them from having to look at what they are doing in relationships and how that feels. What students need to do is develop a style of relating that brings the reward or professional self-esteem desired.

The finished product after that kind of experience ought to be persons whose basic sensitivity to others is keen enough that they are able to adjust their patterns of relating to others in a way that beneficial effects for both are produced. To do that one needs to be able to respond to the other, not on the basis of any preconceived category in which one has placed the other, but on the basis of one's immediate, empathic and empirical, intuitive and conscious judgments about how the other is responding and how one is responding to the other. Hence, one is in fact modifying one's behavior, altering it according to the responses that are present in the other human being. Hopefully, that is the kind of person who comes for training at a recognized ACPE or AAPC certified counseling center. Certainly, we are describing the "ideal CPE graduate," if such a term can be used, the kind of person usually most enjoyable to clinically supervise.

It is probably not irrelevant that the man who was most instrumental in devising CPE, Anton Boisen, had a schizo-phrenic experience and sought the way out of that experience by trusting that it had something important to say to him. Boisen's basic faith statement was that whatever happens to a person has meaning that the person can learn from. In more classically theological language, Boisen's convictions were rooted in the doctrine of Providence. He believed that it is always better to look at oneself and one's own processes than not to. Nothing that one can find there is worse than the absence of that finding.

This philosophy offers a very powerful training experience, keyed by the supervisor. It assumes that the supervisor is going to encourage very intense things to happen, both by structuring the trainee's environment and by consistently insisting that the trainee look in depth at inter/intrapersonal processes while experiencing that structure.

There is the likelihood of a substantial dropout rate from any training program or therapy group that relies on this method, a risk the trainer or supervisor must knowingly accept. An assumption growing out of such an awareness is that there are some people who are ready at a given point in their lives to use this kind of training experience and to move toward being a psychotherapist, and there are some people who are not. To attempt to engage the latter by toning down the intensity of the program fails the former who might actually move on to real excellence as professional counselors.

A major implication of this section is the criteria for acceptability of a counseling trainee. Those criteria are quite similar to ones which apply to a client beginning to explore the possibilities of termination. The major question is this: Are those processes that begin to move in a person when one becomes conscious of oneself already moving, and do they seem likely to be able to continue moving without the constant energizing of the therapist or supervisor? If the potential trainee is at the point where he or she needs external input regularly to keep personal processes moving, that trainee is going to be tempted to use the training too much as therapy, or conversely, to resist it so that healthful movement does not occur. The same is true for the client. Though many clients quite properly remain in therapy long after that process is self-perpetuating in them, it is never fully inappropriate to terminate once that process has begun. It often is fruitful to continue after that has happened, working out the implications of that process through a wide range of relationships. Most importantly, it is never appropriate to end therapy before it has happened.

It is doubtful that there is much point in taking a counseling trainee who is not already actively involved in such processes. If that happens, the training program is constantly going to be trying to do the basic unsettling that should happen before the trainee becomes actively involved in clinical work. This is because the trainee's clients and supervisors are going to be dealing with somebody who has not yet evidenced any commitment to the very process to which the trainee is trying to secure the client's allegiance. That is the one clear contraindication for acceptance into the type of pastoral program this book supports.

Some of the formative thinkers in the pastoral psychology movement have talked about this particular variable as the "soul of the trainee." They look for the soul in interviewing potential trainees as a way of assessing their ability to make their vital energies available as an instrument of personal growth. If trainees cannot or will not do that, they need to be referred either for further personal therapy or, at times, another quarter(s) of CPE—depending, of course, on the ego-strength of the candidate.

Once you have the kind of person you want, the first step in counselor training would seem to be the continued development of relational skills, through the interaction of the supervisory hour, the case conference, the interpersonal relationship group, and the counseling sessions themselves. All of these training experiences are fed back through the same kind of, "How do you relate?" process that typifies CPE supervision—plus the very important new ingredient of beginning to add categories and plans to that basic structure of relational skill.

On the basis of solid relational ability a supervisor can increase a candidate's diagnostic skills and begin to work on treatment plans, as well as raise questions that would help develop the trainee's intellectual sophistication about treatment processes. This is facilitated by the supervisor's comfortable belief that the student will not rely primarily on intellectual categories but on basic relationship skill—the elementary tool of the counselor. We are talking about a way of moving to the goal of the trainee being in full command and contact with his or her intuitive processes, as well as having a high degree of intellectual sophistication about them. It seems clear that most trainees get a substantial dose of cognitive learning through the theological course work they have studied in seminary or in other forms of basic professional training. It is also true that

CPE has tended to open them up intrusively. What we are looking for is a way of nurturing the growing relational and intellectual skills of the counselor that will produce a balanced, therapeutic person at the end of training. We deeply endorse the Greek ideal of *understanding*, not just mere *knowledge*, or factual awareness.

Yet another way of talking about this distinction is to address the difference between inductive and deductive approaches to training. Our suspicion is that once you have done a thoroughgoing deductive training job with a student, you have provided a set of categories on which the student has so much reliance that he or she may never be able to break out of it to trust relational skills. On the other hand, if a student begins with the honing of relational skills to a high degree of precision, that student gains a tool flexible enough to compensate for the rigidities and lacunae or omissions of most deductive schemes. This is clearly where our commitments lie.

An important issue raised by this commitment is the appropriateness of a certain amount of confusion as part of the student's basic training experience. It is not uncommon to hear that some pastoral counseling training programs provide too many opportunities for students to become confused. This criticism eventually points out that the trainee is receiving different messages from consultants representing different professional specialties, and that most supervisors refuse to take *final* responsibility for their students' clinical practice. Realistically, there is no way that the supervisor can assume final responsibility for a trainee's case. The supervisor is not there when the trainee is seeing the client. That means that the trainee must be the person who sifts out from the behavior of the client and from his or her own internal messages the data believed to be the most important to respond to in the session. Our goal is to help trainees learn to relate to that kind of confused situation in which they are the only person who can decide what they will do. (Needless to say, we are very uncomfortable with the notion that the supervisor is the final authority on what the trainee does with the case.)

Some training models are designed with the belief that the trainee needs somebody to depend on for cognitive clarity. We disagree, holding that some confusion is creative. Intellectual dependence on the supervisor seems to delay the learning process. We feel more comfortable with the trainee's dependence on an energizing figure, someone who is going to enable processes to occur for a period of training. The real world is a confused and confusing place. It is finding meaning amidst confusion that ultimately enables pastoral counseling trainees to help clients help themselves. This is a way of saying that it is inappropriate and counterproductive to construct a univocal kind of supervisory relationship or training environment which would encourage the trainee to ask the supervisor what to do in a given situation. Such an autocratic structure does not allow the student to process speculations and fantasies with the supervisor. It does not encourage the trainee to become increasingly aware of the usability, or lack thereof, of his or her typical manner of behavior.

One can see the difference between this approach to training and the kind practiced in many medical, psychological, and social work training programs. Although there are a wide variety of training programs in all those disciplines, they initially tend to focus around basic intellectual categories into which people can be fitted. Then they concentrate on devising appropriate treatment strategies for each category of persons. Only subsequently, far into the student's training, do the issues of a trainee's relational ability begin to emerge with sufficient clarity.

The most common secular training models leave a student without much experience in internal self-corrective processing. The physician, for example, learns an entire categorical system into which all human beings must fit. On meeting a patient, the physician is expected to arrive at the correct classification for the individual being seen. The physician can then deduce the correct treatment scheme and begin to apply it. However, such a strategy leads to dangerous assumptions. Perhaps the most basic of these assumptions is that the categorical scheme is in large part accurate, that it is exhaustive, and that there is going to be a slot in it for every person the prospective counselor sees. It encourages one to spend a great deal of time concentrating on questions of where the person fits and perhaps an insufficient amount of time attending to one's own responses and the kind of behavior that works with the person in question. Ultimately, it leaves the counselor less well prepared to deal with a person who fits poorly into any of the categories, or on the border between two categories. This essentially leaves the therapist in the position of having to depend on a discontinuous cognitive schemata to find the basis for doing therapeutic work.

The senior author suggests that the kind of training that is or should be done in pastoral counseling sets up a habitual inductive process, and that that process is inherently superior to the predominantly deductive one described above. We should be working for self-corrective mechanisms in advanced trainees and in a staff's interrelational skills which enable them to adjust to the behavior of the client, regardless of the category into which the client fits. The first question for us is not then, "Do I know how to treat a pseudo-neurotic schizophrenic?" but "What kind of behavior seems to work with this person I'm talking to, and what is the meaning of my reaction and response?" This allows the trainee a greater and more appropriate form of freedom and flexibility in learning the practice and art of psychotherapy.

A further training implication concerns the kinds of cases trainees are assigned at early levels of training. The belief among our secular consultants has been that you do not refer schizophrenic patients to graduate students or interns until they have read a lot of material about schizophrenia and *"know* what to do." This line of reasoning is open to question, to say the least. Instead, it could be said that one does not assign a trainee a schizophrenic patient until the trainee has mastered personal barriers to relating openly, to taking initiative when it is required, to recognizing when someone else is confused, and to clarifying that confusion with empathy. This means that the criterion is not the intellectual readiness of the counselor for a given kind of client, but the mastery of emotional issues, or at least having identified them, that are problematic for the client. Quite clearly one does not give a seductive male counselor a young, sexy, hypomanic female client—no matter how many books he has read on the seductiveness of hypomanic women. At best, the counselor ought to treat his first hypomanic woman, or at least be assigned to her and meet her for the first time, *before* having read any books on that specific diagnostic type. Having confronted the issues of actually relating to such a person and begun to test out what kind of behavior makes sense and is effective with her would make reading on the subject substantially more useful. In such an instance, reading is appropriate only ex post facto.

This says something about the stage of training at which concepts are introduced, the relative importance given to conceptual learning, and the emotional self-awareness that is at the base of relational skills. Most individuals who enter training, regardless of their CPE or therapy background, are still deficient in relationship skills when they approach their first year of training. It would be a serious error, for instance, to drop an Interpersonal Relationship Group (IPR) and substitute another hour and a half of academic learning. In fact, it might be more fruitful to increase the emphasis on relational skills.

It is certainly true, however, that attention does need to be given to systematically making diagnostic schemata and treatment planning available to students at some point. It is quite important that counselors learn about resistance and insight, that they understand how to handle a termination, that they read something about contracting, and that they examine diagnostic categories. Likewise, it is important that trainees form some expectations about what sort of behavior to anticipate from people of different personality types in response to specific ways counselors might behave. This is not to imply that such reflection or awareness is more important than developing basic relational skills. Trainees cannot really begin to appropriate these issues until they have begun to upgrade their relational skills.

Students who come into our programs from nonpastoral disciplines, no matter how highly skilled they are, are particularly needy for personal skills. They should be in personal psychotherapy and their supervision should always focus around what is going on in their relationship with the counselees. Tapes are wise to use, and questions like, "How did the client feel about what you said then?" should dominate supervisory sessions.

This leads us to the question of how trainees are learning to use their own inner processes in their therapeutic work and how the trainee is learning to be sensitive to the exchanges that do and do not flow between a counselor and a client. The illustration of Jesus at the well with the woman of Samaria is apt. It is obvious that something particular and powerful happened in that encounter. What was important was not the information but the aliveness, genuineness, and openness, the quality of energy that sparked in her the ability to let down her barriers both with Jesus and with the other people in her community. It seems that the most effective treatment is when that kind of contact occurs between people, not focused so much on technique as on the empathic flow between persons which begins to engender new occurrences amongst them.

Imagery borrowed from Gestalt therapy might be useful here. The Gestalt therapist goes with the client down into the latter's feelings, bodily structures, and tensions. Both therapist and client come out of that experience in a changed way. There is a necessary quality in the therapist that one might speak of as "a state of grace" which enables a basic awareness of the client's intrapsychic pilgrimage. That condition of grace is clearly not a matter of what formal religious community a person belongs to or his or her degree of involvement with it. Instead, it is clear evidence of commitment to the process that flows through persons who are in union with a fellowship of redemption that is operative in this world. The therapist contributes the awareness and the reality that, "I've been there, too," not in terms of having struggled with precisely the same pathology or the same limitation that the client has, but in the sense that the therapist, too, has felt the temptation to avoid deep introspection, has struggled and overcome that resistance, and has survived in a greater wholeness.

For the senior author some examples from a Gestalt weekend workshop personally demonstrated the vitality of such a therapeutic relationship. One group participant was working on some material that was very deep and painful. The therapist was able to sense where he was, hold that person in his arms to enable the process to begin flowing, and provide enough safety so that the self-exploration could occur. The contact between persons is very real and powerful in such an event.

Another participant in this workshop had been particularly frightened of his own "craziness." During the workshop, the therapist felt comfortable enough to go to that person and give him a nonverbal signal that freed him to explore the depth and meaning of his fear with great outward expression of emotion. The therapist met the client with respect. Yet the counselor did not maintain a distance but touched the man when he needed to be touched and backed off when he did not need that contact—when he needed to develop his own initiative. Something enabled the therapist to know what was happening in the client and respond to that in an appropriate way. That particular person could go through that experience and relationship with this particular therapist, and it is quite possible that no one else there could have succeeded in that way, either as participant or therapist. What enabled that immensely liberating experience was the sensitivity of the individual and therapist to one another, a sensitivity of a subtlety and complexity that defied diagnostic categories and transcended the results which might have been expected from any approach defined by those categories. In this situation the therapist and the workshop participant were able to trust that the participant's exploration of his own blocks would be a healthful experience, and that neither would be swallowed up in it. This is similar to Boisen's confidence that there was meaning in his own schizophrenia which should not be lost to his readers. Again, the doctrine of Providence is unwise to ignore.

This may be an appropriate place to say more about the theology which undergirds the rationale of what has been described thus far. If ministry is an attempt to help people live their whole lives successfully, to have those lives take on a sense of unity and direction—a wholeness that can be called "holy" or "sanctified" or "saved"—then what are we about in ministry? Whether it is a crisis intervention in the emergency room or a lengthy pastoral counseling relationship, ministry is helping persons cope with the whole of life's value. It is the attempt to reverse aiming our lives toward death, corruption, limitation, and destruction of persons. It is a dedication to life, turning it around so that it does in fact produce redemption, wholeness, and increasing transmission of the richness of experience. We refer to reality bound up in that dimension of being as "salvation." That is what ministry is: the flow of contact and empathetic love for persons—from one individual to another—in the context of a saving, restoring community.

There is a sense in which ministry, pastoral counseling and pastoral psychotherapy included, is an incarnational and sacramental experience. The spirit, that dimension in oneself which enables the deep outreach and contact of processes which flow through us all, is passed from one "believer" to another. Those fortunate enough to have parents who could impart that, or who come in contact with supervisors, therapists, lovers, or friends who impart it, may gain the spirit as a gift that they can transmit, under the proper circumstances and with the right persons, to others. This ultimate "contract" or *contact* with the Ultimate enables them to descend into themselves and find that source of power and growth and flexibility within them. There is a convergence here between the Johannine sense of the circle of life in Christ, the sense of going down into another person and into oneself described by writers in the Gestalt tradition, and Erikson's awareness of the cycle of generations. In all of these experiences there is a circularity, whereby at an appropriate point in one's life one has something to pass on to another, something that has been recognized through an exploration of inner depths and the depths of one's community and faith in life, God, and the self.

Here the issue of awareness of fellowship, or Erikson's issue of intimacy versus isolation, is relevant. From such a perspective, one could say that isolation is the basic "sin," perhaps indeed the only sin. There is a sense in which a person who is isolated is locked into fragmented self-structures, is cut off from the kind of experiences which would challenge him or her to change and enable supportive relationships in which flexibility is possible. Thus, rigidity of character structure is an almost inevitable concomitant of such isolation, and that rigidity bears some deep theological similarities to the biblical notion of idolatry. An appropriate doctrine of God to undergird this thinking is one that sees the Ultimate as a creative force that flows through all events, often at a level below consciousness, breaking up old rigidities and helping people be aware of the sources which provide them with the courage to make themselves available for "new goods," new structures or new experiences. This can happen only in community. The community can then be experienced as a saving circle, or perhaps a spiral of generations.

Thinking of pastoral psychotherapy in this context, and suggesting it as a context in which most modes of psychotherapy might well be considered, the therapist should not be thought of as the possessor of esoteric knowledge about how one keeps a schizophrenic from having hallucinations, for instance. The therapist is a person who has been trained to make his or her own humanness available in a process of creativity and redemption that transcends the self. The therapist is trained to be open and aware as fully as possible for his or her own gratification as well as that of others. The therapist uses intimacy to teach others, by interaction and example, how to acquire that for themselves. The therapist is not set apart but in the midst. Such a professional is an expert on how life can best be joined and shared, rather than how it can be controlled or maintained. This is why the most expert pastoral counselors are also the best psychotherapists available. They are people with a commitment to the possibility of real and substantial betterment of human life and of the potential for that in every person, regardless of the extent of their pathology, their poor prognosis according to MMPI scales, or the diagnostic judgments of similar "objective" measurements.

The key variable at every level is the extent of engagement by trainee, supervisor, and client in his or her own processes. What heals is involvement in the intrapsychic, reflective, working through process, whether that involvement is present at the level of supervision, at the level of the nurturance of consultants and professional staff people, or at the level of the client. In professional staff we expect such a process to be active, continuing, redemptive, and essentially self-perpetuating— with a clear understanding that part of that self-perpetuation comes from our own community. It is expected that the prospective *trainee* coming to us will have some of that process already going and thus will be able to see a major part of the training procedure as a facilitation and enhancement of the ability to perpetuate that process. We usually expect that the *counselee* coming into a center will have only a minimal level of that activity in evidence and will gradually see counseling as an attempt to upgrade it. Consequently, by the time clients are ready to terminate they will be close to the point where they recognize that process and know what contributes to it in themselves, realize when it is working and when it is not, and are well aware of basic responses they can make to keep the process moving. Another way to phrase this is to say that the criteria for termination of a client is very similar to the criteria for acceptability of a counselor trainee.

Closing this chapter is difficult because so many experiences, training rationales, and philosophical positions are acknowledged by pastoral counselors. Yet we feel that most pastoral supervisors would agree that there are similar processes going on at a number of levels within our agencies. The *relationship* between the client and the counselor, the supervisor and the trainee, the supervisory staff itself, and ultimately the relationship between the client and the communities beyond the pastoral center are parallel. The same things need to be occurring within all four dimensions or levels. If we can perpetuate that process among ourselves, and upbuild it to levels of independence and power within our professional fellowship, we can then begin the process of stirring it up, maximizing its consciousness, and strengthening its self-perpetuation in our trainees. Once that happens, they can interrelate with increasing efficiency with clients of various types. Ultimately, those clients will return to the community and enable that kind of living in their marriages, families, and institutions. When that process is in action, then the counseling center and its trained staff are providing the service that they are ordained, commissioned, accredited, licensed, and paid to offer.

P A R T

FIVE

EVALUATION AND RESEARCH

C H A P T E R

15

Pastoral Counseling Centers and Evaluative Research

Steven C. Nahrwold, John L. Florell, and David M. Moss III

It seems appropriate that the concluding section of this volume is focused on the merits of research and the significance of experimental processes for pastoral counseling centers. So often experimental reflection is relegated to an insignificant status and not affirmed as a valuable mode of formulating practical speculations and verifying clinical constructs in the construction of well-reasoned projections regarding center policies, organizational models, and pastoral services. When careful research is not conducted, hindsight is the typical vista used to assess "fortunate" advances or explain away failures in the intra/interpersonal ministry of such centers. Each of the preceding chapters is an outgrowth of cautiously implemented research projects and experimental designs specifically tailored to explore issues like center models, related legal concerns, styles of quality control, philosophical rationale, and monetary factors.

Evaluative research can provide pastoral counselors or psychotherapists with qualified tools to closely examine what form of ministry is most often needed in a particular environment. Insightful research adds strength to our attempts to help people help themselves. A "map" can develop providing self-cohesion and wholeness—a dimension which pastoral counseling affirms as an elementary expression of the doctrine of Creation. In other words, research may be considered from a number of perspectives, including theological vantages integrally tied to the provision of pastoral care.

In this chapter theology will not be an explicit topic of discussion, however. Our concentration will be an examination of several research constructs and resources that can be practically employed by pastoral counseling centers. We present this material with the understanding that evaluative research geared to improve the delivery of pastoral psychotherapy services touches only one arena of the expanding health care delivery system through which persons may find qualified psychotherapists. Consequently, we have a deep sensitivity for the virtual "nightmares" that state licensing bureaus, accreditation agencies, and insurance companies must confront. It is out of this appreciation that we join them in questioning: "What is *quality* health care?" "Is intensive service limited to a certain dimension of psychological disorders or is extensive care to be offered for a broad range of emotional problems?" "Who is qualified to deliver aid in either instance?" "Are, for example, paraprofessionals—given their specialties—better suited to deal with partial maladies than, say, psychiatrists or clinical psychologists?" "If so, are these counselors to be included or excluded from official accreditation and insurance payments?" "Who should decide?"

Pastoral counseling centers have a critical stake in the answers to these questions and therefore in the evaluative research from which their related solutions will be derived. But along with such issues as program certification, evaluative research can provide pastoral counseling centers with important information relevant to program planning, implementation, and modification.[1] Thus, research, often thought of by those who work in clinical settings as a luxury, something done by students or "high powered" people with computer banks at their disposal, is an important, practical, and necessary undertaking for those concerned with the quality of pastoral counseling, its maintenance, improvement, and justification to the wider field of mental health.

Evaluation and Controversies

Most evaluation of social programs, including mental health, falls into two general categories. The first is quality

257

control, or *process evaluation*. For example, how efficiently and consistently does a delivery system provide continuity of care within established guidelines. The second is evaluation of services, or *outcome evaluation*. In other words, what measurable effects does the delivery system have on client outcome or community well-being?

Variation among social programs makes for a great diversity of evaluation purpose and method as well as some complex problems. There is disagreement among authors as to the nature of evaluation research itself. For Alkin, the distinguishing element of evaluation as opposed to other types of research lies in the preconceptions of the evaluator.[2] Comparison of "what is" with "what should be" is obviously a subjective element. Weiss states that "what distinguishes evaluation research is not method or subject matter, but intent—the purpose for which it is done."[3] Other authors emphasize the importance of method and adherence to techniques of traditional scientific research, preferring a single-factor approach to a holistic approach.[4] Within the past several years there has been a growing number of authors who propose a broader definition of evaluative research. The consensus is that different purposes call for different approaches. Modification of the traditional scientific method has been called for in order to accommodate the peculiar nature of social agencies serving the public interest.[5]

By 1957, only two books on evaluation had been written.[6] Since the fifties, the enormous growth of government-sponsored social welfare programs has generated a great need for social welfare program evaluation. A plethora of theories and methods has arisen in the past decade and a half to fill that need. The literature at present is so abundant that a thorough review would cover volumes. As it is such a new field, there are significant problems both in theory and practice. Schulberg points out, "There is a striking difference between high quality and sophistication of theory and low quality of actual research of programs."[7] Evaluation studies are generally easier to formulate and criticize than to carry out. It has even been suggested that evaluation would be simpler and more practical if nonresearch trained field workers carried it out.[8]

Much of the present controversy centers around the value of a holistic versus a specific, or single-factor, approach. Some say evaluation should concentrate on the net effect of a center because of the unwieldy multiplicity of factors and variables. Moreover, the tighter a specific hypothesis is, the more limited it is in application and utility. Others stress that part observations and little experiments should not be devaluated, for they can contribute to the evolution of an integrative theory.[9] Similar to many behavioral researchers, many theorists propose an evolutionary, building-block approach to evaluation research focusing only on limited manipulable behavioral variables of change rather than on holistic, subjective, and symbolic evidences of change and effect.

In addition to this controversy of approach, there are other questions to be answered by the researcher attempting to do effective evaluation within the context of a mental health agency such as a pastoral counseling center: How to formulate adequate operational definitions of concepts such as "mental health," "cure," "effective psychotherapy," etc.; how to clarify and operationalize a center's goals; how to substantiate and duplicate intuitive judgments such as "I think" or "I feel"; how to reduce distortion due to selective perception of the evaluator; how to adapt research methods to account for the dynamism, constant change, and adaptation of the center itself; how to compensate for concurrent counter effects and parallel effects to the center's program; how to do research of high quality and utility with limited financial resources; how to reduce defensiveness toward evaluation and implementation of results; who should evaluate, for whom, and for what purpose?

Developing a Research Project in a Pastoral Counseling Center

In line with the questions and limitations listed so far, one must keep in mind evaluative research does not give a final answer about what is being studied. Rather, evaluative research allows one to get a general sense of what is happening in the area being studied at the time of the study.[10] The conduct of evaluative research involves two basic questions: (1) What are the goals of the program to be evaluated; and (2) What will the center do with the data when the research is complete? To be effective the researcher has to know the alternatives available for changing the program or services offered if the results are negative. Otherwise the research will be of little use. Another issue concerns whether the research will result in quality control information or in data that will help to deliver the center's service in a finer, more efficient manner. The research ought to touch issues in which the staff is interested. Successful research is based on having an empathetic sensitivity for the needs of the staff and, as a consequence, being able to build in things that are important to them. This is the best way to identify the problem area(s) that are to be researched.

The next step is to read other studies that are related to the problem to be researched. These can provide ideas on how to conduct the research project and may also provide ready-made measuring instruments, designs, or hypotheses. Then it is necessary to define the problem to be investigated in as clear terms as possible. This will help in the formulation of a testable hypothesis or theory tentatively believed to explain how the service under investigation works. Also, presumptions should be stated in a way that will dictate how the data are to be interpreted—if the results are "this," it will mean "that."

After this comes the construction of the research design. Questions to be answered are: Who will be the subjects? How will they be selected? What is being tested? How will behavior be observed and change evaluated? What instruments will be used to evaluate change? In the kind of research that is done by pastoral counseling centers, the subjects will primarily include the staff, the counselees, students, and/or workshop participants. Selection can be randomized, using a random table of numbers, or all the people in one category can be studied.

Categories such as age groups, religious affiliations, and other demographic factors may be used to group subjects.

When the subject population is determined, the decision must be made as to what kinds of change in behavior, attitude, or skill will be observed and how that information will be obtained. There are three basic ways to gather information. The first is the self-report method. This is probably the simplest, least expensive method of gathering data, but it is also one of the least accurate in that subjects can influence their scores in undesirable ways. A second method is to observe the subjects in action or to measure change by testing them before and after treatment. The third method is indices measurement, which utilizes records or accounts that were intended for another use (e.g., intake records), so the subjects do not know they are being observed for a research project.

The more ways of observing the subjects, the stronger the research will be. For example, in a study of counselees' reactions to a certain mode of therapy, the researcher might observe counselees going into and leaving counseling sessions, ask what they felt about the therapy, and ask the therapist how the counselees reacted during the sessions. This would yield three different points of view or observations to help evaluate the therapy. The three together are more powerful than any one type of observation alone.

After the basic design has been formulated, the researcher needs to select the method by which the results will be analyzed. Simple statistical procedures are available such as the *t*-test or chi square, which are explained in most elementary statistics books. However, it is even easier to use simple counting methods like the positive-change, negative-change, no-change model where one counts the number of subjects in each group to determine what changes, if any, have occurred and how strong the changes have been for a group as a whole.

After the research has been planned and carried out, the final step is to evaluate the data and interpret the results. This is probably the most difficult step as it involves drawing

261

conclusions about what the observations seem to mean. It is important at this point to try to consider what else might have caused the results other than the proposed theory. If another explanation makes as much sense as the theory originally proposed, the research loses power. Where possible, it is helpful to control or screen out rival explanations. For example, if a two-week marriage enrichment workshop is being evaluated, the participants might be asked not to read any outside books on the subject. This would help control for possible outside or rival explanations for the increase in knowledge of the workshop participants.[11]

Evaluative Research Designs and Their Applicability in Pastoral Counseling Centers

The basic steps in developing a research project have been described above. From this outline there have arisen a wide variety of evaluation methods and designs. A review of some of the major research techniques will now be presented and their practical use in pastoral counseling centers considered.

The classic research design which uses experimental and control groups, randomized inputs, and beyond-chance statistical difference in results is usually touted as superior to all others. In outcome studies, it is one of the methods of choice because it offers the most reliable data regarding causal relationships between techniques or practices and outcomes.

The controlled experiment is, however, often difficult to use in action settings such as pastoral counseling centers. Continuity and control over other variables are hard to maintain. It may be difficult to find a control group. Also, there is the ethical problem of denying service or a specific treatment to people coming for help. Those in control groups may drop out prematurely, a factor over which the experimenter has little or no control. The Hawthorne effect also has a contaminating effect on those who are aware of their participation in an experiment.

In the past few years, the experimental model has come under attack because it is too restrictive and aseptic to be generalizable to the real world. For this reason, research in an action setting has begun making use of quasi-experimental designs.[12] They allow some uncontrollable variables but take advantage of what opportunities there are to control against threats to logical soundness. These designs are often more practical and realistic in settings where "pure" classical experiments are unfeasible. Of course, the results sometimes must be stated in more qualified, tentative terms. A good rule of thumb is always to ponder other plausible explanations and discount them by logical assessment, if possible.

Quasi-experimental designs include: Time Series, which involves a series of measurements of output at periodic intervals before the program begins and then after it ends (it assumes that the flow of clients over a period of time will remain relatively stable and that significant change is due to the program); Multiple Time Series, which is a variation on the Time Series design in that it includes successive measurements during a program in addition to before and after; Nonequivalent Control Group, one of the most common designs in practice, in which no effort is made to randomize or match clients, so a reasonably similar comparison group (e.g., a similar centers' clients) is used as a control; Patchwork Designs, in which one controls whatever is necessary and possible to control (e.g., if a researcher feels that age is the only factor that would account for differences in patients' response, control of only this factor would be attempted at the exclusion of other variables.

Quasi experiments are easily done in a pastoral counseling center. A good example of this type of experiment would be giving some clients who entered therapy tension-relieving exercises along with their regular therapy and comparing them to a control group entering therapy that received therapy only. By comparing anxiety tests given before and after ten weeks of therapy, the effectiveness of the tension-relieving exercises on client anxiety could be assessed. Obviously, in this example, one could not control who comes into therapy or when they would begin therapy. However, the treatment, relaxation exercises, can be given to some new clients and withheld from others. By comparing the group that receives relaxation exercises and therapy with the group that receives only therapy, certain conclusions could be drawn about how helpful the relaxation exercises were in augmenting regular therapy in terms of relieving anxiety.

The problem with this kind of research is that there may be other things that explain the differences. For instance, the therapists used would have to have more or less the same amount of counselees in both the control group and the treatment group. The therapists would have to use basically the same kind of therapeutic approach on their clients in each group. The therapists would have to be kept in the dark about which clients were getting the special treatment so that they did not treat the treatment-group clients differently from the control-group clients. That is to say, the way that the two groups were treated would have to be kept as equal as possible to try to eliminate as many rival explanations as possible.

Evaluation researchers have devised several alternate designs which do not fit into regular experimental or quasi-experimental categories. One of these is the laboratory, or computer simulation.[13] No attempt is made to recreate "reality." Variables from clinical situations are abstracted and are often assigned a mathematical value in the attempt to predict outcome. Some laboratory experiments try to create an entire program, "set it in motion," and observe the behavior of people. Most of these are highly questionable and tentative.

A still popular form of evaluation is the case study approach. In this category are included one-shot case studies, involving a short one-time inspection by a group of experts or professional colleagues[14] and long-term studies by an individual or group. The National Institute of Mental Health still considers case studies an important means of evaluation.[15] Usually comparison is done afterward with other similar centers. *The Mental Hospital* by

Stanton and Schwartz is a classic example of a comprehensive, intensive, insightful long-term case study. In such studies, one often does not need to know much about a program or agency before one begins the evaluation. The structure and organization of the research may develop during the evaluation (and technique may shift as needs arise) or after the inspection is complete.

The case-study or group-case-study approach is one of the most common methods used in pastoral care and counseling. One case or several cases with similar elements are studied in depth to try to tease out why people behave in certain ways or why they have certain attitudes. Usually such elements as the presenting problem, age, sex, religious affiliation, background, socioeconomic status, the dynamics of pathology, family, medical, work, and religious histories, marital information, relation to children or family members, and self-assessment are included in such studies. The advantages of this method are that a center usually has the information on hand to conduct the study; it is relatively inexpensive in terms of time and money; and it has pragmatic value to the pastoral counselor and counselee. The disadvantages are that it is inevitably somewhat subjective, and there are insufficient numbers in the research sample to justify valid generalizations about other counselee responses.

Cost-benefit analysis is often viewed as an alternative to experimental evaluation research. It relates program costs to output costs. However, measuring benefits in terms of dollars is not that easy. It sounds appealing to compare programs in terms of "A dollars for B hours of labor to achieve benefits for C number of patients." But what are considered important benefits? And how are intangible benefits such as heightened self-esteem or reduced anxiety convertible into dollar terms? Even when comparisons are done with other programs having the same "benefits," it is almost impossible to determine if the "benefits" have the same quality and intensity. Patient goals or benefits, therefore, are usually described in some measurable

265

terms such as increase in total center income. There is also a problem with comparing achievement of goals. More input may be necessary to achieve reduced goals for disadvantaged people than for more advantaged clients (in terms of education and social class). Also, what should be included as benefits from curing a drug addict for example? The list could include cost to society in terms of welfare payments, law enforcement, prison costs, hospital treatment, and the like.[16] Furthermore, what numerical value should be assigned to benefits? And will the benefits be permanent? Are they ascribable to other causes? The list of problems goes on. Nevertheless, economic analysis and comparison of various programs remains an important and politically useful form of evaluation.

Keeping in mind its limitations, cost-benefit analysis can be a useful means of evaluation within pastoral counseling centers. If staff members log how they spend their time over a given time period, it will give the administrator a pattern of the work habits of each staff member and of the center as a whole. This information can be helpful in terms of evaluating efficiency, arranging staff schedules, and letting the staff know how others on the staff are using their time. For the more sophisticated administrator, cost analysis can help evaluate programs in terms of a time-spent per cost-per-hour-invested basis. Programs that have high overhead with little monetary return may be eliminated from a center's programs or reevaluated and revamped to make them more profitable or productive in terms of the time-cost ratio.

If a center uses a computer billing service, one may be able to study the aging of accounts to make sure clients do not get too far behind on their payments. It also can help counselors be aware of their counselee's behavior in relation to payment.

An intriguing technique of evaluation is the Goal Attainment Model.[17] This model proposes that evaluation be done within the framework of goals determined and reached. It is a versatile model, useful in measuring a wide variety of goals provided they are not too global or abstract. Goals may be for therapists, patients, adminstrative activities, or program services.[18] For instance, a particular patient-therapist goal is determined. A measurable scale is set up specifying a t-score for the patient in terms of overall goal attainment. Goals are scored from most successful attainment ($+2$) to the least successful (-2). This procedure reportedly helps to differentiate problems, structure therapy (or any other procedure), and clarify outcomes. One problem with this model is that it may not allow for the dysfunctional assignment of more resources than are necessary for achieving a goal.[19] Goal achievement is not the only consideration; evaluating the input used to achieve a goal is also an important consideration when researching a program.

Several books and monographs have concluded that the best evaluation is that which is a systematic, ongoing part of a program.[20] Evaluation should be a built-in feature assessing a program's effectiveness, making judgments, and offering suggestions for change. Most pastoral counseling centers do not have this feature, at least not to any degree of effectiveness. Pastoral counseling centers usually rely on administrators eyeballing monthly summaries and whatever regular record keeping is performed.

One of the sources of information for continuous assessment of a center is the collection of basic statistics on the delivery of services. This is a simple descriptive data-gathering type of research which reveals the kinds of problems the center is dealing with, the turnover of counselees, number of hours of service, and so on. The purpose of this type of research is to describe in an orderly fashion the services the center is delivering.

This type of research can be used in a number of ways. In terms of public relations, the data can be used to give the percentage of marriage counseling, family counseling, child therapy, and other kinds of therapy. In a counseling service with several different centers, the services rendered by each center can be compared. In terms of staff efficiency, counselors can be evaluated on how long they keep their counselees, the percentage of client turnover, and the number of new clients each counselor gets monthly. In terms of efficiency rating an earning-per-time-spent ratio can be established.

Continuous research on delivery of services fits nicely into the overall planning of a counseling center in terms of decision-making about the kinds of educational programs that may be useful to the staff and in terms of future planning for expansion of services to the areas of most need. If a center finds that 50 percent of its counseling is marriage counseling, it might plan to schedule educational events that will help the staff be better marriage counselors. It also may be an indication that churches in the area or the community at large might benefit from a series of marriage enrichment workshops. The Virginia Institute of Pastoral Care (VIPCare) service statistics have been used in establishing new centers in areas where there seems to be a strong demand for services. With this type of research, they are able to allocate counselors to those centers with a strong growth potential and to tell the communities served about the needs that the center is meeting in their community.

Another method, continuous evaluation of service, focuses more on the quality than on the quantity of services. There are a number of ways to evaluate services. One of the easiest is to ask people to rate the kind of counseling they have received in terms of satisfaction with the results of therapy, expectations, acceptance, how counselees felt during counseling, the structure that the counselee perceived being used, how influential the therapist was, attitudes of client and counselor, and their responsiveness to each other. This method can help the counseling center get a profile of why clients come, what their complaints are, how they feel, and what styles and methods they respond to best. The same basic method can be used to research both counselors and counselees at a center. The therapists can relate their goals, how they feel while they are doing therapy, how they relate to their counselees, and what they perceive as bringing about change in the therapeutic process. This kind of basic self-observation, when correlated with the client's perception of the counseling process, gives counselors helpful insight into how well they are reaching their clients and how they might improve services. It also provides much needed input from the consumers of the center's services.

Another aspect of the continuous evaluation approach is peer-review research. Typically in intake, staffing, and case conferences the counselor's work is evaluated in some way by peers. By simply logging the kind of feedback each counselor gets in such conferences, both the counselor and the center get a view of the counselor's strengths and weaknesses over a period of time. Such information can be valuable in assessing how well a counselor learns from consultation sessions and whether further education is needed. It also may provide a profile of the kind of consultation that is given by staff and outside consultants. If the consultants are stagnant in their approach, or the staff members are unresponsive to the consultants' presentations, there may be a need to bring in new consultants or change the consultation procedure.

Another type of service a center may want to analyze is the training it conducts. Two parts of the training process might be investigated: first, how do the supervisors train the trainees to be pastoral counselors; and, second, how are a trainee's skills assessed? Other than the formal supervision of supervisors in the supervisory training of professional organizations like ACPE or AAPC, there is little done in the way of evaluation of the supervision that students receive. It is almost as if once credentials are obtained, it is assumed that the supervisor will do good supervision. For those who train students to do pastoral counseling in an ever-changing and complex field, this is a dangerous assumption.

Research can help clarify what is happening in the supervisory process. Various methods are used in the evaluation of supervision. Tests for competency in counseling can be given before and after a certain period of training, at least on a content basis. Ongoing monitoring can be done by asking the students and the supervisors how they perceive each supervision session. A checklist might be constructed for supervisors and a similar one for students.[21] If the two checklists correspond closely, then it can be assumed that students and supervisors are congruent in their assessment of the supervision process. But if they are not similar, the reasons for the discrepancies should be investigated. The monitoring of supervision on a session-by-session basis can enable a center to evaluate if the supervision conforms with good counseling and supervision theory. Such research helps supervisors and students grow and learn from the ongoing process in which they are participating. Research has shown that behavior change is more likely to occur when feedback is immediate. The advantages of feedback in the supervision process means that changes can be made immediately in teaching methods that do not seem to be effective. It means the students have input into their supervision process that they might not have without the research. Such research makes both the supervisor and the student responsible to each other.

Another form of researching supervisory effectiveness is to analyze the student's performance before consultation or accreditation committees. These committee members can provide a more objective assessment of a student's performance on a limited basis. There is a wealth of information that can be very helpful to training centers if they would just avail themselves of it.

An additional important area of continuous evaluation is from the people who refer clients to a center. This is a vital group for every center to be aware of, and it is important that the center knows how they feel about the services it is rendering. Too often the procedure is to wait and see if they refer someone else to find out if they are satisfied with the services that the center is providing. Again, straightforward questioning can be one of the easiest, most effective ways of finding out how referrals are made to the center. Information on why the referral was made, how the client was referred, what follow-up contacts were made about the referred client, who initiated the follow-up, and whether the referring professional was satisfied with the referral would be useful to a center in several ways. First, such a questionnaire would communicate concern on the part of the center for the professional or layperson making the referral. Second, the information can help counselors educate referring persons who may have unrealistic expectations of the counseling center. Finally, it might indicate how referral could be increased or made more effective.

Another phase of a center's functioning that might benefit from continuous evaluation would be workshops that are offered by the staff or sponsored by the center. There are three areas that it would be helpful to research. First, discovering the attitude of the participants about the workshop that they have attended would be helpful. Finding what the participants liked and disliked could be the key to a successful workshop program. Second, finding how effectively the workshop informed, educated, or helped develop skills is important. A simple before and after testing on content or attitudes could be helpful in assessing how effectively the workshop got across its message. Third, finding what other types of educational offering the workshop participants are interested in in terms of subjects, workshop leaders, and times can be invaluable in planning a workshop schedule.

At times, centers do not have the resources or inclination in terms of expertise, time, or funds for continuous evaluative research. It is at these times that having an outside expert or student come in can be beneficial. Contracting to have research done can be relatively inexpensive, particularly if a center is located near a large educational facility or is interested in evaluating common services that others may have already done. Almost any graduate program has students who may be interested in doing research in a center, and there are research services offered by institutions like VIPCare, which will assist pastoral counseling centers in doing research on a contract basis. The advantage of this type of educationally or professionally contracted research is that a center does not have to worry about developing and analyzing the research. It can also offer more sophisticated methods and analysis than a center could do alone. In addition, there is the advantage of being able to do pure research, that is, research that does not have any practical application at the time that it is done, but may be of benefit in the future or contribute to the field.

One research project that is presently under way and promises to be a very valuable source of information for the entire pastoral counseling movement is being undertaken by the Institutes of Religion and Health (IRH) in New York. They are conducting the first substantive research evaluation of pastoral counseling centers and, more specifically, the effectiveness of a particular model of centers which they are establishing. This project proposes to develop not only an effective organizational model for pastoral counseling centers, but also a viable method of ongoing research evaluation. Ten new centers will be established. It was believed that fewer would not provide enough generalizable data, and more would be too difficult to coordinate.[22] Starting the evaluation with new centers rather than with those already established gives this research an important advantage not usually available to other evaluators. The researchers explain:

More than measures of effectiveness are needed to encourage utilization of the new model by others. If good records are not made prior to and during the process of setting up the centers, it is difficult, if not impossible, to reconstruct the procedures followed and the problems met and solved, to isolate these characteristics of the community which seem related to differential effectiveness, to evaluate the achievements at different stages of development, and then to prepare materials which will help others learn from the experience gained in the process.[23]

Evaluation will attempt to measure goals which have been determined for each model center. These goals are predetermined characteristics of quality service and a quality delivery system.[24] The most important source of evaluation data will be gained from the routine face sheet which will be used by all centers and filled out by everyone receiving service, direct or indirect. It is precoded for data processing. Among other things, this face sheet will help determine if the center is serving people not receiving service elsewhere, serving people most in need of help as judged by the initial community survey, and many other questions regarding utilization rates.

In addition to face-sheet data, information will be collected on services rendered. Types of service, characteristic of those who receive them, number and types of referrals, etc., will be included. The face sheet and service reports will also help determine to what extent people are being reached who have never received prior service, the number of people served who cannot afford other kinds of available help, and those served who are dissatisfied with other agencies. Further information on termination will be gathered, and follow-up interviews will be made with randomly selected subjects no longer involved with the center. The directors of each center will be asked to evaluate every major program at the center and will be assisted by a director of evaluation at the IRH.

Besides formal collection of data on standardized sheets, the researchers will gain much additional information in a variety of ways. First, follow-up questionnaires and interviews, by telephone if necessary, will be used with former clients to get their evaluation of the service. Staff input will be gathered as well. Special additional in-depth studies will be made of some selected clients who received one of two alternative forms of care. Other in-depth studies will be conducted to determine if specific goals are being met—particularly, community acceptance, liaison with other professionals, and impact on specific community problems. An index of acceptance by other professionals in the community will be evaluated periodically. Information on this will be gathered by interviews and questionnaires. Differences in attitudes toward the center will be noted. Other procedures will be used to evaluate the training programs and seminars provided by the centers. Cost-accounting procedures will monitor the entire economic operation and jugments will be made regarding various types of sources of funding. Cost-accounting data on the use of staff time will provide information on the cost-benefit of various programs.

Routinely collected data from standardized reports will be evaluated within each center for standard periods of time (e.g., every six months). Comparisons of past and present will help formulate a pattern of development. Data from other studies at each center will be evaluated independently and then together with other centers. Finally the supervising staff at the IRH will arrive at a consensus regarding rank order of the ten centers in terms of their overall performance. Factors contributing to success will be isolated by nonparametric statistical procedures. If, however, all centers are equally successful, then the data collected will be only of descriptive value.

The evaluation made on each center will give consideration to specific characteristics of each community in which the center is located. Disasters and other special occurrences will also be noted. Hence, the gathering of data on each community prior to establishment of a center is important. Indices of social disruption, leadership, level of sophistication, and so on, will be obtained. These community profiles will also be updated periodically to note any changes which might affect the services and programs of the center.

Of interest is the importance the IRH places on the personality, training, and experience of the center directors and their being an important factor in success. Hence, levels of success will be related to the characteristics of each director in most cases.

Responsibility for data collection and analysis will be in the hands of a central director of evaluation, the center director, a research coordinator, and a program implementation consultant. They will establish procedures for data collection. Each will have training pertinent to their role. The director of evaluation will work closely with the center directors to actively engage them in the evaluation process at all levels. Most of the record-keeping will be done by relatively untrained personnel or volunteers in order to save funds. Thus, the record-keeping procedures are constructed and organized in such a way that these individuals can manage the task.

The IRH believes most initial data analysis will be quite simple. Tabulation of types of service and number of clients will be done manually or by computer, depending on the number involved. Between groups, analysis will use chi-square values. Before-and-after measures of attitudes, etc., will use techniques such as tests between correlated means. Analysis such as this will be done periodically. When enough results are compiled, periodic reports will be made through AAPC newsletters and the *Journal of Religion and Health.* In addition, a manual designed for those interested in establishing pastoral counseling centers will be published.

Recently a new type of evaluation research has been proposed. Nearly all present types of research evaluation employ a goal-model approach or the identification of goals and the measuring of variables which assist or hinder in the achievement of those goals. This is the case with most outcome studies. The research is analytical, reducing wholes to more discrete isolated parts and examining the relationship between those parts, hopefully to find a cause-effect relationship. The assumption is that since parts are simpler, they are more amenable to understanding. When the understanding of the parts is achieved, it will be possible to understand the more complex whole. The proposed model differs from this traditional approach. It is very complex and still more theoretical than practical at this time, but is nevertheless worth considering.

Inspired somewhat by Ludwig von Bertalanffy's *General Systems Theory,* the proposed model called "systems analysis" attempts to analyze not just identifiable parts and variables but the whole process by which a complex system such as a social agency functions.[25] Organizations such as counseling centers are fluid, complex systems, continually adapting and changing with respect to their environment. Furthermore, every whole system is an entity different from the sum of its parts, and these synthetic wholes cannot be explained by reductionist summaries of their parts. Expansion, technology, reciprocity, and self-regulation are more characteristic of systems. Causality may be circular with many variables in an indeterminate reciprocal relationship. Systems are dynamic, active, and open; not static, reactive, and closed.[26] Social organizations not only achieve official goals, they have to acquire resources, coordinate subunits, and adapt to their environment. These preoccupations get tangled up with and limited by the achievement of program goals. There is an increasing awareness of bureaucracies and government programs which continue to exist long after the need for them dies and which probably spend more energy in maintaining their own survival and organization than in serving the public. They seem to have a life of their own quite apart from achieving the intended social goals and benefits. To overlook the complex structure of such organizations is unrealistic and artificial.

A distinction should be made here between systems analysis and evaluation. Most systems analysis is descriptive; evaluation is the often subjective judgment based on such analysis. The systems model relies heavily upon the evaluator's extensive knowledge and understanding of an organization.[27] The demands this places upon the evaluator in terms of knowledge makes it difficult to imagine its practical application at present.[28] It has been suggested that descriptive analysis of organizations' internal systems be combined with statistical studies of input and output.[29] In spite of its present difficulties, the systems model is seen as particularly promising for situations with a high degree of complexity of variables and their relationships.[30]

All systems have certain features in common, as does the evaluation of those systems. First of all, information is the basis of all activity. It is translated into energy which affects the environment and in turn reenters the system as new information. Second, all systems have three levels of activity: the skill or task level,[31] the organizational level,[32] and the interpersonal level.[33] Systems analysis must consider all three levels of activity. Evaluation must also consider all three but is usually done after the systems analysis. Evaluation involves value judgments, measures outcome, and is done over a longer period of time than analysis; yet it still employs a systems analysis paradigm.[34]

Thompson and Rath propose a common language and framework for a systems analysis and evaluation model. The system, containing its three subunits—skill and task competence, organizational solutions, and interpersonal functioning—is evaluated, and the planning and control that come out of the evaluations is fed back into the system, completing the circuit.[35]

The procedure for systems analysis begins with problem formation, which determines objectives and criteria. These, in turn, along with resources, constraints, and alternatives, determine the analytical procedure. The results are then evaluated by a decision-maker who decides, with the use of ranked alternatives and scenario, to either accept an alternative, redo analysis, or drop the project.[36]

This model has three underlying concepts. First, utilizing the categories of time and space, there is the concept of the "cloud of variables" which proposes that all possible variables affecting the system be suspended, or held for consideration, and their interdependence noted.[37] Second, all variables may be defined and given different weights, or numerical values, by different researchers in different disciplines. The orientation and values of the decision-maker can transform the nature of the variables. Thus, the nature of the variables in the mind and interest of the decision-maker is important. In fact, if all variables could be translated into this concept, some of the instability could be reduced.[38] Third, the Confidence-Utility concept accounts for purposeful decisions made within the organization or system.[39]

277

Decision can be described as changes [jumps] in the state of confidence in the individual with respect to some value [utility] of interest. . . . The primary value of this concept is that the purposeful variables in a system can be described in terms of a simple two-dimensional metric—with changes in state of confidence, with respect to some variable, we have achieved a "fact"; to the extent we have diverging states of confidence [or different utilities] we must recognize that we are dealing with a "value."[40]

A very interesting, even captivating, type of organizational evaluation is psychoanalytic evaluation. It does not purport to be comprehensive, but instead a valuable addition to a comprehensive evaluation. It might be considered a logical extension of the systems approach. If organizations are dynamic wholes different from the sum of their parts, analogous to biological units, then maybe they can have "corporate personalities" and psychodynamic conflicts similar to individual persons.[41] The current popularity of various types of psychohistory of individuals, political movements, nations, or institutions is doubtless an attempt to humanize, perhaps anthropomorphize, as well as understand forces that have and still do shape our culture.

The method of such evaluation is largely subjective and generally relies on interview, field observation, and organizing the emotional impressions of the researcher. Available records are sometimes the only source. Research of this type done in relation to churches and a nursing home persuasively demonstrates that institutions can manifest, through corporate behavior of members and institutional structures, complex defense mechanisms to deal with preconscious or unconscious fears and wishes.[42] As individual dynamics are reactions to inner and outer environment so also organizations have dynamic reactions to inner and outer stresses and cues. In fact, they can evolve into a rigid personality structure which influences all behavior.

A final word needs to be spoken in regard to information gathering. Whatever method of evaluation is chosen, there are several means of gathering data. The most popular is the questionnaire. Questionnaires have the advantage of allowing a large number of people to be sampled with a nominal investment of time and money. However, questionnaires are difficult to design. They are often poorly worded, ambiguous, and too long.

In designing an effective questionnaire, the first step is to state the goal of the questionnaire and how the data will be analyzed. Essay questions should be avoided whenever possible because they are often difficult to interpret and codify. If possible, different responses should be anticipated and listed as multiple choice alternatives.[43] It is helpful in *designing* a questionnaire to give a small group of people, who represent the sample to be surveyed, open-ended, essay type questions from which multiple-choice alternatives can be constructed.

Questions that can be answered true-false are easiest to evaluate and interpret. The more choices that are given, the more the possibility of variation is increased. It is also a good idea to avoid leading questions where the desired answer is obvious.

There are two elements to be kept in mind when developing a questionnaire. First, there will be some people who will not respond to the questionnaire. In most questionnaire research a 60–70 percent return rate is considered good. Stamped, self-addressed envelopes and a follow-up letter or telephone call usually help increase the return rate. The second consideration is anonymity. In research circles it is generally considered that people will be less candid if they can be identified. It is important to assure the respondents that their identity will be protected in some way (e.g., "Your name will only be used to code responses and will not be used in any reports or be made known to other persons.").

Many of the pitfalls of questionnaire research can be avoided by using direct observation techniques such as the interview, case study, or record-statistical study. These techniques are especially useful when the sample is not large or as a preparatory study for a questionnaire or survey project to be used on a larger group.

The strength of the interview method is that data will be available on every person sampled, so the researcher will have more of a sense of what each respondent means when they answer questions. Some of the weaknesses of this method are that interviews are time consuming and expensive, may give more information than desired, and if several interviewers are used, there may be a different perception of what some of the questions mean among the different interviewers. Thus, it is important that interviewers agree on what each question means. Other elements in the preparation of an interview would be to state the goals of the interview, how the data gathered will be analyzed, and how the questions will be asked.

The advantages and disadvantages of the case-study approach and record-statistic approach have been dealt with in the general discussion of research designs.

Conclusion

This chapter has attempted to point out some of the practical aspects of doing research in a pastoral counseling center in terms of developing a research project, using pragmatic designs, practical means of investigation, and more sophisticated methods. The benefits of such research include quality control information and evaluation of services rendered. Despite the problems involved in determining standards of quality and evaluation, some national agencies and organizations have devised lists of principles and priorities by which they would determine quality service. These include the National Institute of Mental Health,[44] American Psychiatric Association,[45] and the American Association of Pastoral Counselors.[46]

Evaluative research enables a pastoral counseling center to deliver better services and plan for the future. Also, research is a way of learning more about how to help people and how to use resources already available to their best advantage, whether it is in the area of consultation, training, or referral sources. Research provides the data for speculation about the nature of behavior change and about the nature of persons. In relation to professional identity, those involved in pastoral counseling ought to be able in some way to articulate their basic view of persons, which in turn influences the methods of counseling and training that are used. Thus, the benefits of research accrue not only to individual centers, but also to the field of pastoral counseling as a whole. A number of nationally prominent pastoral care and counseling organizations have banded together to sponsor the Joint Council on Research.[47] This organization sponsors and encourages research in pastoral care and counseling. It also sponsors the *Pastoral Care and Counseling Abstracts* which abstracts current published and unpublished research in the field. This can be both a resource and a forum for the person in the pastoral counseling center. It is hoped that increasingly research will be reported to the *Abstracts* so that all can benefit from what has been done in our field.

We also hope that our message regarding the merits of evaluative research will further encourage pastoral counseling centers to engage in responsible modes of assessment. Research is one of the simplest, most respectable ways of evaluating and learning about pastoral counseling. As we said at the outset, each of the previous chapters in this book are products of careful research and reflection. However, the issues that they underscore, like the models and constructs they describe, are ongoing concerns that necessitate re-evaluation. In other words, research in the field of pastoral counseling and psychotherapy is dynamic. As the pastoral psychology movement grows, research projects are needed to continue to offer insights that assess its strengths and weaknesses. It is from such evaluative or reflective perspectives that maturation occurs. In fact, *maturity*, in so many ways, is the basic concern of this anthology as well as a principal ethic of all pastoral research.

Notes

1. Marvin Alkin, "Evaluation Theory Development," *Evaluation Comment*, 2:1 (1969), p. 5.

2. Alkin has defined evaluation as "the process of ascertaining the decisive areas of concern, selecting appropriate information, and collecting and analyzing information in order to report summary data useful to decision makers in selecting among alternatives." *Ibid.*, pp. 2, 3.

3. Carol Weiss, *Evaluation Research* (Englewood Cliffs, N.J.: Prentice-Hall, 1972), pp. 6-7. Weiss cites a use for a decision-making, *program* derived questions, judgmental quality, action setting, role conflicts (between evaluator and administration), and a lack of general publication of results as differences between *evaluation* and other research.

4. Carstairs states, "Most authors deplore the tendency to evaluate global results; better to focus on particular elements and measure their effectiveness." G. M. Carstairs, "Problems of Evaluation Research," in R. H. Williams and L. D. Ozarin, eds., *Community Mental Health, An International Perspective* (San Francisco: Jossey-Bass, 1968), p. 47.

5. Howard and Krause support this contention with the following points: "1. Traditional scientific method does not concern itself with the issues of conflicting interests, but evaluation of a service program in the public interest (as distinct from evaluation in some special interest) must consider the diverse commitments of the various groups or parties affected by or invested in that program; 2. Even aside from conflicting interest, decisions to expand, curtail, modify, continue, or terminate a service program cannot be logically derived merely from the results of controlled experiments, and the basis of this inferential uncertainty in research may differ from party to party; 3. Even if a controlled experiment could yield pragmatically decisive results, what is evaluated is qualitatively changed by the introduction of the research, though the intrusion differs for each party; 4. The inherent effect of publication of evaluation researches, done in the open, public, honest manner of full disclosure associated with the ethic of science, is often destabilizing for its host action program, because the various interest groups affected by a program can each use the findings 'politically' to further their own often conflicting demands on the program or its funding source." Merton Krause and Kenneth Howard, "Program Evaluation in the Public Interest: A New Research Methodology" (A revised version of a paper presented at the Society for Psychotherapeutic Research, Philadelphia, Pa., June 1, 1973), pp. 1-2.

6. Paul Lemkau and Benjamin Pasamanick, "Problems in the Evaluation of Mental Health Programs," *American Journal of Orthopsychiatry*, 27:1 (1957), p. 55.

7. Herbert Schulberg, *et al.*, eds., *Program Evaluation in the Health Fields* (New York: Behavioral Publication, 1969), p. 20.

8. Otto Klineberg, "The Problem of Evaluation," *International Social Science Bulletin*, 7:3 (1955), p. 347.

9. Lemkau uses the analogy that "knowing some behavior of a person is important even though we cannot be certain what it indicates regarding the total personality." Lemkau and Pasamanick, p. 56.

10. Due to limitations of skill, time, and finances, most evaluations are compromises and limited in their scope, which has led Bloom to state that most evaluations are little more than descriptive rather than truly evaluative. Carstairs, p. 48.

11. For further discussion on basic procedures and questions with which evaluation research must concern itself, refer to:

Alkin, 2.

Donald Campbell and Julian Stanley, *Experimental and Quasi-Experimental Designs for Research* (Chicago: Rand McNally, 1971).

Evaluation in Mental Health, published by the Public Health Service (Washington, D.C.: U. S. Government Printing Office), Publication 413, p. 7.

J. C. Glidewell, *et al.*, "Methods of Community Mental Health Research," *American Journal of Orthopsychiatry*, 27 (1957), p. 72.

M. Jahoda and E. Bernitz, "The Nature of Evaluation," *International Social Science Bulletin*, 7:3 (1955), p. 354.

Weiss.

12. For an excellent discussion of the variations of experimental and quasi-experimental designs see Campbell and Stanley.

13. Joseph McGrath, "Toward a 'Theory of Method' for Research on Organizations," in Schulberg *et al.*, p. 143-44.

14. Donald Campbell, "Factors Relevant to the Validity of Experiments in Social Settings," in Schulberg *et al.*

15. *Evaluation in Mental Health*, see note 11, p. 23.

16. Weiss, p. 86.

17. Originated by Thomas Kiresuk, Ph.D., Chief Clinical Psychologist and Director of Research and Program Evaluation, Hennepin County Mental Health Center, Minneapolis, Minnesota.

18. *Planning Creative Changes in Mental Health Services: Use of Program Evaluation* (Department of Health, Education, and Welfare, Publication No. 73-9145, Washington, D.C., 1973), p. 8.

19. Amitai Etgioni, "Two Approaches to Organizational Analysis: A Critique and a Suggestion," in Schulberg *et al.*, p. 109.

20. P. Hesseling, "Principles of Evaluation," *Social Compass*, 11:6 (1964), p. 22.

21. *Evaluation of a Model for the Utilization of Community Pastoral Counseling* (A proposal for the National Institute of Mental Health, Grant No. MH 24288, by the Institutes of Religion and Health, New York, 1975).

A checklist like the one shown below might be used.
1. What counseling themes were discussed during the session?
2. What did the student want from the session?
3. How well motivated was the student?
4. How helpful do you feel you were to your student this session?
5. To what extent did your student show progress or regression?
6. What pastoral elements were dealt with in this session?
7. What were your goals for this session?
8. How did you act toward your student(s) this session?
9. How did you feel during the session?
A similar checklist can be used for students.

22. *Ibid.*, p. 12. A long, detailed outline of procedure for "Clinical Center Establishment" is given in their prospectus. It involves such items as site selection, community contacts, advisory board, director and staff, services rendered, etc.

23. *Ibid.*, p. 41.

24. *Ibid.*, p. 18.
   Goals include:
   1. Autonomous and self-supporting as soon as possible.
   2. Psychiatric or clinical psychological supervision of pastoral counselors where needed.
   3. Low starting costs ($18,000 total), minimum need for subsidy, and low-cost provision of service.
   4. Efficient service delivery.
   5. A mutually supportive relationship with other health maintenance organizations.
   6. To develop strong ties with the whole community and its leadership.
   7. Adaptability to provide service relative to specific community needs.
   8. To provide some preventive mental health.
   9. To be susceptible to continuous evaluation and assessment.
   10. To help train pastoral counselors and make a contribution to the entire pastoral counseling movement.
   11. To have a well-trained director with broad administrative and therapeutic skills.
   12. To demonstrate the particular values of pastoral care.

25. Schulberg states that the systems approach is nonexperimental and emphasizes that "programs are complex social systems . . . in which all variables are reciprocal and dependent." He adds that "the system model of evaluation is not concerned with specific goal achievement, but with the distribution of resources to all needs and the allocation of funds . . . even to non-vital activities." Schulberg *et al*, pp. 19, 9.

26. Ronald R. Lee, lecture notes, May 1973.

"Hence, in describing a system we may talk about:
1) *input*—the input of energy from the environment.
2) *throughput*—the transformation of energy within the system.
3) *output*—the release of energy back into the environment.
4) *negative entropy*—the storing of energy within a system which causes internal fluctuations.
5) *cycles*—of input and output.
6) *self-regulation and feedback loops.*"

27. Etgioni, pp. 103-4.

28. Weiss, p. 30.

29. Williams and Ozarin, see note 4, p. 205.

30. Charles Thompson and Gustave Rath offer an illuminated overview of the system's approach to evaluation. They suggest that this method provides "a method of orderly progression to the solution for problems which appear intransigent because of the complexity of the variables and their relationship . . . an approach which in a reasonably complete and orderly form identifies and accounts for all of the important variables, suggests the process or sequence which should be followed to carry out the decisions (manipulations) which are likely to achieve the results desired, and includes provisions for evaluation." Charles Thompson and Gustave Rath, "Making Health Systems Work" (A paper presented at the annual meeting of the American Academy of Pediatrics, October 20-24, 1973, in Chicago, Illinois), p. 1.

31. *Ibid.*, p. 4. This includes not only clerical, technical, and professional skills (from secretary and janitor to therapist) but more refined levels of activity and types of evaluation such as operations research, forecasting, cost-benefit analysis, attitude surveys, quantitative research, and any other skills used to assist organizations.

32. This relates jobs, skills, and tasks to each other. It includes formal and informal organizational structures, rules, customs, procedures, and so on. The authors add that "often organizational skills must be included (such as) . . . organizational models, formal organization, span of control, lines of communication, job assignment, job descriptions . . . matrix management . . . patient's assignments, career trees, examination and accreditation." Thompson and Rath, p. 6.

33. *Ibid.*, p. 10. This is an important level in terms of agency success or failure. It involves techniques in relating to people and all forms of psychotherapy and group dynamics used by the staff with both clients and themselves to avoid serious intra-agency conflicts.

34. For a pictorial presentation see Thompson and Rath.

35. *Ibid.*

36. *Ibid.*

37. All systems are highly complex. They exist in the real world in space

and time and are made up of a large number of variables stretching from remote past to remote future. This means that "all possible variables of potential interest can be aggregated in a conceptual schema without introducing problems of definition, of classification, of inclusivity and exclusivity or of hierarchies, and each variable may then be further tested for relevance on the simple basis of its present or potential relationship with the system under consideration." *Ibid.*, p. 12. Parameters may then be set with lines denoting causal relationships between independent and dependent variables within the overall "cloud of variables."

38. It can be said that all variables have one thing in common, they exist in the form of information available to the senses or memory of one or more persons. Hence they are to be analyzed not only in relation to the system, but in relation to the person who knows them, who has the information.

39. Thompson and Rath, p. 15.

40. *Ibid.*, pp. 16-17.

41. The idea of a corporate personality is not new. As Lee suggests, "the analogy of the state as a person goes back into antiquity with Plato's Republic, and . . . the idea of the corporate personality is to be found in the Old Testament itself." Ronald Lee, "Patterns of Institutional Behavior," *Iliff Review*, 26:1 (1969), 14. Freud also approached institutions and cultures as projections of human psychology by identifying group fantasies, defenses, taboos, and so on. Instead of material forces shaping institutions, as many today believe, human psychology is made the primary force. Recent authors who also advocate this view include Erik Erikson, Eric Hoffer, W. R. Bion, and Robert Cole.

42. Lee, 7-8.

43. IRH, NIMH, p. 13.

> For example:
>
> Did you feel your counseling session was helpful to you?
> Yes _____ No _____
> If yes, what element do you feel was most helpful? (Please mark only one.)
>
>   ____a.   Relief of tension.
>   ____b.   Reassurance about what I was doing.
>   ____c.   Better ability to feel my feelings.
>   ____d.   Better self-understanding.
>   ____e.   Better able to express my feelings or problems.
>   ____f.   Better self-control over my moods and actions.

44. The NIMH has established the following list in decreasing order of priority:

1. Consultation with other public health or health-related agencies.
2. In-service training for staffs of other agencies.

3. Community development.
4. Counseling and guidance for people with emotional problems.
5. Provision of follow-up and other rehabilitative services.
6. Research in program development.
7. Mental health education of the public.
8. Individual therapy for persons with manifest psychotic or neurotic symptoms.
9. Case funding, diagnosis, or referral of persons to whatever therapy resources are available.

Guidelines for the Federal Grant-in-Aid Programs to Support Mental Health Planning (Department of Health, Education, and Welfare—NIMH, 1963), p. 244.

45. The APA has established the following principles to assist centers to develop programs, and accreditation agencies to develop policies and criteria in evaluation of quality. The overall principle from which all others are derived is this: "The Association holds that every patient has the inalienable right to receive treatment appropriate to his illness, under conditions that protect his privacy and dignity, and with essential humanity." Derived from this belief are the following principles:

1. The primary functions of any psychiatric facility are to diagnose, to treat, and to restore mentally disordered persons to an optimal level of functioning and return to the community.
2. The dignity and rights of all patients are to be protected.
3. The facility has a competent ethical staff.
4. Services are integrated with other community services and are responsive to community needs.
5. The facility cooperates with standard-setting and re-imbursement requirements of various third-party payors in order to provide for its patients the economic protection of health insurance.
6. The facility keeps accurate, current, and complete clinical and administrative records.
7. The facility has written policies, procedures, and plans.
8. The physical plant of the facility provides a safe, wholesome environment that enhances the program.
9. The facility is available, accessible, and appropriate for the care of all potential patients.
10. The facility promotes a climate that makes possible the establishment of significant relationships between staff, patients, and their families.

Standard for Psychiatric Facilities: A Revision of the Standards for Hospitals and Clinics (American Psychiatric Association, Washington, D.C., 1969), pp. 2-3.

46. The AAPC has established standards for pastoral counseling centers, which can be found in its *Handbook*.

47. Member organizations include: Association for Clinical Pastoral Education, American Association of Pastoral Counselors, College of Chaplains, Association of Mental Health Chaplains, Catholic Chaplains' Association, Army Chaplains and Navy Chaplains.

CONTRIBUTING AUTHORS

G. Edward Alley, M.Min.

Administrative Director, Indiana Counseling and Pastoral Care Center, Indianapolis; Adjunct Faculty, Christian Theological Seminary, Indianapolis; Fellow, American Association of Pastoral Counselors; Clinical Member, American Association of Marriage and Family Therapists; formerly, a minister for United Methodist congregations in northern Indiana.

*Richard E. Augspurger, Ph.D.

Executive Director, The Institute for Living, Winnetka; Diplomate, American Association of Pastoral Counselors; Clinical Member, American Association of Marriage and Family Therapists; Professional Affiliate, National Alliance for Family Life; Editor, *Abstracts of Research in Pastoral Care and Counseling.* Formerly, Director of Pastoral Counseling and Research, Virginia Institute of Pastoral Care, Richmond; Coordinator of Counseling Services, Kendall College, Evanston; minister to United Church of Christ congregations in Glenview and Winnetka, Illinois; publications include numerous research critiques and book reviews.

Richard G. Bruehl, Ph.D.

Private Practice of Pastoral Psychotherapy, Nashville; Assistant Professor of Pastoral Theology, Vanderbilt Divinity School; Assistant Clinical Professor of Psychiatry, Vanderbilt School of Medicine; Diplomate, American Association of Pastoral Counselors; Clinical Member, American Association of Marriage and Family Therapists; Member, American Academy of Psychotherapists. Formerly, Director, Nashville Counseling and Consultation Center; National Chairman, Centers and Training Committee, American Association of Pastoral Counselors; minister to United Methodist congregations in Indiana and Illinois; publications include articles in various professional journals and anthologies.

*John C. Carr, Ph.D.

Senior Editor of this volume; Executive Director, The Pastoral Institute of Edmonton, Alberta, Canada; Adjunct Faculty Member, St. Stephen's

*Editorial Committee Member

College, Edmonton; Member, Editorial Advisory Committee, *The Journal of Pastoral Care*; Member, American Association of Pastoral Counselors; Clinical Member, American Association of Marriage and Family Therapists; Assistant Supervisor, Canadian Association for Pastoral Education; Vice-chairman, Advisory Board, Behavior Management Services, Edmonton. Formerly, a minister of Presbyterian parishes in Canada.

Carl W. Christensen, M.D.

Private Practice of Psychiatry, Northbrook; Psychiatric Consultant, Community Pastoral Counseling and Consultation Center, Lutheran General Hospital, Park Ridge; Adjunct Professor of Pastoral Psychology and Counseling, Garrett-Evangelical Theological Seminary, Evanston; Associate, Department of Psychiatry, Northwestern University's School of Medicine; Assistant Clinical Professor of Psychiatry, Abraham Lincoln School of Medicine, University of Illinois Medical Center; Member, American Psychiatric Association. Formerly, lay consultant, Mission Boards of the Methodist, American Baptist, and United Presbyterian churches; publications include articles in various professional journals and anthologies.

*Emily Demme Haight, Ph.D.

Pastor, Grace-Cortland Methodist Church, Maple Park, Illinois; Adjunct Staff Counselor, Community Pastoral Counseling and Consultation Center, Lutheran General Hospital, Park Ridge; Member, American Association of Pastoral Counselors; Adjunct Faculty, Garrett-Evangelical Theological Seminary, Evanston.

John L. Florell, Ph.D.

Director, Pastoral Counseling and Consultation Services, The Health Center, Bloomington; Adjunct Professor, Illinois State University; Editor, *Journal of Pastoral Care*; Diplomate, American Association of Pastoral Counselors; Clinical Member, American Association of Marriage and Family Therapists; Member, Association of Clinical Pastoral Education; Member, American Psychological Association. Formerly, Director of Research, Virginia Institute of Pastoral Care, Richmond; Editor, *Pastoral Care and Counseling Abstracts*; National Research Chairman, American Association of Pastoral Counselors; parochial service, United Presbyterian Church; publications include research articles and methodological commentaries.

Brian W. Grant, Ph.D.

Training Director, Indiana Counseling and Pastoral Care Center, Indianapolis; Affiliate Professor of Culture and Personality, Christian Theological Seminary, Indianapolis; National Chairman, Centers and Training Committee, American Association of Pastoral Counselors; Supervisor, American Association of Marriage and Family Therapists; Licensed Psychologist, Indiana. Formerly, minister to Disciples of Christ congregations in Indiana;

publications include theoretical articles for professional journals and
Schizophrenia as a Source of Social Insight.

*Richard E. Guest, Ph.D.

Administrative Director, Des Moines Pastoral Counseling Center; Consultant, Iowa Children's and Family Services; Pastoral Consultant, Iowa Annual Conference of The United Methodist Church; Member, United Methodist Church's North Central Jurisdictional Task Force on Nurture and Assessment; Fellow, American Association of Pastoral Counselors; Clinical Member, American Association of Marriage and Family Therapists. Formerly, minister to United Methodist congregations in Colorado.

*John E. Hinkle, Jr., Ph.D.

Associate Editor of this volume; Professor, Pastoral Psychology and Counseling, Garrett-Evangelical Theological Seminary; Graduate School Faculty, Northwestern University; Director, Assessment Services, Garrett-Evangelical Theological Seminary; Consulting Staff Member, Community Pastoral Counseling and Consultation Center, Lutheran General Hospital, Park Ridge; Editorial Board Member, *The Christian As Minister*; Diplomate, American Association of Pastoral Counselors; Clinical Member, American Association of Marriage and Family Therapists; Member, American Academy of Psychotherapists; Licensed Psychologist, Indiana. Formerly, Administrative Director, Indiana Counseling and Pastoral Care Center, Indianapolis; Project Director, "Pastoral Care and Mental Health," closed circuit television series, Indiana; Affiliate Professor of Clinical Pastoral Education, Catholic Seminary Foundation, Indianapolis; Adjunct Professor, Christian Theological Seminary, Indianapolis; Missionary, Mindanao Central District and Iligan City, Philippines; Associate Pastor, First Congregational Church of Evanston; publications include research studies and theoretical articles in various professional journals.

Jan Lindemann, M.S.W.

Psychiatric Social Worker, Outpatient Clinic, Larue D. Carter Memorial Hospital, Indianapolis; Consultant, Indiana Counseling and Pastoral Care Center, Indianapolis; Member, Academy of Certified Social Workers; Clinical Supervisor, graduate students in social work.

*David M. Moss III, Ph.D.

Associate Editor of this volume; Executive Director, The Seabury Institute for Pastoral Psychotherapy, Atlanta; Pastoral Consultant, All Saints' and Holy Innocents' Episcopal churches, Atlanta; Clinical Supervisor, Christian Outrach to the Handicapped, Chicago; Artistic Photography Editor, *Pilgrimage: The Journal of Existential Psychology*; Book Review Editor, *Journal of Religion and Health*; Diplomate, American Association of Pastoral Counselors; Clinical Member, American Association of Marriage and Family Therapy; Member, American Orthopsychiatric Association; Member,

Pastoral Counseling Centers

American Psychological Association (Division of Psychoanalysis); Member, Assembly of Episcopal Hospitals and Chaplains; Life Member, Association for Clinical Pastoral Education; Member, National Association of Family Conciliation Courts; Member, *Counseil International sur les Problèmes de l'Alcoholism et des Toxicomanies*; Member, Society for the Scientific Study of Religion. Formerly, Clinical Staff, The Center for Religion and Psychotherapy of Chicago; Adjunct Faculty, Garrett-Evangelical Theological Seminary, Evanston; Editorial Board Member, *Plumbline: Journal of Ministry in Higher Education*; Associate Chaplain and Pastoral Consultant, St. Thomas à Becket, Northwestern University, Evanston; Chairman, Research Committee, Central Region, American Association of Pastoral Counselors; Chairman, Episcopal Diocese of Chicago's Commission on Alcoholism; Senior Staff Counselor, The Community Pastoral Counseling and Consultation Center, Lutheran General Hospital, Park Ridge; Assistant Rector, St. Chrysostom's Episcopal Church, Chicago; Field Education Supervisor, Seabury-Western Theological Seminary, Evanston; publications include monographs, research reports, interdisciplinary articles, and reviews in professional journals and anthologies.

*Steven C. Nahrwold, Ph.D.

Director, Employee Counseling Service, Continental Illinois Bank and Trust Company of Chicago; Member, Association of Labor and Management Administrators and Consultants on Alcoholism. Formerly, Pastor to Missouri Synod Lutheran Church parishes in South Dakota and Chicago; Member, National Advisory Committee on Drug Abuse Benefits, Blue Cross-Blue Shield; publications include professional papers on the ethical considerations of industrial mental health care programs.

Blaine B. Rader, Ph.D.

Executive Director, Samaritan Counseling Center, Battle Creek; Editorial Board, *Journal of Supervision and Training in Ministry*; Certified Consulting Psychologist, Michigan; Certified Marriage Counselor, Michigan; Registered Psychologist, Illinois; Diplomate, American Association of Pastoral Counselors, Clinical Member, American Association of Marriage and Family Therapists; Member, American Psychological Association. Formerly, Educational Coordinator and Senior Staff Counselor, Community Pastoral Counseling and Consultation Center, Lutheran General Hospital, Park Ridge; Chairman, Central Region, American Association of Pastoral Counselors; minister to United Methodist parishes in Dayton and Detroit; publications include research studies and theoretical articles for progressive journals.

George Siskind, Ph.D.

Private Practice of Psychotherapy, Indianapolis; Research Psychologist, Larue D. Carter Memorial Hospital, Indianapolis; Training Consultant, Indiana Counseling and Pastoral Care Center, Indianapolis; Associate Professor

Contributing Authors

Department of Psychiatry, Indiana University Medical School; Member, Indiana State Board of Examiners in Psychology; Consultant, Disability Determination Center, vocational Rehabilitation Division of Indiana; Clinical Member, American Association of Marriage and Family Therapists; Member, American Psychological Association; Member, Indianapolis Hebrew Congregation. Formerly, Director, Psychology Department, Larue D. Carter Memorial Hospital, Indianapolis; Instructor, Purdue University Extension Division, Indianapolis; Chief Psychologist, Marydale School and Diagnostic Center, Indianapolis; Secretary, Professional Standards Review Committee, Indiana Psychological Association; publications include research studies and theoretical articles in a variety of professional journals.

BIBLIOGRAPHY

Alkin, Marvin. "Evaluation Theory Development." *Evaluation Comment*, 2:1 (1969).

American Association of Marriage and Family Therapists. *Register*.

American Association of Pastoral Counselors
"AAPC Report of National Research Committee." Unpublished, 1974.
Directory of Consultants for Pastoral Counseling Centers.
Directory of Pastoral Counseling Centers.
Handbook, 1978. "Code of Professional Ethics." "Standards for Pastoral Counseling Centers."
Registry of Training Programs in Pastoral Counseling.

American Psychiatric Association
Standards for Psychiatric Facilities: A Revision of the Standards for Hospitals and Clinics, 1969.

American Psychological Association
Biographical Directory.
Psychological Abstracts.

Barton, Walter E., and Sanborn, Charlotte J. *Law and the Mental Health Professions: Friction at the Interface*. New York: International Universities Press, 1978.

Bennett, David. "Clinical Pastoral Education, Personal Faith, and Sense of Vocation." *Pastoral Counselor*, 7:1 (1969).

Caldwell, Joe E. "Issues of Identity, Models and Methods in Supervision." *Pastoral Counselor*, 5:2 (1967).

Campbell, Donald, and Stanley, Julian. *Experimental and Quasi-Experimental Designs for Research*. Chicago: Rand McNally, 1971.

Clark, Maurice. "New Trends in Pastoral Care and Counseling." *Journal of Pastoral Care*, 23:2 (1969).

Clinebell, Howard. "The Challenge of the Specialty of Pastoral Counseling." *Pastoral Psychology*, 15:143 (1964).

———. "The Future of the Specialty of Pastoral Counseling." *Pastoral Psychology*, 15:158 (1965).

Department of Health, Education, and Welfare. *Planning Creative Changes in Mental Health Services: Use of Program Evaluation*. Publication No. 73-9145. Washington, D.C., 1973.

294

————. National Institutes of Mental Health. *Guidelines for the Federal Grant-in-Aid Programs to Support Mental Health Planning.* Washington, D.C., 1963.

Dickens, Arthur Geoffrey. *Reformation and Society in Sixteenth-Century Europe.* Norwich, Jarrold & Sons, 1966.

Directory of the Association of Family Conciliation Courts.

Eliot, Thomas Stearns. "The Rock." *Collected Poems: 1909–1935.* New York: Harcourt Brace & Jovanovich, 1963.

Ernst, Morris L., and Schwartz, Alan U. *Privacy: The Right to Be Let Alone.* New York: Macmillan Company, 1962.

Erwin, Sam J. "Civilized Man's Most Valued Right." *Prism* (1974).

Faber, Heije. "Is the Pastor a Psychotherapist?" *Journal of Pastoral Care,* 27:2 (1973).

Fleming, Joan, and Benedek, Theresa. *Psychoanalytic Supervision: A Method of Clinical Teaching.* New York: Grune and Stratton, 1966.

Florell, John L. "Results of AAPC Research Relative to Insurance Payments and Internal Revenue Questions." Richmond: Virginia Institute of Pastoral Care, February, 1975.

Foster, Leila M. "Do You Want to Share Your Therapy Tapes With the Court?" *Professional Psychology* (November, 1974).

————. "Illinois: A Pioneer in the Law of Mental Health Privileged Communications," *Illinois Bar Journal* (August, 1974).

————. "Priveleged Communications: When Psychiatrists Envy the Clergy." *Journal of Pastoral Care,* 30:2 (June, 1976).

Gallup Report #114, *Religion in America.* Princeton, N. J., 1975.

Glidewell, John C., *et al.* "Methods of Community Mental Health Research," *American Journal of Orthopsychiatry,* 17 (1957).

Goldstein, Abraham S., and Katz, Jay. "Psychiatrist-patient Privilege: The GAP Proposal and the Connecticut Statute." *American Journal of Psychiatry,* 118:8 (1962).

Gurin, Gerald, *et al. Americans View Their Mental Health.* New York: Basic Books, 1960.

Henry, William, *et al. The Fifth Profession.* San Francisco: Jossey-Bass, 1971.

Hesseling, P. "Principles of Evaluation." *Social Compass,* 11:6 (1964).

Hiltner, Seward. "American Association of Pastoral Counselors—A Critique." *Pastoral Psychology,* 15:143 (1964).

————. " 'Credentials' for Pastoral Counseling?" *Pastoral Psychology,* 11:110 (1961).

Hinkle, John E., Jr. "The 'Robin Hood' Policy: Ethical and Practical Issues Growing Out of the Use of Fee Scales in Pastoral Counseling Centers." *The Journal of Pastoral Care,* 31:2 (1977).

Houck, John B., and Moss, David M. "Pastoral Psychotherapy, The Fee-for-Service Model, and Professional Identity." *Journal of Religion and Health,* 16:3 (1977).

Houck, John B. "The Professional Identity of Pastoral Counselors." Unpublished Ph.D. dissertation. Chicago: Illinois Institute of Technology, 1974.

Bibliography

Hurst, James C., *et al.* "Current Fee Charging Practices and Perceptions in College and University Counseling Centers." *Student Development Report*, vol. II. Fort Collins: Colorado State University, 1974.

Illinois Revised Statutes. Chapter 51, Section 48.1. *Communications to Clergymen*. Approved August 17, 1961.

Institutes of Religion and Health, *Evaluation of a Model for the Utilization of Community Pastoral Counseling*. A proposal for the National Institute of Mental Health. Grant No. MH24288. New York, 1975.

Internal Revenue Service. "How to Apply for Recognition of Exemption for an Organization." Publication No. 557.

Jahoda, M., and Bernitz, E. "The Nature of Evaluation." *International Social Science Bulletin*, 7:3 (1955).

Jester, Harold. "The Pastoral Counseling Center Ministry." *The Christian Ministry*, 5:3 (1974).

Johnson, Herbert J. "Don't Confide in Me." *Christian Advocate*, 10:2 (1966).

Johnson, John R. "Book Review—*Referral in Pastoral Counseling* by William B. Oglesby, Jr." *The Saint Luke's Journal of Theology*, 22:4 (1979).

Joint Council on Research. *Pastoral Care and Counseling Abstracts*.

Jorjorian, Armen D. "Reflections upon and Definitions of Pastoral Counseling." *Pastoral Psychology*, 23:224 (1972).

Klineberg, Otto. "The Problem of Evaluation." *International Social Science Bulletin* 7:3 (1955).

Kohut, Heinz. *The Search for the Self*, 2 vols. Ed. Paul H. Ornstein. New York: International Universities Press, 1978.

Krause, Merton, and Howard, Kenneth. "Program Evaluation in the Public Interest: A New Research Methodology." A revised version of a paper presented at the Society for Psychotherapeutic Research, Philadelphia, Pennsylvania (June 1, 1973).

Lee, Ronald R. "Patterns of Institutional Behavior." *Iliff Review*, 26:1 (1969).

———. "Referral As an Act of Pastoral Care," *Journal of Pastoral Care*, 30:3 (1976).

———. "Totemic Therapy." *Journal of Religion and Health*, 18:1 (1979).

Moss, David M. "The Early Pastoral Psychology Movement: An Interview with Seward Hiltner." *Pilgrimage*, 6:2 (1978).

———. "Pastoral Psychology in a Historical Perspective: An Interview with Carroll A. Wise." *Pilgrimage*, 4:2 (1976).

———. "Priestcraft and Psychoanalytic Psychotherapy." *Journal of Religion and Health*, 18:3 (1979).

Myers, Robert L. "State Licensing Pastoral Identity." *Journal of Pastoral Care*, 30:2 (1976).

National Register of Health Service Providers in Psychology. Baltimore: Port City Press.

New Hampshire Pastoral Counselors Licensing Act.

Nichols, William C. *Marriage and Family Counseling: A Legislative Handbook*. Claremont: American Association of Marriage and Family Counselors, Inc.

Oates, Wayne E. "Association of Pastoral Counselors—Its Values and Its Dangers." *Pastoral Psychology*, 15:143.

Oglesby, William B., Jr. *Referral in Pastoral Counseling*. Philadelphia: Fortress Press, 1968.

Piaget, Jean. *Main Trends in Inter-Disciplinary Research*. New York: Harper & Row, 1973.

Public Health Service. *Evaluation in Mental Health*. U.S. Government Printing Office. Publication No. 413.

Rader, Blaine B. "Supervision of Pastoral Psychotherapy." *The Journal of Pastoral Care*, 31:3 (1977).

Schulberg, Herbert, *et al.*, eds. *Program Evaluation in the Health Fields*. New York: Behavioral Publications, 1969.

Shireman, Joan. "Client and Worker Opinions about Fee-Charging in a Child Welfare Agency." *Child Welfare*, 54:5 (May, 1975).

Slovenko, Ralph. *Psychotherapy, Confidentiality, and Privileged Communications*. Springfield, Illinois: Charles C. Thomas Press, 1966.

Stanton, Alfred H., and Schwartz, Morris S. *The Mental Hospital*. New York: Basic Books, 1954.

Taggart, Morris. "The Professionalization of the Parish Pastoral Counselor." *Journal of Pastoral Care*, 27:3 (1973).

Thompson, Charles, and Rath, Gustave. "Making Health Systems Work." Presented to the American Academy of Pediatrics, 1973.

The Virginia Code Commission. *Virginia Code*. vol. 7A. 1950.

Von Bertalanffy, Ludwig. *General Systems Theory*. New York: G. Braziller, 1969.

Weiss, Carol. *Evaluation Research*. Englewood Cliffs, N.J.: Prentice-Hall, 1972.

Weiss, Stanley, and Fleming, Joan. "Evaluation of Progress in Supervision." *Psychoanalytic Quarterly*, 44 (1975).

Wigmore, John H. *Evidence in Trials at Common Law*. Revised edition, vol. 8. Section 2285. Boston: Little, Brown, 1961.

Williams, Richard Mays, and Ozarin, Lucy D., eds. *Community Mental Health, An International Perspective*. San Francisco: Jossey-Bass, 1968.

Wise, Carroll A. "The Pastor As Counselor." Pastoral Counselor, 5:2 (1967).

———. *Pastoral Psychotherapy: Theory and Practice*. New York: Jason Aronson, 1980.

Wong, S. "A Descriptive Study of Garrett Graduates." Unpublished. Garrett Theological Seminary, 1971.

I N D E X

Index of Names

Index of Subjects

Bill of Rights (U.S. Constitution), 133, 135, 139
Billing, 102-3, 104, 161, 266
Board of directors, 27-28, 36, 144, 152, 203
Business manager, 92

Canadian Association for Pastoral Education, 22
Career development centers, 108
Case conferences
 as diagnosis, 156-59
 as quality control, 160, 163, 244, 269-70
 confidentiality of, 133
 interprofessional, 66-67, 82, 197
 staff responsibility, 153-54
 trainees and, 71, 74, 244
Caseload, 35, 70, 100-101, 110, 153, 216
Case study approach, 264-65, 279-80
Catchment area, 49
Catholic Chaplains' Association, 288
Catholic charities, 35
Causal relationships, 262, 275-76, 286
Certification (*See also* Accreditation), 72, 75, 96, 131, 132, 139-41, 163, 184-85, 191, 242, 257
CHAMPUS, 146
Chaplaincy, 32-34, 96, 105, 107
Christian Church (Disciples of Christ), 119
Church attendance, 46
Clinical pastoral education, 63, 235, 240-42, 244-45, 248
College of Chaplains, 288
Common law, 135-38
Community mental health services, 27, 102, 145, 162, 187, 217, 218, 287
Community needs
 determination of, 28, 85, 111, 274
 role in development, 39, 41-52, 55, 221, 268, 284, 287
 role in training programs, 57-58, 60-62, 71
Community service directory, 188
Competence
 as supervisor, 229
 clinical practice, 110, 161
 fees and, 116, 118, 121
 licensing and, 142
 of counselors, 19, 31, 51, 155, 174, 220, 269
 of consultants, 167, 177-80, 186-90, 192-98

secretarial, 106
Computers, 257, 264, 266, 275
Confidentiality, 33-35, 47, 68, 104, 106-7, 113, 131-39, 161, 168, 175, 212
Congregations, 31-32, 34, 42, 45, 79, 93, 97, 103, 107, 116, 123, 163
Congress, 136
Consultation, 18, 20-21, 51, 87, 133, 281
 authoritarian working relationships, 25, 27, 59, 68, 98, 177-83, 191-94, 198
 organizational, 52, 54, 80-82, 108
 pastoral, 64, 152, 221, 235-36
 psychiatric, 26-28, 33, 35, 64, 86, 102, 156, 158, 160, 165-76, 228
 psychological, 157, 177-83, 190-99, 216, 219, 228, 246
 remuneration for, 80, 93, 102, 169, 175, 180-81
 social work, 102, 158, 177-90, 198-99, 228, 286
Continuing education, 58-59, 69, 273
 for pastoral counselors, 64-65, 103, 108, 153, 163, 169, 182, 236
 for pastors, 34, 62-63, 75, 103, 221
 for consultants, 190
Continuous evaluation of services, 268-71, 284
Contracted services, 71-73, 102-3, 115, 118-21, 183, 197-99, 248, 271-72
Control group, 262-64
Cost analysis, 100, 110, 266
Cost benefit analysis, 265-66, 274, 285
Cost of delivered services, 120, 124, 128-29
Council on Social Work Education, 184, 186
Counselors-in-Training, 58-75, 91, 194, 233-34, 239-54, 269-70, 281
Countertransference, 67, 174, 232, 234
Credentials, 122, 178-80, 183-86, 198, 209, 269
Credit, 74-75
Crisis intervention, 27, 33, 41-42, 51, 162, 251

Data analysis, 261-62, 274-75
Data gathering, 50, 261, 267, 274, 278-80
 interview, 47-48, 73, 155-56, 171, 209-11, 213-16, 261, 273, 278-80
 questionnaire, 42-46, 48, 117-18, 200, 271, 273, 279-80

Index of Subjects

Psychoanalytic evaluation, 278
Psychoanalytically oriented psychotherapy, 151, 167
Psychological testing, 21, 93, 102-3, 107,
156-57, 193
Psychologists (See also Consultation)
as consultant, 26, 86, 277-83
as counselor, 44-45, 203
clinical, 21, 103, 170, 207, 217,
227-28, 246
legal issues, 95, 96, 139-41, 145
perspective of, 66
Psychotherapy (personal), 66-67, 118,
121, 160, 231, 235, 244, 249

Quality Control, 17, 20, 150, 154, 165
evaluative research and, 256-60, 272
relationship of consultant to, 87, 93,
174-76, 196
relationship of fees to, 125-26, 129
relationship of training to, 57-60, 68,
69, 71
standards of, 88, 142
tools for, 158-61, 163, 226
Quasi-experimental designs, 263-64
Receptionist, 104, 106, 128, 210
Record keeping, 85, 163, 267, 275, 287
financial, 103-5, 110, 113, 160-61,
168, 176
clinical, 113, 159, 160-61, 168, 216,
261
Record statistical approach, 279-80
Recruitment of trainees, 61, 64, 72-73
Referral, 20, 21, 200-223
as treatment, 154-55, 157-61, 172
chains, 27, 30, 48, 64, 96, 103, 162
of trainees, 244
pastor as, 25, 75, 93, 105
procedures, 86, 104, 200-223
role in evaluative research, 270-71, 273,
281, 287
role of centers in, 32-37, 84-86, 97, 101,
143
role of consultant in, 180, 182, 184,
187, 189
self-, 25, 105
Research
evaluative, 103, 159, 256, 288
projects, 113, 161, 170, 185
study results, 63, 84, 116-20, 121, 163
Resources
center as, 87-88
consultant as, 170, 192
development and, 39, 46, 85, 280-81

financial, 125, 259
mental health, 79, 172-73, 184, 187,
200, 203, 221, 287
personnel, 151-52
research, 257, 276-77
testing, 156
Rogerian counseling, 151
Role playing, 160
Roman Catholic Church, 119, 230

Salary, 26, 35-36, 91, 110-11, 115,
123-24, 153, 169
commissioned, 99
cost of living increases, 102
negotiated, 99, 102
percentage, 30-31, 100-101, 103, 109,
119
proportional, 33, 99-101
salary plus percentage, 101
Salvation Army, 35
Satellite centers, 87, 107, 109-12
Schizophrenia, 242, 247, 252
Scholarships, 27, 98, 113
Secretary-Bookkeeper, 103-4, 106, 133,
209
Self-employment, 112
Seminary, 32, 61, 63, 72, 74, 107, 120,
169, 244
Sexual equality, 22
Sin, 227, 240, 252
Social work (See also Consultation), 21,
200, 227, 246
correctional, 185-87
family service, 96, 102, 140, 185-86,
188, 216
medical, 186-87
psychiatric, 44-45, 66, 115, 145, 159,
170, 177-90
Socio-economic levels, 25, 31, 36, 71,
92, 94, 111, 112, 119, 124, 265-66
Statutory law, 135-38
Steering committee, 52-53, 55
Suicide prevention service, 205
Supervision, 18, 21, 25, 30, 64
clinical, 31, 73-74, 82, 86, 93, 98, 137
confidentiality of, 168
evaluation of, 159-61, 269-70
focus of, 240
group, 65-66, 108, 185, 196-97, 230
individual, 65-66, 69, 108, 121, 196-
97, 230
role in professional development, 118
role in training, 59, 71, 242-49, 251,
253-54

303